NINETEENTH-CENTURY
SPANISH AMERICA

NINETEENTH-CENTURY SPANISH AMERICA

A Cultural History

Christopher Conway

Vanderbilt University Press
NASHVILLE

© 2015 by Vanderbilt University Press
Nashville, Tennessee 37235

First printing 2015

This book is printed on acid-free paper.
Manufactured in the United States of America

Book design by Dariel Mayer
Composition by Vanderbilt University Press

Library of Congress Cataloging-in-Publication Data on file

ISBN 978-0-8265-2059-3 (cloth)
ISBN 978-0-8265-2060-9 (paperback)
ISBN 978-0-8265-2061-6 (ebook)

For Desirée Henderson

CONTENTS

LIST OF ILLUSTRATIONS

ACKNOWLEDGMENTS

It took more than a village to write a book like this; it took many years of the love of family and friends, the kindness and interest of peers, the inspiration of my teachers, the example of authors I admired, and many life experiences. I hope a trace of those riches remains in this book. I begin by thanking the University of Texas at Arlington for providing me with a research leave that allowed me to write for seven months without interruption—this, after several years of other kinds of support, large and small. Several colleagues at my institution went out of their way to help me do my best work. My friend and former department chair A. Raymond Elliott selflessly supported my research agenda for many years, helping create some of the conditions that made this project germinate. Antoinette Sol, who was also my chair, volunteered for extra department service in order to give me time to finish the last two chapters of this book, to say nothing of always being a trusted friend. I thank my dean, Beth Wright, for championing my scholarship and for answering the questions I had about nineteenth-century French art. I am also grateful to Kimberly van Noort for helping me navigate my career in ways that were vital to my happiness and productivity. Becky Rosenboom and Melissa Miner made it a priority to encourage and help me, whether it was with travel, course scheduling, or anything else that affected my working conditions at the university. I can't thank them enough for being there for me. I also acknowledge the fantastic staff of the UTA Interlibrary Loan Department, for cheerfully and efficiently procuring hundreds of rare books for me.

Over the years, several teachers and mentors have played a key role in nurturing my love of Latin American studies. This book is, in some ways, an homage to them. I thank my high school teachers Janice Kornbluth, Larue Goldfinch, David Rathbun, and Josefina de la Cruz for nourishing my love of books and writing. At the University of California, Santa Cruz, my professors made me fall in love with Latin American culture and literature, as well as the study of world history. I don't think I'll ever stop idolizing them, even though twenty-five years have passed since I sat in their classes: Roberto Simón Crespi, Marta Morello-Frosch, and Norma Klahn. They tower in my heart. I also thank Bruce Thompson, whose brilliant, yearlong survey of European history and warm mentorship will never be forgotten. In my PhD program at the University of California, San Diego, I am proud to have been the pupil of Jaime Concha, Susan Kirkpatrick, and Max Parra. Their rigor as teachers, their warmth as mentors, and their confidence in me helped me succeed and made me feel a sense of belonging.

I am grateful to Julio Ortega and Stephanie Merrim for helping me when I was their junior colleague in the Department of Hispanic Studies at Brown University. They opened new doors and built my confidence as a scholar and teacher. How to thank Beatriz González of Rice University, who for over twenty years has been reading my work and collaborating with me? Her work and her generosity gave me confidence and made my scholarship better. I also thank John Charles Chasteen of the University of North Carolina at Chapel Hill, for his friendship, and for his trust, advice, and expertise. I'll never forget how an encouraging word from him several years ago made me believe in my work and in myself when I was struggling. His fantastic books and love of writing pushed me to be more creative in the chapters that follow. Pamela Murray of the University of Alabama at Birmingham offered insights that improved this book, besides being an exemplary, supportive colleague. I thank my friend Juan Carlos González Espitia of UNC Chapel Hill, who assisted with this project and other ones that came before it. I also thank Ronald Briggs of Barnard College and Víctor Goldgel-Carballo of the University Wisconsin–Madison for reading parts of this book in manuscript form. My Venezuelan friends Alejandro Contreras, Luis Felipe Pellicer, Rafael Guillén, and the extended Guillén family in Caracas opened their homes to me and showered me with countless hours of conversation and encouragement. Matthew Wyszynski of the University of Akron has been one of my most constant and loyal readers and confidants. Douglas García has been following me around the country for over twenty years—

visiting my classes, sleeping on my couches, and valiantly listening to me talk about my projects. I thank him for cheering me, and reading parts of this book, and always asking to see more. *Gracias hermano*.

I reserve an especially warm thank you for William Acree of Washington University, who, more than any other colleague, helped me write this book. His tireless encouragement and interest in my work, his ability to analyze some of the questions I tackle in these chapters, and even his skepticism about my canonical appreciation of Jorge Isaacs were instrumental in helping me finish. Billy made the writing of this book so much less solitary than it could have been.

I thank my editor at Vanderbilt University Press, Eli Bortz, for believing in this project and in me, and for shepherding this project from speculative inception to concrete completion. In particular, Eli helped me find a voice for the Introduction, which I did not know how to write at first. The anonymous evaluators of this book made excellent, constructive comments and helped improve it significantly. If they would allow it, I would name them here. My copy editor, Peg Duthie, did a magnificent job tightening up my prose, notes, and bibliography. I am also deeply grateful for three research assistants who helped me tremendously: April Young Burns, Francisco Laguna-Correa, and Julia Ogden. One of my most talented MA students, April spent three months helping me get this project off the ground in 2011. Francisco, a talented fiction writer and a promising scholar, helped me in 2012, finding many of the sources cited in Chapters 2 and 3. Julia, an excellent young historian, worked with me for over a year, tracking down sources for several chapters and taming my bibliography. Her unerring instincts about what kinds of sources I needed was key to my timely finishing of the manuscript, and to some of the better passages in this book. Last but not least: Christian Nisttahuz, one of my most talented undergraduate students, read the Introduction and helped me work up the courage to make some much-needed edits.

I am also indebted to several people who helped me make this book attractive. Michael Hironymous, from the Rare Books Department of the Nettie Lee Benson Collection at the University of Texas at Austin, went out of his way to be a friendly and helpful contact in the process of procuring illustrations and scanning them. Paul Frecker, of Nineteenth Century Photography, was equally helpful and kind in helping me illustrate the pages that follow. I owe a special debt of gratitude to Wolfgang Wiggers, another fantastic private collector whose enthusiasm for this project helped me bring high-quality Mexican photographs to my readers.

Ana C. Cara of Oberlin College is an excellent scholar, and a kindred spirit, so she generously shared a delightful photograph of Cocoliche with me. I thank the staff at the University of Virginia for their work scanning illustrations. I also thank Randy Smith of the Peter H. Raven Library of the Missouri Botanical Garden, for providing illustrations and permissions. At Vanderbilt University Press, I thank Dariel Mayer and Joell Smith-Borne, for helping me understand how to assess illustrations for publication and much more.

I have thought a lot about my late parents, John and Magdalena Conway, while writing the chapters that follow. It was thanks to them that I had the privilege of growing up in Spain, Costa Rica, and the Dominican Republic. It was their courage and spirit of adventure that enabled me to fall in love with the Spanish language and with Hispanic culture. Their joy in exploring the world, and choosing the path less traveled, lives on in me, and in everything that I write.

Finally, my most important thank you is for my partner of nearly twenty years, Desirée Henderson, to whom this book is dedicated. I thank her for showing me new worlds, and for letting me introduce her to my own. I thank her for teaching me, and for helping me stand in good times and bad. How to forget the drums we heard in Choroní? Or the wild horses we saw at the entrance to the sundrenched ruins of Pumamarca? There is not enough gratitude for that and everything else we continue to share.

Te estoy buscando América y temo no encontrarte,
tus pasos se han perdido entre la oscuridad . . .

(I'm searching for you America and I fear I won't find you,
your steps have been lost in the dark . . .)

—RUBÉN BLADES

INTRODUCTION

Cultures

In October 1841, Brantz Mayer, a thirty-two-year-old lawyer from Baltimore, Maryland, arrived in Mexico City to take his post as secretary to the US legation in Mexico.[1] His hotel, the Gran Sociedad (Grand Society) was on the corner of Espíritu Santo and Refugio Streets, two blocks from the main plaza. Like other colonial structures on the block, the hotel was a two-story building with a spacious interior patio. Inside was a café that served snacks, ice cream, and liquor, and a fancy dining room that offered French meals twice a day. On the second floor there was a gaming room with billiards and card tables. The hotel was aptly named because it was frequented by the crème de la crème of Mexican society. On theater nights, couples dropped by the café for refreshments, and in the afternoons and evenings men of leisure filled the gaming room with their cigar smoke as they played cards.

After checking in, the eager traveler exited the Grand Society to take a walk and explore. As he wandered down the street, enveloped by the hubbub of city life, Mayer tipped his hat to the upper-class women, who wore expensive gowns and sported small, delicately embroidered pieces of fabric over their heads. He observed women of lesser means—clad in unadorned petticoats and plain dresses, and wearing colored shawls called *rebozos*—walking alongside barefoot Indians in misshapen, soft hats and torn clothes. Horse-drawn coaches rolled down the cobblestone street as groups of people crossed the thoroughfare.

Not far from the hotel, on Tacuba Street, Mayer sauntered along a row of street stalls that sold produce, drinks, and religious items. One shop in particular, a butcher's stall, caught his eye: it was built out of four large boards, and had large cuts of beef hanging from the ceiling, garlands of linked sausage streaming across the boards, and a fierce-looking live rooster tied to the front counter. On the back wall of the structure was a cheaply printed image of the Virgin of Guadalupe, who had miraculously revealed herself to the Mexican peasant Juan Diego in 1531, and who had been the spiritual counsel and comfort of the Mexican people ever since. The dark, curly-haired butcher in his bloody leather apron was laughing as he spoke to the women in *rebozos* at his counter. He took out a small guitar and began to sing, making his customers laugh, but Mayer was too far away to understand the words. He pulled his pocket watch from his vest and realized he should get back to the Café de la Gran Sociedad for his appointment with other members of the US legation. He turned away from the butcher's stall and walked back up the street, pausing once again to tip his hat to another lady of distinction, and trying to ignore the pleading children in rags at his heels.[2]

I describe scenes from Brantz Mayer's arrival in Mexico City to use them as a metaphor for the subject matter of this book. Only a few blocks from his hotel, Mayer had encountered the rich and contrasting tapestry of mid-nineteenth-century Mexico, where different classes of people crossed paths and rubbed shoulders. He saw the accoutrements and spaces of privilege at the aptly named Grand Society and caught a fleeting glimpse of how the humbler classes lived and moved around the city. In light of these dramatic contrasts, limited to a few blocks of Mexico City in 1841, the idea of summarizing and interpreting nineteenth-century Mexican culture, to say nothing of Spanish American culture in general, seems impossible. After all, culture is everywhere around living people, in the organization of space, in variations of language, in pastimes and belief systems, and much more. Culture's vast scope, variability, and changeable nature make it resistant to faithful re-creation, even if it had somehow been preserved in its entirety and undistorted in the historical record. And yet the contrast between the Grand Society and the butcher's stall on Tacuba Street is a useful starting point for telling the story of nineteenth-century Spanish American culture. The coexistence of a culture of refinement and privilege with a culture of the street provides us with a framework for thinking about culture in a dynamic and complex way.

This book explores the cultural forms that encapsulated the worldviews, lifestyles, and ideologies of Spanish American elites and commoners in the nineteenth century. By "cultural forms" I mean artifacts of human creation that are associated with both the fine arts and popular culture. The fine arts encompass literature, theater, music, dance, and painting, all of which have been associated with refinement and exclusivity in the modern Western world. Popular counterparts to these kinds of art forms—sensationalist novels and crime stories, neighborhood musicians, fandango dancers, and circus and other street entertainments—are generally accessible to more people because they are not tied to financial privilege or restricted to one class of people alone. The chapters that follow tell the story of both these kinds of culture: they tell the story of the literary tastes and reading habits of elites, the popularity of cockfights and street entertainments among commoners, and the ways that different classes of people viewed each other through cultural expression. This book examines trends and patterns in the production of cultural objects and explores the networks, institutions, and belief systems that framed and gave meaning to cultural creation.

At its simplest, the argument here is that nineteenth-century Spanish American culture was forged through the opposition and intertwining of tradition and modernity. Republican statesmen, journalists, and writers used the idea of culture as an instrument to shape attitudes and promote social stability. Writing novels and plays, going to the theater, and enjoying classical music showed that a society was developing and improving itself. Cultural elites did not tire of promoting these activities, producing a vast body of print that celebrated culture's regenerative powers, although they did little to include the majority of the people in their cultural communities. Indeed, elite pastimes were not an option for the majority of people because they were expensive and required forms of cultural literacy that were tied to financial privilege and high levels of education. The exclusivity of elite culture fostered prejudice among its practitioners, who frowned on the culture of commoners because they considered it indecorous, primitive, or contrary to their Europeanized ideology of progress. By the same token, the cultural expression and entertainments of commoners challenged the values and protocols of the elite and affirmed local identities and their distinctive voices and sensibility. This was not a uniform or organized resistance but rather an authentic expression of a different way of living and seeing the world. The popular theater, the circus, and puppet shows highlighted heroes who shared the language of the man and woman of the street, and whose spicy wit could and did criticize elites or bear witness to social injustice. If the culture of the educated was defined by restraint, and by a quest for order through new, Europeanized cultural forms, the culture of commoners was both freer and more steeped in the traditions of the past.

All the above may seem to cast the Grand Society and the butcher's stall in opposition. While the divergences between the two are pronounced, cultural life was also very much about the convergence of the two; elite and popular culture were not located on unmovable, separate tracks, but rather on intertwined pathways. In 1852, for example, in a magazine article titled "Operas and Bulls," the Mexican journalist Francisco Zarco complained of the popularity of bullfights among women of refinement, and expressed nostalgia for the days when elites frowned on this lowbrow entertainment. However, in a clever inversion of the usual opposition between the civilized culture of the elites and the "barbarian" entertainments of the masses, Zarco ended his article by attacking the indecorous and rude behavior of people who attended the opera. He complained of how they crammed dozens of family members into narrow theater stalls, chattering and laughing loudly. He griped that this suffocating mass of compressed and unruly humanity was an assault on other theatergoers, like an invasion of US soldiers or a pirate attack.[3] For him, attending the opera was not in itself proof of refinement if patrons didn't know how to behave properly during the performance or appreciate its moral superiority over bullfights. If a society's entertainments crystallized its soul and essence, Zarco wrote, the fact that Mexican elites patronized both operas and bullfights underscored that they were lacking in character and refinement. Zarco's humorous essay reminds us that we should not draw a simplistic and rigid opposition between so-called high and low culture. Elite and popular cultural forms exist in a shared continuum rather than in separate locations; cultural objects and expressions from opposite ends of the spectrum come together and move apart. They are rarely locked in place.

This book argues that binaristic thinking is too simplistic to describe how culture works. In the chapters that follow, I propose a more process-oriented definition, one in which binaries break down through contact and blending. For nearly a century, cultural theorists have tried to define this process of combination, beginning with the influential work of the Cuban ethnographer Fernando Ortiz. Ortiz's most famous book, *Cuban Counterpoint: Tobacco and Sugar* (1940), explored the cultural diversity of the island through the interaction of different classes of people, different cultures, and two different kinds of agricultural production: tobacco and sugar. Ortiz denied that dominant cultures simply stripped culture away from a subordinate group (deculturation) to force it to acquire the culture of the powerful (acculturation.) Instead, Ortiz coined the word *transculturation* to describe a more complex process by which different cultures come into contact and create something new. He used the analogy of human procreation to summarize this idea: transculturation was a coupling of cultures that gave birth to new cultural forms that carried within them the genetic make-up of their parents.[4] The idea of transculturation, much debated to this day by scholars, encourages us to think about culture in terms of change, redefinition, and creation, and not in terms of rigid binaries like high/low, Hispanic/Indian, white/black, and so on.

Two Views of the Tiger of the Plains

The contrast between different kinds of culture and values, and the ways that they blend together, can be illustrated by competing representations of a military chieftain from Argentina, Juan Facundo Quiroga. In particular, the story of Quiroga's infamy illustrates the dominant cultural paradigm of nineteenth-century Spanish American elites, who equated their culture with civilization and refinement, and the culture of rural and uneducated people with barbarism. Facundo's story also demonstrates that different kinds of culture dialogued with each other, often in surprising ways.

Juan Facundo Quiroga was born into an influential cattle family in the landlocked province of La Rioja in northwestern Argentina. After playing a supporting role in the Wars of Independence as the captain of a local militia, and foiling a prison escape by captured royalists in the town of San Luis in 1819, he emerged as a charismatic local caudillo. In 1825, when the faraway port city of Buenos Aires and its Unitarian faction enacted measures to bring the interior of the country under centralized control, Quiroga stood against it alongside other caudillos of the interior, who identified themselves as Federalists. For six years, under red or black banners adorned with the motto Religion or Death and the symbol of a cross or a skull and bones, Quiroga waged war against the Unitarians and became the most feared Federalist chieftain of the interior. He was known as the "Tiger of the Plains."

After the defeat of the Unitarians in 1831, Quiroga retired to Buenos Aires as one of the three most powerful military pillars of the Argentine Federation, alongside Estanislao López and Juan Manuel de Rosas. In November 1834 he accepted a commission to travel to Córdoba Province to resolve a dispute between Federalist governors. After reconciling the men, Facundo Quiroga and his secretary began the long journey back to Buenos Aires on the Camino Real in February 1835. Despite receiving multiple warnings that his political enemies were plotting his assassination, Quiroga continued on his journey in a four-wheeled coach drawn by a train of four horses, with a small party of peons, drivers, and a few mail carriers. On a desolate plain called Barranca Yaco, a dozen gauchos in blue ponchos led by a man named Santos Pérez stormed the carriage and slaughtered the whole group.[5] The killers stripped the bodies naked and plundered the luggage. When one of Pérez's men pleaded with his commander to spare the life of his nephew, a boy who was apprenticed to the driver of Quiroga's coach, Pérez promptly shot the man and personally slit the child's throat.

This was not the end of Quiroga, however, because he went on to live on in myth, legend, and history as one of Argentina's most memorable political and military figures. In particular, the life and death of Quiroga provide us with a compelling lens for examining the beliefs and experiences of his Federalist supporters. In one oral tradition, glossed by the historian Ariel de la Fuente, Quiroga appears at a village wedding and witnesses the bride declaring her true love for a man in the crowd who is not the groom. Quiroga orders his officers to hang the girl from a tree and has her true love shot immediately. In this tale, as de la Fuente explains, Quiroga plays the role of a powerful father figure who defends the institution of marriage and the patriarchal privilege of families to arrange marriages, regardless of the personal preferences of grooms and brides.[6] Similarly, the songs that have been preserved about the assassination of Quiroga underscore how local troubadours viewed the leader as a defender of religious values. In one song, titled "Quiroga Lost His Life," this theme is accented by a fictional addition: it places a priest in Quiroga's party on Barranca Yaco and has the assassins mercilessly shoot him down. In another song, "The Virgin of Rosario," Santos Pérez and his men are depicted as a band of Herods—a reference to the king of Judea who ordered all the children in Bethlehem to be slaughtered in an attempt to eliminate the newborn Jesus. By that logic, the song casts Quiroga and his party as murdered innocents. In "The Song of Juan Facundo Quiroga and the Gaucho Santos Pérez," we hear how the singer struggles to sing about the hero's death: "The Virgin Mary appears and requests / that I don't carry on with my song—/ its memory is so sad / you should not listen to it." At another point he cries: "My beloved Virgin, don't let him / die in Barranca Yaco—/ send him to La Rioja, / send him to chew tobacco over there."[7]

These oral traditions demonstrate that Quiroga was respected in parts of Argentina by rural peoples who supported the Federalist cause and who depicted him as a religious martyr and a hero. At the same time that these traditions took shape, a different kind of story about Quiroga emerged through the publication in 1845 of one of the most influential books of nineteenth-century Spanish America intellectual history: *Facundo: Civilization and Barbarism*, by Domingo Faustino Sarmiento. Like Quiroga, Sarmiento was an imperious man with a larger-than-life personality. He hailed from San Juan in Argentina, which neighbored Quiroga's La Rioja, and came from a devout Catholic family of modest means that supported the Federalist cause. He had been a child prodigy who had learned to read at age four and who demonstrated an insatiable passion for learning and self-betterment. One of Sarmiento's idols was the North American Benjamin Franklin, whose credo of hard work, order, and economy formed the basis of Sarmiento's self-image as a man of humble origins who had pulled himself up from his bootstraps through duty to family, learning, and a principled life of the mind.[8]

Sarmiento experienced a profound political conversion that turned him away from Federalism when he was fifteen years old. He was managing his family's modest country store in San Juan when a mounted Federalist force of six hundred gauchos rode into the town. From the doorway, he watched the men ride through the dusty, unpaved streets between the rows of one-story adobe houses. The fierce, sunburnt men looked monstrous because they were wearing large rawhide chaps that they used to protect their bodies and mounts from the thorns of the chaparral. Their horses nervously reared and jostled for space, startled by the friction of these shields bumping against each other. The restless hooves kicked up dust that enveloped the loud-voiced riders whose wild hair and ragged clothes made them look mad and diabolical. "This is my version of the road to Damascus," Sarmiento said, comparing his epiphany to the Christian conversion of Saint Paul. "All the ills of my country suddenly became evident: Barbarism!"[9] The gaucho force of Federalists was a vision of chaos. Sarmiento spent most of the rest of his life trying to counter barbarism with the idea of civilization and its attendant concepts of order, hierarchy, and rationalism.

In 1845, after nearly being killed by a Federalist mob in San Juan, Sarmiento found himself living in exile in Chile, where he worked as a schoolteacher and a journalist. In May, he began writing a major work condemning the savagery of Argentina's Federalist dictator, Juan Manuel de Rosas. Interestingly, Sarmiento chose Quiroga, who had been dead for a decade, as the focus of his book, instead of Rosas. This was because Quiroga provided a life story with a beginning and an end (unlike Rosas, whose story had not yet reached its denouement), and because Sarmiento was probably more familiar with Quiroga, whose theater of war was closer to his native San Juan than the province of Buenos Aires where Rosas had emerged. Sarmiento cast himself in the role of a necromancer who brings Facundo back to life to reveal the barbaric essence of Rosas and the geographical, cultural, and historical forces that defined Argentinean barbarism.

The parts of *Facundo* that tell the story of Quiroga's life demonize him. Sarmiento compared Quiroga's long, curly black hair to the snakes of Medusa's head, and described several emblematic scenes of terror: Quiroga setting fire to his father's house, Quiroga personally slaughtering fourteen royalists in San Luis with an iron bar, Quiroga ordering two hundred lashes upon one of his officers for telling a joke that wasn't funny, Quiroga cutting open his son's head with an axe, and Quiroga severing the ears of one of his mistresses. Sarmiento also dwelled on the ways in which Quiroga's actions parodied civilization and its protocols. In a mockery of military parades, Quiroga rounded up the well-to-do men of La Rioja at eleven o'clock at night and forced them to march and maneuver in formations until morning, while his officers yelled at them and beat them with batons. Through such anecdotes, the veracity of which have been lost to time, Sarmiento underlined Quiroga's disdain for the rituals of power, discipline, and association that characterized civilized societies.

Sarmiento framed these compelling, dark exploits of Quiroga with a broad argument about what constituted civilized, modern life. He argued that civilization and its beneficent spirit of progress were defined by certain qualities that Quiroga's savagery negated—qualities visible in commercial activity (in both the manufacture and the sale of goods), the rule of law (in the existence of laws, and of administrative bodies for their enforcement), municipal organization (in the structure of government), education (both in schools and in clubs dedicated to the pursuit of learning), ideas (in writing, print, and the free exchange of ideas), a European style of dress and manners, selfless civic spirit, the maintenance of order, and the initiation of new ventures (i.e., entrepreneurialism). Barbarism and its arbitrary rule of terror destroyed all these indicators of order. Barbarism is anathema to anything other than brute force, terror, bloodlust, and pleasure. It is also anathema to European traditions of mind and culture, which Sarmiento considered seminal for the germination and growth of civilization.

Sarmiento's book about Quiroga became an influential indictment of Federalism in Argentina and was canonized as classic literature in part because of his distinguished career as a writer and his term as president twenty-three years after the book's publication. He succeeded in defining Quiroga for posterity. The more charitable versions of Quiroga's life that we saw in the songs about his death faded into relative obscurity as the printed words of Sarmiento were read and reread, generation after generation inside and outside of Argentina. Regardless of who told the truth—here I am not concerned with the truth of Quiroga, but his image—the voice of the unschooled singers told a story that was different from the one told by Sarmiento. One notable difference was that the singers did not print the songs they sang to preserve them on paper; their Quiroga was the stuff of ever-changing oral traditions, moving across time and space from singer to singer. Another key difference was that their interpretation of Quiroga was conditioned by a different political loyalty (Federalism) and a more traditional (in this case, religious) worldview that had little use for the European ideas of progress that informed Unitarian ideology and Sarmiento's own political thinking.

Is it really accurate, though, to use the opposition between orality and print to contrast the Quiroga of songs to Sarmiento's biography of Quiroga? Immediately after Quiroga's assassination, Federalist printers published numerous accounts, homages, and lithographs about their hero, and some of this print in all probability contained some songs that circulated throughout the interior and entered into the repertoire of regional singers. By the same token, Sarmiento's work, despite its erudition, gets much of its vigor from popular legends and accounts about Quiroga's life, a fact that the author readily acknowledges in more than one passage of his book. Indeed, one researcher has determined that Sarmiento's account of Quiroga's assassination at Barranca Yaco was based on a song about the event.[10] Did Sarmiento have a printed copy of the song or had he heard it? Was he working off of a prose account based on the song? We can't be certain, but the idea that the songs belonged exclusively to orality and that Sarmiento's book was opposed to orality is misleading. What is clear is that the contrast between the Quiroga of oral tradition and

Sarmiento's Quiroga points to the existence of different kinds of culture that were bound together. Sarmiento's vilified Quiroga was informed by an ideology that prized modern ideas culled from European political and cultural thought, while the people's Quiroga was an archetypal symbol of religion and good versus evil. Each cultural expression informed the other, enacting a dialogue about divergent interpretations of politics and identity.

Civilization and Barbarism in Nineteenth-Century Spanish America

Sarmiento classified Argentinian, and by extension, Spanish American culture, along two neatly oppositional categories: civilization and barbarism. For the majority of Sarmiento's intellectual contemporaries and the generation of writers that came to prominence in the last quarter of the century, the dichotomy of civilization and barbarism was a structuring theme for assessing underdevelopment and exploring ways for overcoming it. Francisco Bilbao, in his landmark work *Chilean Sociability* (1844), argued that the *guasos*, or the solitary and primitive horsemen of Chile, embodied backward and fanatical beliefs that threatened Republican values. He evoked the image of marauding *guasos* armed with swords and axes on the streets of Santiago during the War of Independence, their mouths foaming with rage and their eyes burning with hatred as they dragged furniture and other spoils of war through the streets. In contrast to this embodiment of anarchy, Bilbao presented the patriotic, Republican forces of the future: "See the other camp, see those glorious men, see the culture of civilization, see the men of city . . . the enlightened men. . . . See the rifle grasped by the man of industry, and then compare them."[11] Bilbao and other proponents of the civilization and barbarism dichotomy commanded writing, reading, and print, allowing them to define what kinds of culture were good for society and what kinds were harmful.

As we can see, the drive to civilize was, in essence, the drive to modernize—to prod Spanish American societies onto the same road to perfectibility that European societies and the United States were supposedly traveling. At the end of the century, this impetus was institutionalized through positivism, a philosophy that sought to use rationalism and science to mold society in the name of progress. The French sociologist

Auguste Comte developed the theory of positivism in a multivolume work titled *Cours de philosophie positive* (Course in positive philosophy; 1830–1842), which argued that knowledge and societies evolve through three well-defined stages: (1) A theological period dominated by a deity or deities, (2) a metaphysical period characterized by appeals to abstraction or broad ideas, and (3) the positive age, in which knowledge is shaped through a scientific understanding of the laws of nature and society. In Mexico and Venezuela, positivism was instrumental in systematizing scientific inquiry, developing educational models and, most importantly, buttressing the policies of their rulers, Porfirio Díaz and Antonio Guzmán Blanco.[12] Influential positivists throughout Spanish America believed that historical change could and should be driven by the purposeful, modernizing actions of men and states rather than vague, ungraspable forces operating outside of human influence. It was an ideology that appealed to elites in many nations because it promoted peaceful evolutionism rather than violent revolution, and because it provided a framework for reasserting ethnic prejudice in scientific terms.[13] Racism was an age-old problem, but positivist anthropology made it scientifically defensible and rational. In short, positivism renewed the civilization and barbarism dichotomy, refining and rationalizing it at the end of the century.

Not all thinkers embraced the elitism of the civilization and barbarism dichotomy. One of Sarmiento's contemporaries, Juan Bautista Alberdi, accused the "educated barbarians" of being more destructive to Argentina than rural caudillos like Facundo Quiroga and Juan Manuel Rosas. They "contracted loans for sixty millions of hard pesos, allowed the public debt to absorb half the national budget with interest payments, levied taxes higher than those paid in England" and "allowed insecurity to reign in the city and countryside alike."[14] José Hernández, one of Sarmiento's Federalist foes, wrote that city people and their prejudices against the gaucho were barbaric. His poem *The Gaucho Martín Fierro* (1872), which celebrates a noble and persecuted gaucho, helped to fuel a rejection of the formula of civilization and barbarism in Argentina and Uruguay, where cheaply printed stories about victimized gauchos became wildly popular. Another powerful criticism of the civilization and barbarism equation came from the Cuban journalist, poet, novelist, and political organizer José Martí. When he was sixteen years old, Cuban authorities arrested Martí for speaking out against the monarchy and put him in chains in a labor camp where he witnessed atrocities and suffered physical and psychological injuries. After he was freed at age eighteen,

Martí began his remarkable travels around the world: to Europe, Venezuela, Guatemala, Mexico, and the United States, where he served as a foreign correspondent for major Spanish American newspapers. In his short life—Martí died on a Cuban battlefield, fighting to liberate his homeland—he saw firsthand the corruption and the pettiness of governing elites in Spanish America, as well as the colonialist ideology of US policy makers. In his groundbreaking article "Our America" (1891), he sought to propel Spanish America in a new direction. "There's no battle between civilization and barbarism," Martí wrote, "but rather between false erudition and nature." He argued that the civilization and barbarism mindset had shackled Spanish America to foreign precepts; to decolonize and defend itself against the political and economic interests of the US and European powers, Spanish America needed to pursue a political philosophy based on local solutions for local problems, as well as to embrace its own humble origins with pride. "Make wine from plantains," the Cuban famously proclaimed. "It may be sour, but it's our wine!"[15]

Contrasts and Continuities in Nineteenth-Century Spanish America

The phrase "Spanish America" is used by scholars as shorthand for a plurality of "Spanish Americas," each of which may be divided into increasingly smaller categories of identity, such as nations, provinces, ethnicities, and social classes. The broader the geographical or analytical category, the greater the risk of overgeneralizing and distorting the object of study. What this means is that a truly hemispheric approach to Spanish American culture in any historical period is ultimately a dramatic study in contrasts. Cultural variation reflects ethnic diversity and the intersection of place and history. In the Caribbean, African culture has left a deep mark, whereas in Guatemala and Peru, the enduring presence of indigenous people and languages has created distinct cultural patterns. Literacy rates in late nineteenth-century Argentina and Uruguay (near 70 percent) were at least ten times higher than that of other Spanish American countries, meaning that print culture in the Southern Cone was more impactful and widespread than elsewhere. Baseball became popular and politically significant in Cuba, which had close geographical and cultural ties to the United States, but much less so on the South American mainland. The musical form of the *corrido*, a narrative song related to medieval Spanish poetry, could be found in places like Chile and Argentina in the middle of the nineteenth century, but it consolidated itself as an enduring tradition only in Mexico, where it thrives to this day. I could go on listing such differences and variety *ad infinitum*.

Yet, it is also true that there are some important patterns of cultural continuity in nineteenth-century Spanish America that allow for this book's general synthesis. Spanish American societies were bound together situationally and culturally by their shared colonial past under Spanish rule, by their emancipation at the beginning of the nineteenth century (with the notable exception of Cuba and Puerto Rico), by bloody struggles between conservatives and liberals, and by Catholicism. Mexicans, Colombians, Venezuelans, and Peruvians read many of the same books, enjoyed many of the same pastimes, and held many of the same beliefs about the future and how to get there. For example, most elite Spanish Americans from north to south learned about what constituted good manners from a single conduct manual by the Venezuelan Manuel Antonio Carreño, the *Manual de urbanidad y buenas maneras* (Manual of refinement and good manners; 1854). In several countries, bullfighting endured as a holdover of Spanish tradition, provoking parallel cultural debates about class, identity, violence, and national development. Theatergoers in Buenos Aires, Caracas, and Mexico City saw local plays that were similar in theme and style, and they enjoyed the same fashionable plays and operas from Europe. These and other examples of cultural continuity are the subject of this book, which identifies cultural commonalities and structures of shared experience. My argument is not that there is one Spanish America, but that nineteenth-century conversations about culture and its definition established an identifiable pattern across the hemisphere.

One of the transnational cultural continuities for mapping nineteenth-century Spanish American culture is the binary of culture and barbarism, which I outlined in the previous section. Another is the clash between conservative and liberal factions, which made the century a period of constant civil war over how territories should be geopolitically organized and governed. At first, up to the middle of the century, the warring concepts of conservatism and liberalism were not at the forefront of people's political self-identification. Instead, political factions formed around the push and pull between monarchism and Republicanism, and especially between Federalism and centralism. In major cities, men also associated politically through Masonic lodges and patriotic societies. In the second half of the century, the terms "conservative" and "liberal" became more widespread. Political liberalism was generally characterized by a secularist outlook, capitalist policy, and the pursuit of European cultural models. Political conservatism tended toward older models of economic and cultural practice, including economic protectionism and the defense of church privilege. The liberal/conservative divide was also linked to the conflict between Federalism and centralism. In mid-nineteenth-century Mexico and Colombia, Federalism was identified with liberalism, and conservatism with political centralism. In Argentina, however, the liberals who fought Quiroga were centralists and the more conservative Federalists advocated regional autonomy. To complicate matters further, in Venezuela, the true conservatives were called "liberals" and the true liberals "conservatives." Lest we lose hope in finding solid ground to stand on, what is certain is that liberals were generally the champions of the idea of progress and were deeply committed to using Europeanized culture to promote it in every area of Republican life. For this reason, political liberalism and its cultural proposals play a key role in this book.

A third cultural continuity is the idea of the nation. The cultural critic Benedict Anderson coined the influential phrase "imagined community" in 1983 to describe nations as a kind of collective fiction that citizens experience as something personal and binding. He defined the nation as a limited and sovereign political community that is "*imagined* because the members of even the smallest nation will never know most of their fellow-members, meet them, or even hear of them, yet in the minds of each lives the image of their communion . . . as a deep, horizontal comradeship."[16] In Spanish America, the nineteenth century saw newly independent republics questing for positive representations of the national self, national histories about their past, and celebrations of civic pride and duty. Manuel Antonio Carreño's influential conduct manual, cited above and addressed at length in Chapter 3, included a chapter on patriotism that described the "imagined" community of the homeland in deeply personal terms: "Our families . . . our friends, all the people that saw us born . . . who love us and form with us a community of affect, happiness, suffering and hope, everything exists in our homeland, all is inside of her, and it is in her that our destiny and that of our most valued aims are joined together."[17] The powerful blending of a political idea, the nation, with feelings was a vital foundation for the intellectual, literary, and cultural programs that Spanish American liberals spearheaded. For them, a nation's progress was not only a set of concrete processes based on agriculture, industry, finance, and the law, but an intangible, spiritual journey of self-improvement and self-discovery that built and enhanced the idea of patriotic citizenship. One caveat is in order, however: the enthusiasm for the idea of the *patria grande* (the nation or large homeland) was not shared by the masses who were rooted and loyal to some kind of *patria chica* (a smaller or narrower form of communal identity, centered on a particular place or a social strata).

The urban ideal is another concept that is integral to understanding nineteenth-century Spanish America writ large. Cities provided a dramatic stage for the literal and figurative confrontation between civilization and barbarism. The Mexican liberal Ignacio Manuel Altamirano once wrote that what was important about writing newspaper articles about the elite entertainments of Mexico City was that such texts provided models and instructions for readers who lived outside of the city, or for invalids who lived in the city but could not leave their homes to partake of city entertainments. In other words, the city was a school of progress and a symbol of modern civilization. Cities also expressed resistance to the new, highlighting the clash between different types of culture, one prescriptive (order) and the other anarchic (disorder). The paradox was that the people who embraced cities as magical templates for transforming society (city-as-order) also turned away from them in disgust because of the chaos and contradiction that cities embodied (city-as-disorder). The Uruguayan cultural and literary historian Angel Rama argued that Spanish American cities have always been "inventions of the mind" that applied abstract ideas to a messy and resistant reality.[18] His phrase the "lettered city" does not refer to brick-and-mortar cities but to the city as a metaphor of political and administrative power, and to the network of intellectuals and statesmen whose social and urban planning designed, regulated, and promoted the idea of the city.

The civilization and barbarism construct, conservatism and liberalism, nationalism, and urbanism are categories that help us understand nineteenth-century Spanish American culture. They all speak to the overarching theme of modernity, which was championed by governing elites who enacted it piecemeal through new laws and buildings, and new kinds of economic practices. Intellectuals also promoted it by prescribing certain kinds of culture and criticizing other kinds, all of which was done in the name of progress. These contrasting interpretations of what was modern and what was not help us understand the different kinds of artifacts and cultural conversations that appear in this book.

A Capsule History of Nineteenth-Century Spanish America

This book is a cultural history of the nineteenth century. By itself, any period spanning one hundred years is not meaningful. The idea of a century only makes sense when historians make interpretive arguments about its meaning and characteristics and justify its unity. In this book, I define the nineteenth century as beginning in 1830, after the end of the Wars of Independence, and ending in 1910, the year that the Mexican Revolution began. In this period of uneven political and cultural reawakening, we can identify general patterns and evolving conversations about the meaning of culture, like the ones outlined above. Before I proceed to explore how these themes manifest in a variety of cultural domains, it will be helpful to sketch the general contours of nineteenth-century Spanish American history.

The first and most important step in understanding the period is to look at the Wars of Independence, triggered by the Napoleonic invasion of Spain in 1808. The toppling of King Charles and his replacement with Napoleon's brother, Joseph Bonaparte, created a crisis of legitimacy in the Spanish Empire. The New World colonies adamantly rejected the French king and began to experiment with local self-rule while they waited for the restoration of the Spanish monarchy in the person of Charles's heir, Ferdinand. When the Spanish monarchy was restored in 1813, Spain was torn by political conflict between conservatives and liberals, while across the Atlantic, factions of monarchists and anti-monarchists fought civil wars over whether the New World should be independent or not. King Ferdinand, newly installed on the Spanish throne, tried to regain control but the colonies secured their independence by the 1820s, with the notable exceptions of Cuba, Puerto Rico, and the Philippines, which the United States wrested away from Spain in the Spanish-American War of 1898. (After a period of US military occupation, Cuba and the Philippines became independent whereas Puerto Rico remained under US supervision.) On the mainland, the Wars of Independence were indeed a fight against Spanish colonialism, but they were was also the beginning of decades of civil war that pitted conservatives and liberals against each other. One of the greatest heroes of Independence, Simón Bolívar, "the Liberator," surveyed the dawn of the era of Independence in 1829 with a bitter and prescient pessimism. He declared that treaties and constitutions were worthless papers, elections were pretexts 1. life in Spanish America was miserable.[19]

When we look at the chaotic period spanning Indep- 1880s we can sympathize with Bolívar's bitterness. Constant tween conservatives and liberals, or between centralists and crippled the building of democratic institutions and the everyda the majority of the people. Another disruptive influence was caudi. a phenomenon in which military men seized political power or influ- ice through charismatic populism and regional armies. These fearsome war- riors, like Mexico's Antonio López de Santa Anna, Argentina's Facundo Quiroga or Venezuela's José Antonio Páez, identified themselves as either conservative or liberal, or both, to such a degree that our understanding of this binary collapses under ambiguity and contradiction. In Mexico, the push and pull between centralists and Federalists crippled the coun- try to such a degree that the country could not maintain unity when it fought a war with the United States in 1846. In Argentina, a similar pat- tern held: Federalists fought for much of the century against the central- ist Unitarians of Buenos Aires over how the country should be governed. The Federalists nominally held power through the rule of the caudillo Juan Manuel de Rosas between 1835 and 1852, after which the Unitar- ians fought their way back into power. Beginning in the 1860s, Argen- tinian politics overcame constant civil war and forged some semblance of national unity. This general pattern of conflict and stabilization was reproduced throughout Spanish America: in Colombia, Venezuela, Peru, Chile, and the Central American republics.

International wars were another plague on the house of Spanish America, but they also stoked the fires of nationalism, one of the defin- ing ideological characteristics of the century. One of the most destructive international wars of the century took place in 1864–1870 between Para- guay and the allied powers of Argentina, Uruguay, and Brazil. The con- flict was initially provoked by the rivalry between Paraguay and Brazil, but soon drew Uruguay and Argentina into the war. The overwhelming superiority of the Triple Alliance devastated Paraguay, which was crippled for decades after its defeat. In 1879, Chile fought a war against Peru and Bolivia because of a dispute over mineral rights on the border between Chile and Bolivia. Interventions by foreign powers also disrupted Spanish American politics and economics, as in the case of the US-Mexico War (1846–1848), the French invasion and occupation of Mexico (1862–1867), the War of the Pacific between Spain and the allied powers of Peru and Chile (1879–1883). These wars disrupted politics and commerce but also encouraged populations to identify themselves as heroic, nationalist collectivities ready and willing to fight for their homelands.[20]

In light of all these civil wars, foreign interventions, and wars with neighbors, it isn't surprising that economic stagnation defined the middle part of the century. The militarization of Spanish America that began with the Wars of Independence made tremendous economic demands on the newly liberated republics. Not only was it extremely expensive to raise, maintain, and keep armies, constant skirmishing encouraged the unchecked spread of violence in rural areas, disrupting commerce and agriculture and inhibiting foreign investment.[21] During the colonial era, Spanish American economies had been limited by the Spanish Crown's trade monopoly with the New World and by an overdependence on the mining of precious metals at the expense of other kinds of economic production and trade. Despite the liberalization of trade after Independence, the new republics struggled to assert their economic interests and protect local producers against cheaper foreign products from abroad.[22] Hacienda owners also had difficulties in keeping a stable rural workforce, which led to oppressive forms of debt peonage designed to tie rural laborers to the land through antivagrancy laws. If a peon could not prove who he was and where he belonged, he could be arrested and forced to work at a nearby hacienda. The most successful exporting sectors of this period were mining in Chile, guano in Peru, and beef from the Southern Cone, while coffee, cacao, sugar, and tobacco production advanced in Colombia, the Caribbean, and Central America. In many places, however, economic activity was limited to subsistence agriculture and internal trade between hacienda owners and nearby towns. There weren't safe roads to move goods long distances, or trains to move volume. Yet, for discerning eyes, especially European and North American ones, there was tremendous potential for integrating these underdeveloped economies into the Atlantic economy.

Things began to change politically and economically by the last quarter of the century. In many countries, civil war subsided and was replaced by a period of relative stability and reconstruction. Enlightened but autocratic reformers like Presidents Porfirio Díaz of Mexico, Antonio Guzmán Blanco of Venezuela, and Rafael Núñez of Colombia, among others, single-mindedly and aggressively pursued foreign investment, the build-

ing of railroads, and the construction of modern sewa[...]
streets, and imposing buildings and monuments. These [...]
ists I mentioned above. In their quest to bring foreign [...]
countries, and to facilitate its ability to generate wealth, [...]
used their agents and the military to crush peasants an[...]
who dared to challenge the power of foreign companies [...]
talists. In Gabriel García Márquez's novel *One Hundred Years of Solitude*
(1967), a masterpiece of Spanish American literature that is considered an
imaginative retelling of the unfolding of Colombian and Spanish American history, there's an unforgettable scene (based on a true event from
1928) in which hundreds of peacefully protesting agricultural workers are
massacred by soldiers defending the interests of a US banana company.
This was the nightmarish dimension of what historians have named "the
neocolonial period," which began at the end of the nineteenth century
and extended into the early twentieth. The well-known phrase "Banana
Republic," used to refer to small, weak countries that export bananas or
a single fruit crop to the developed world, and which we associate with
violence, poverty, and government corruption, was the invention of late
nineteenth-century neocolonialism. Neocolonialism was indeed about
European and US financial penetration of Spanish American economies,
but it was also an internal phenomenon that pitted local elites against the
disenfranchised in the name of the security, wealth, and advances that
foreign investment brought to those on top of the heap.[23]

My quick sketch highlights some general trends, but also leaves
out a wide swath of geography and historical and cultural experiences.
For one thing, the nineteenth-century history of the largest country in
South America, Brazil, does not fit into our general framework because
it achieved independence peacefully under the authority of a Portuguese
prince, Emperor Pedro II of Brazil. It was not until the end of the century
that it became a republic like its Spanish American neighbors, and without the destructive and protracted civil wars that defined their Republican experience. The Republic of Texas (a hybrid of Spanish and North
American culture) and other frontier zones of northern Mexico (including California, Colorado, Arizona, and New Mexico) were absorbed by
the United States after the US–Mexico War of 1846–1848. Many of the
inhabitants of this vast territory were Mexicans, but they spent the second half of the nineteenth century becoming something new: an under-
class of Hispanic North Americans weathering a flood of land-hungry

glo prospectors, settlers, farmers, and cattlemen. Spanish America did not end at the Río Grande, but was well established in what became the western and southwestern parts of the United States.

This Book

In the chapters that follow, I explore the interlocking worlds of Brantz Mayer's Grand Society and the butcher's stall, or the divide between the cultural concepts of civilization and barbarism. Previous histories of Spanish American culture, such as *A Cultural History of Spanish America* (1962) by Mariano Picón-Salas, and *El continente de los siete colores* (The seven-colored continent; 1965) by Germán Carrera Arciniegas, are valuable handbooks but they are primarily grounded in intellectual and literary history, meaning that they exclude popular culture. The excellent *The Poverty of Progress* (1980) by E. Bradford Burns, from which I draw inspiration, shows how elites celebrated their culture at the expense of the culture of the masses, but it does not present a panoramic view of culture. Moreover, Burns emphasizes the social prejudice inherent in the elite culture of liberalism, whereas I underline how elite and popular culture intersected and blended together, regardless of the ideology of the communities involved in cultural practice. Since the publication of *The Poverty of Progress*, a boom in interdisciplinary studies, gender studies, and new approaches to race and class has produced a rich bibliography— too vast to detail here—on modern Spanish American culture, but not a general, international synthesis like the one that appears in these pages. This book stands on the shoulders of this rich bibliography of specialized scholarship but it aims to do something different: to provide an accessible framework for talking about culture across national borders.

At the outset, readers need to know that the story I tell here privileges cities in general, particularly Mexico City, Lima, Bogotá, Santiago, Buenos Aires, Caracas, and Havana. This is not only a function of limitations of space, but also a deliberate choice that reflects a focus on the intertwining of modern cultural forms and traditional ones. As I show in Chapter 1, cities were the stage on which the most visible and dramatic encounters between imported culture and local culture took place. Cities in general, and the biggest ones in particular, are a kind of laboratory where we can detect the trends, combinations, anomalies, and movement that show the interplay between different kinds of culture.[24] This book, like any primer on a big subject, cannot be exhaustive, and the privileging of cities is key for building an interpretive framework for a broad understanding of the dawn of modern Spanish American culture.

A few personal words on style and audience are in order. When I was an undergraduate student, I tried to transpose the lessons I learned from cultural histories about Europe and the United States to my study of Spanish America because I did not have a general introduction to its cultural history. Since becoming a scholar, I have continued to look for a broad cultural synthesis that addresses Spanish America's unique patterns and diversity. I wrote this book to meet that need, for myself and others looking for an accessible introduction to the subject. To this end, I use a direct expository style, uncluttered by references to scholarly debates and theories, which are instead presented in endnotes and "Suggestions for Further Reading." I also privilege description, visuality, and anecdote, to try to render the past as vividly as I can. To write a book that features clowns and larger-than-life bullfighters and rural musicians, and to make it uninteresting or jargony, would simply defeat the purpose of the whole enterprise. Finally, I believe that every introductory book should stimulate its readers to seek out other books and research. I hope these pages will serve that purpose: to invite the reader to dig deeper, ask more questions, and formulate new answers. Let's go.

CHAPTER I

Cities

CITIES ARE REAL PLACES OF HABITATION, commerce, and administration, but they are also symbols of authority, progress, and underdevelopment. For our purposes, cities are important because they were the staging ground for implementing new ideas from abroad in places still conditioned by traditional ideas and practices. Urban planners populated urban space with their utopian imaginings and struggled to overcome the often chaotic and dispiriting realities of city life, if they even acknowledged them at all. One panegyrist of the city of Buenos Aires, for example, wrote that all "manifestations of progress and social life at its most refined" were embodied in the city, giving it a physiognomy of material and moral greatness.[1] A Chilean commentator observed that country life, characterized by small, isolated, and scattered human populations, was a barrier to the circulation of ideas and the spread of progress. "Cities," he wrote, "and all kinds of towns of substance, foster justice and the rule of law."[2] Because nineteenth-century Spanish American cultural and political history was defined by the desire to become modern, we could argue that cities embodied modernization better than any other idea or place. They were laboratories for grafting foreign ideas onto local environments, and making progress visible through buildings, monuments, tree-lined avenues, and parks. In Spanish America, as in Europe, the nineteenth century was the age of the city.

The nineteenth-century Spanish American urban experience was defined by tremendous change: cities and their populations grew at an astonishing rate, breaking down the colonial city and replacing it with something more expansive and difficult to control. But what was the colonial city? Inspired by the ancient Roman architect Vitruvius, whose treatise *De architectura* was well known in sixteenth-century Spain, New World colonial cities were designed on a grid pattern with a central plaza that prominently featured buildings symbolizing the authority of the church and of the state.[3] City planners situated unhygienic establishments, like slaughterhouses, on the periphery of cities or near rivers, to ensure sanitation. The Crown also dictated that central plazas be rectangles half as long as they were wide, and out of which four major streets should radiate outward. After these general considerations, urban space was divided into lots called *solares* and distributed by way of a lottery to merchants and then to residents of means and distinction. The driving force behind these and other dicta was order, an idea that was intimately tied to the concepts of political power and administration. In one representative sixteenth-century ordinance, for example, Spanish authorities instructed a conquistador to ensure that any town he founded "appear well-*ordered* as regards the space designated for the central plaza . . . because where such *orders* are given from the outset, *orderly* results will follow."[4] Against the unknown vastness of the New World, cities were supposed to be sites of repeatable and recognizable architectural structures, as well as of political and cultural patterns of collective behavior.

Until the end of the nineteenth century, to look out from any natural promontory over any Spanish American city was to see a low skyline of one- and two-story buildings punctuated by the bell towers of churches and a cathedral. Caracas, nestled in a mountain valley twenty miles from the Caribbean coast, was dwarfed by El Ávila Mountain, looming majestically over it at nearly nine thousand feet above sea level. Mexico City, Havana, and Lima also kept low architectural profiles until the twentieth century. One traveler to Montevideo in 1891 called it a bustling city of stucco and bright colors laid out in a chessboard pattern over undulate ground, allowing the pedestrian to enjoy layered vistas of buildings and shimmering glimpses of the River Plate. Most of the buildings were flat-roofed and low, with the exception of the new Hotel Victoria, which rose above the skyline.[5] Around the same time, a traveler described Bogotá as a squat city of terra-cotta roofs surrounded by mountain ranges and lined with straight, narrow cobblestone streets busy with covered carriages.[6] It wasn't that impressive, he wrote, but it was charming.

The size of the populations that lived in cities matched the modesty of their skylines. At the end of the eighteenth century, most cities had populations under one hundred thousand: Lima (sixty thousand), Buenos

Aires (forty thousand), Santiago (forty thousand), Bogotá (twenty thousand), and San José [Costa Rica] (fourteen thousand).[7] Two of the largest cities in the New World at the dawn of the nineteenth century were Mexico City and Havana, which had populations of around one hundred thousand, but this number paled in comparison to the nearly two hundred thousand inhabitants of Madrid, the half a million in Paris and the nearly one million inhabitants of London.[8] Throughout the century, the cities grew and became more crowded. The population of Mexico City and Havana rose to over two hundred thousand, Bogotá and Lima hovered at one hundred thousand, and Buenos Aires reached over half a million, quickly surpassing a million in the first quarter of the twentieth century.[9] This demographic growth happened in tandem with urban renewal and change. The rhythms of life accelerated. Railroad tracks and steam engines multiplied. Buildings rose higher, monuments appeared, and streets became wider. The plazas bustled with foodsellers, tobacconists, and ambulatory *santeros* who sold figurines representing Christ, the Virgin Mary, and the saints. A Venezuelan essayist sarcastically wrote in 1877 that he knew his country was progressing because he could not move forward when he tried to walk the streets of Caracas; there were building supplies littering the sidewalks and throngs of workers digging ditches, to say nothing of hundreds of supply mules blocking his way.[10] In the pages that follow, we'll explore this world of change and delineate key themes of the urban experience. We'll find that the urban ideal was an optimistic and forward-thinking one, but that it was also haunted by the horrors of poverty, violence, and disorganization. In other words, the cultural meanings associated with nineteenth-century city life were the product of Sarmiento's famous formula of "civilization" and "barbarism."

The City of Light

In 1875, the French writer Victor Hugo praised the cultural superiority of Paris in comparison to other European cities by calling it the "Ville Lumière" or the City of Light.[11] The word for "light" in French, as in Spanish, denotes intelligence, rationalism, knowledge, and culture. To illuminate a city with light—to make it more like Paris—was to structure, beautify, and rationalize it in order to promote the vitality, customs, and industry of its inhabitants. Indeed, this relationship between the city and the metaphor of light was common knowledge among educated city dwellers in Spanish America. In an 1850 letter to the municipal government of the Chilean city of Valparaiso, a group of concerned citizens wrote that "lights" were the most effective kind of police for improving life in the poorer suburbs of the city. "Light convenes everyone to order," they wrote, and "every streetlight is a night watchman who works for free."[12] The city of light was a rational and civilized city, one defined by order and symmetry. In a similar vein, Mexican commentator from Guadalajara wrote that a country's state of progress could be measured by the conditions of its streets. Straight, smooth, and ordered cobblestone streets modeled on those of Europe's capitals were both a thing of beauty and an inducement for a city's inhabitants to interact in civilized ways.[13]

Nineteenth-century European ideas about urban planning were a product of capitalism, the industrial revolution, and the astonishing poverty and crowding that emerged in growing cities. Urban planners agreed that the health of the city organism required both infrastructure and new symbolic spaces and ornamental fashions. What was needed were wider streets to improve the circulation of people and goods, mechanisms for delivering water and removing waste, and buildings, plazas, and monuments to represent modern values. When European urban planners reconstructed their cities to meet these goals, Spanish American travelers and governments took notice and sought to emulate them. In particular, they found inspiration in Paris and the work of Georges-Eugène Haussmann, whom Emperor Napoleon III appointed to the position of prefect of the Seine in 1851, with the charge of repairing the chaotic and unsanitary conditions in Paris. Haussmann ordered the construction of wide and imposing streets like the Boulevard de Sébastopol and the Avenue de l'Opéra, as well as secondary streets, razing slums and older buildings in the process. These changes helped to unify the city, relieving congestion and improving access and circulation. Haussmann's other notable achievements included the building of numerous city parks, waterworks, and sewage systems. His accomplishments were so well known that Spanish American commentators praised their own visionary and successful urban planners by explicitly comparing them to Haussmann.[14] Indeed, most of the major changes to the nineteenth-century Spanish American city were inspired by Haussmann's Paris, such as the Paseo de la Reforma in Mexico City, the Avenida Mayo in Buenos Aires, and the Paseo Calvario in Caracas. Beautiful urban parks such as Santiago's Santa Lucía, the park of Palermo Buenos Aires, and Lima's Exposición were also inspired by the parks of the French capital.[15] To "Haussmannize" a city was to mod-

Figure 1.1. Street scene, Lima, Peru, circa 1880.
Digital image courtesy of the Getty's Open Content Program.

ernize it, which meant widening streets, razing slums, erecting monu-mental buildings, creating sewer systems, and building parks to infuse cities with health.

Benjamín Vicuña Mackenna, one of Chile's most distinguished intel-lectuals and political figures, sought to implement some of Haussmann's ideas during his tenure as city manager of the Chilean capital of San-tiago in 1872–1875. Twenty years earlier, during a turbulent period of con-flict between conservatives and liberals, Vicuña Mackenna had fled the country to avoid arrest and traveled widely in Europe and the United States, learning a great deal about different kinds of cities. He repeat-edly marveled at cities with parks and straight, orderly streets lined with trees that breathed freshness into the air. The European city that best cap-tured Vicuña Mackenna's definition of the perfect urban habitat was Ed-inburgh, Scotland. Cities like Paris and London were indeed impressive, and worthy of imitation in many ways, but they were also big, bustling, and overwhelming. For Vicuña Mackenna, Edinburgh struck a perfect balance between the old and the new, and between nature and civilization. "Without having the majesty and size of a large population," he wrote, "it's nonetheless a city of small palaces and gardens, clean and brilliant on its exterior, with a small-town spirit that is tranquil, laborious, and intelligent, without the noise and tumult of carriages, men, and business."[16] When Chilean president Federico Errázuriz Zañartu called on the former exile to oversee the urban renewal of Santiago, Vicuña Mackenna saw an opportunity to try to recreate in Chile some of what he admired about Edinburgh and other European cities.

Vicuña Mackenna developed an ambitious, Haussmannian blueprint for reimagining Santiago that can be broadly summarized as follows: redirecting or channeling rivers in or near the city, building new roads and making road improvements, developing waterworks, removing structures associated with the urban working classes (like unseemly saloons and markets) and replacing them with new and improved ones, and building new schools and parks. One of his most ambitious proposals was to divert the Mapocho River, which transected Santiago from east to west into two districts.[17] Although the Mapocho supplied water to the city's fountains, it was not potable, requiring the channeling of drinking water from outside the city, as well as many water carriers who sold drinking water door-to-door from large earthen jugs carried on their backs or on donkeys. Not only was the Mapocho polluted with sewage, but it was also prone to dangerous flooding in the wintertime. Vicuña Mackenna's proposal to divert the river would have improved the city's flood defenses, helped to manage the flow of sewage, and integrated the district on the north bank to the southern district, which was the seat of the city's political and commercial interests. He also envisioned an artificial lake in the city's center that could be created through a system of dams and channels, to help purify the air and make urban life more sanitary. Unfortunately, these impressive waterworks were not realized during Vicuña Mackenna's tenure as city manager, but President José Manuel Balmaceda oversaw the successful construction of a channel to divert the Mapocho River between 1888 and 1891.

Another of Vicuña Mackenna's proposals, which was only partially completed by 1875, was the construction of a large avenue that would encircle the southern district of the city. He believed that this band, called the *camino de la cintura* (beltline road), would help demarcate the city proper and distinguish it from the poorer parts of town to the north.[18] By drawing this boundary, the core of Santiago could better protect itself from the slums on the outside, and improve traffic congestion in the center of the city. Although this beltline road did not transect Santiago like Haussmann's Boulevard de Sébastopol did Paris, it was not unlike that famous French street because it was a bold attempt to unify urban space and improve the circulation of people and goods. Vicuña Mackenna also planned to place a series of circular pathways along the *camino* for people to use for leisurely walks or paseos.

One of Vicuña Mackenna's most interesting projects was the Paseo de Santa Lucía, a one-acre park situated on an outcropping of volcanic rock in the northeastern part of the city, at the end of the Avenida de las Delicias.[19] One traveler described the lush, wooded park, with its summit overlooking Santiago, as a "garden in the air," full of "beautiful grottoes and cozy nooks" from which visitors could catch vistas of the city or commune with nature.[20] At the top of the hill was an outdoor theater, a restaurant, ample patios and terraces, and pathways through gardens. Vicuña Mackenna considered it the premier park in the city, which it undoubtedly was, and an exceptional rival to any of the great city parks of Europe. One telling detail about the park and the expectations that Vicuña Mackenna and his collaborators brought to its planning was a structure that was ultimately excluded from its final design. In 1872, Manuel Aldunate prepared a watercolor for Vicuña Mackenna and the city council of what the completed park might look like. At the center of the summit of Santa Lucía Hill, Aldunate had put a tall, electric lighthouse with an imposing spiral shaped tower: Let there be light.[21]

The City of Monuments

While debating a bill related to urban planning on the floor of the Argentine Congress on August 1, 1883, a congressman declared that it was quite obvious what the function of monuments was in cities that aspired to be centers of civilization and culture: they served as pleasant destinations for foreign visitors, and places of congregation for all. It was there, he argued, at the foot of bodies of bronze or stone, that the people absorbed culture and learning.[22] In the previous section, we learned about how Paris inspired the construction of wide streets, infrastructure, and parks in nineteenth-century Spanish American cities. But the city was more than an architectural challenge relating to water lines, sewers, and the best way to relieve traffic congestion; it was also a vessel for shaping the experience of its inhabitants through ritual and collective memory.

By standing before a monument, a citizen could experience a sense of belonging to a historical community defined by seminal events and actors; in turn, this feeling encouraged loyalty to the nation and comradeship with fellow citizens. This subjective experience can be illustrated by an essay that the Cuban patriot and Pan-American writer José Martí wrote for a children's magazine about the importance of hero worship. In the opening lines of his article, Martí described a weary traveler who, upon arriving for the first time in Caracas, rushes to the Plaza Bolívar to see the equestrian statue of the Liberator at its center. In light of Martí's eloquent character and beliefs, to say nothing of his own stay in Venezuela, it is fair to surmise that he was describing his own experience when he wrote that as the traveler stood alone among the tall and pleasant-smelling trees of the plaza, weeping as he looked up at Bolívar atop his bronze horse, the statue seemed to come alive and move toward him the way a father might do to welcome a long-lost son. Martí wrote that the traveler had done well in rushing to see the monument of the Liberator "because all Americans should love Bolívar like a father."[23]

The paradox of monuments was that although they were inert constructions of stone and metal, they were nonetheless designed to provoke and reflect intimate feelings like those experienced by Martí and so many others. Monuments were designed to be catalysts of memory, and instruments for defining national identity. The equestrian statue of Bolívar in Caracas, as well as other nineteenth-century monuments in the city, illustrate the dramatic and contradictory ways that these objects interacted with politics and culture. The statue of the Plaza Bolívar was inaugurated in 1874 by order of President Antonio Guzmán Blanco, who controlled Venezuela between 1870 and 1888. Guzmán Blanco, like his Mexican contemporary Porfirio Díaz, was nominally liberal because of his pursuit of foreign investment and urban projects to improve and modernize his capital city. But he was also a ruthless autocrat and an egomaniac who was intent on celebrating himself as the supreme heir, if not the equal, of Simón Bolívar himself. The rhetoric and iconography of his regime instructed the population that to speak of Bolívar's glory was to speak of Guzmán Blanco's, and vice versa—a form of auto-propaganda that did not sit well with political opponents who were loyal to the memory of Bolívar but not to their president's policies and administration.

In 1878, while Guzmán Blanco was traveling in Europe, the Venezuelan congress repudiated its former leader and called for the destruction of statues he had erected to himself in Caracas. When Guzmán Blanco was restored to power in 1879 by his allies, the new congress repudiated the previous one and called for the restoration of the destroyed monuments and the erection of new ones in his honor. Then, in 1889, after the definitive fall of Guzmán Blanco's regime, his statues came down again.[24] Most dramatically, President Juan Pablo Rojas Paúl was forced to ring the statue of the Liberator in the Plaza Bolívar with soldiers, to protect it from mobs who were enraged by the inscription on its pedestal, which read: *General Antonio Guzmán Blanco President of the Republic Erects This Monument in 1874*. A military officer resolved the standoff between rioters and the military by covering the inscription with a new one on a piece of white fabric that read: *A Grateful Nation Erects This Monument in 1874*. Later, the original stone panel with the offending inscription was removed from the pedestal and replaced with a new one containing the new inscription.[25] The lessons learned from this are clear. On the one hand, reviled leaders may erect nationalist monuments, but they do not own them; the people will adopt them as their own. Second, for a monument to endure, its subject had to be a heroic figure, probably distant in time, who was widely accepted as foundational to all factions. The further back in time a hero's death was, the more universal he could become. In short, the politics of monuments was a deep and symbolic one, more akin to religious fervor than to the push and pull of magistrates, presidents, and individual regimes.

Besides representing great men, nineteenth-century Spanish American monuments also represented abstract ideas, such as Independence, or arguments about the ethnic origins of a nation. In 1877, for example, a statue to Christopher Columbus was inaugurated in Mexico City on the Paseo de la Reforma. The monument emphasized the Spanish component of Mexican identity as a vital and valuable element of modern Mexico. (Although Columbus was not Spanish, he functioned as a Hispanic figurehead because he spearheaded the discovery and exploration of the New World by the Spanish Empire.) Also, the placement of four religious figures associated with Christianity and the evangelization of the New World at Columbus's feet presented a benevolent argument about how Christian values had contributed to the making of the Mexican people.[26] Ten years after the erection of this statue, we see the inauguration of nineteenth-century Mexico City's greatest historical monument on the same street, but with a cultural message that challenged the script of identity embodied by the Columbus monument. The statue to the last emperor of the Aztecs, Cuauhtémoc, was erected in 1887 after eleven years of planning, meaning that its inception had coincided with the placement of the statue to Columbus. The monument symbolized the will of the Mexican government and of cultural elites to publicly identify the nation as a whole with the Aztecs, who were now institutionalized as distant but noble forebears worthy of veneration. It did not matter that most of the same supporters of this monument saw the living descendants of the Aztecs and other pre-Columbian peoples as degraded and inferior; what mattered was that Mexico, like the nations of Europe, could make a symbolic claim on an ancient, heroic past. Mexican nationalists had been invoking the heroic example of the Aztecs since the Texas War of 1836, but the erection of an imposing monument in the heart of the city, along one of its widest and most beautiful streets, represented a bold, public, and visible staging of Mexican pride about its indigenous past.[27] Moreover, by incorporating ornamental elements from pre-Columbian structures on the monument, its designers sought to create the illusion of exotic authenticity, as if the structure had been built by the Aztecs in 1520 and not by Mexicans in 1887.

Our brief survey of a few monuments, and the idea of the monument, can't do justice to the dramatic life stories of most Spanish American monuments. Yet, it is clear that monuments are not as static and unmovable as they might appear at first glance. Monuments talk and tell stories. They dialogue with other monuments, as well as with culture, politics, and the lives of ordinary people. Even a twentieth-century foreigner can be affected: on arriving in Caracas for the first time, I found myself moved while standing in front of the equestrian statue of Bolívar; when I told a Venezuelan friend about it the next day, her eyes teared up with pride over the power of her Liberator.

The Dark City

Inside of the Haussmannian city of hygienic urban design and the monumental city of patriotic fervor and inspiration was a very different city, one that was defined by disorganization, poverty, and crime. The utopian cities dreamed by Vicuña Mackenna and his Spanish American contemporaries were instruments for transforming this dark side of the city, the very existence of which challenged optimistic assessments and predictions of national and cultural progress. In Vicuña Mackenna's prescriptions for renewing Santiago, he referred to the slums to the south of the city, primarily populated by Africans, mulattoes, and mestizos, as a completely barbaric city alongside the enlightened, opulent, and Christian city of Santiago. He was disgusted by the bustling community of the working poor, with its crowded straw dwellings called *ranchos*, its haphazard mud streets, and its nauseating pools of waste and garbage. He called it an "immense sewer full of vice, crime, and pestilence—a true field of death."[28] If the City of Light, as embodied in Vicuña Mackenna's Paseo de Santa Lucía, represented a striving upward, toward spiritual and scientific ideals, the Barbaric City affirmed the baser impulses and appetites of the human body that middle- and upper-class people rejected completely.

The problem of poverty and crowding, common to all nineteenth-century cities in the Western world, was not only a question of poverty creeping inward from the periphery into an uncontaminated city, but also an expansion of poverty from within. This was accompanied by a general coarsening of urban culture that writers and statesmen found anathema to civilized life. Carlos Prince, who chronicled life in Lima, was offended by the crowding of carriages on the street and the bodies of the poor, which roughly jostled ladies and gentlemen trying to walk the streets. The speech patterns of the urban poor, with their habit of combining words and dropping consonants, was also repugnant to him, especially in the Plaza del Mercado, where people haggled over the price of foodstuffs.[29] Similar sentiments may be found in the book *La miseria en Bogotá* (Poverty in Bogotá; 1867) by the Colombian writer Miguel Samper Agudelo, who theorized and contextualized the concept of urban corruption instead of simply complaining about it. Like Prince, he recoiled in horror at the language of the urban poor, and the impossibility of finding peace or security in public. Samper argued that such horrors were not a simple function of inferior classes of barbaric people, but of broader historical, political, and sociological processes that promoted backwardness rather than progress. Most notably, he argued that the never-ending civil wars between liberals and conservatives in Colombia had made the acquisition of wealth and the growth of industry impossible. Although Samper was a liberal, when he wrote this book he had come to the conclusion that some had taken liberalism's egalitarianism too far, damaging the moral authority of the church and stirring up class resentments that wounded the moral fabric of the Colombian people. Politics had become a cynical and violent game of power, not the expression of rational beliefs and actions. "Time will tell which liberals have been loyal to the true cause of liberty," he wrote, "and which, using and monopolizing the term liberal, have adopted doctrines that are opposed to the rights of the people."[30] Whatever the merits of Samper's analysis—political conservatism was hardly a paragon of virtue in Colombia or anywhere else—it was common for Spanish American critics of the modern city to associate its moral decadence with modern life and values, concepts that were generally championed by liberal thinkers as an improvement over the dark age of Spanish colonialism.[31]

Analyses of the Dark City became more scientific at the end of the century, with hygiene (or, better said, the lack of hygiene) becoming the primary basis for assessing urban poverty and its impact on the moral fabric of the city and the nation. The growth of cities and the increasing visibility of tenements and slums in both city centers and suburbs made poverty seem like an existential threat. The crowding of the poor in cramped living quarters without sanitary services created breeding grounds for diseases that did not discriminate between rich and poor or anyone in between. Infectious diseases like cholera and typhus killed thousands in nineteenth-century Mexico City and Havana in waves of epidemics. Guillermo Prieto vividly described the horror of an 1833 outbreak of cholera in Mexico City by writing about eerie, empty streets, churches packed with wailing people, colored banners on doorways indicating someone inside was infected, and the creaking wheels of the death carts hauling away dead bodies. He shared his experience of walking into a deserted house, with all of its interior doors swinging open and closed as the wind blew through the open windows. He was chilled to the bone by the emptiness, as if the terror of death still hung in the air.[32] One of the most dramatic medical catastrophes of the century occurred in Buenos Aires in 1871, when fourteen thousand people died of yellow fever in the city, provoking a desperate, city-wide panic.[33] Throughout Spanish America, such infectious diseases, as well as smallpox, scarlet fever, and dysentery, sowed panic among people and resulted in city improvements in sewage removal and waterworks. But these terrifying diseases also helped to promote metaphors of death and destruction that demonized the urban poor, especially people of color, as subhuman carriers of infection to be feared, regulated, and controlled.

Disease was inexorably linked to nineteenth-century urban realities, specifically forms of habitation defined by extreme crowding, cheap construction, poor ventilation, and standing sewage. Such neighborhoods went by different names in different countries: in Peru, they were known as *callejones*; in Argentina, Uruguay, and Chile they were *conventillos*; in Havana, *solares*; and in Mexico, *casas de vecindad*. In what follows, we take a closer look at the *callejones* of Lima and the *conventillos* of Buenos Aires. The word *callejón* means "alley" in Spanish, and the tenements that carried this name were whitewashed enclosures that consisted of two rows of cramped, single-story apartments transected by a narrow, unpaved alleyway. A brave outsider could enter the *callejón* by way of a modest arch to find crowds of people in the corridor between the apartments, including women cooking over charcoal fires, and men and women drawing water from a measly supply, via the communal fountain that also served as a latrine. Chickens, roosters, and rats ran loose, as did barefoot, skinny children. The neighborhood might have a patron saint, who stood in effigy on a wall niche, and whose feast day was celebrated by the inhabitants of the *callejón*. Depending on its size, a *callejón* might include anywhere from fifteen to forty apartments packed with families of the working poor. On Malambo Street, the *callejones* were primarily black, and commentators complained that they were criminal, diseased, and dangerous, but there were *callejones* for every ethnicity. The notorious *Callejón de Otaiza* was exclusively Chinese and served not only as housing for Chinese immigrants, but also as a destination for those seeking opium, gambling, and brothels.[34] When *callejones* grew so that multiple alleyways became interconnected, creating a maze-like structure, they were called *solares*. Such living arrangements were not new—they had existed since colonial times—but what was distinctive about Lima in the second half of the century was the explosive growth of such living arrangements; approximately half of the entire population of the city—seventy thousand people—lived in these cramped and dangerous slums, which were prone to a high incidence of infectious diseases and crime.[35]

In Argentina, *conventillos* were of two kinds. The first was a large colonial house in disrepair reorganized to accommodate large numbers of the working poor. The other was the twin of the *callejones* of Lima: a building consisting of two rows of single-room apartments facing each other across a narrow alley. In both cases, the sanitary conditions were deplorable and people lived practically on top of each other. In 1883, one Buenos Aires journalist described the desperate living conditions in the twelve- or fifteen-square-foot apartments of the *conventillos* by emphasizing their diverse uses:

> It's the bedroom of the husband, of the wife, and their *cría*, as they say in their expressive language; the *cría* are five or six suitably dirty kids. It's the dining room, the kitchen and pantry, the playground,

the temporary place for depositing excrement; the trash heap; the store of dirty laundry and, if there's any, of clean clothes; the home of the dog and the cat; storage for kindling; and the place where a candle or a lamp glows at night. In short, each one of these rooms is a pandemonium where four or five people breathe the same air, against all hygienic prescriptions, common sense, good taste, and the very requirements of the human organism.[36]

At the time the journalist wrote these words, Buenos Aires had a population of nearly three hundred thousand, and over one quarter of its inhabitants lived in such habitations.[37] Paying four pesos to rent an apartment, a member of the urban working class who averaged a monthly salary of twenty pesos could afford to live there with his wife and children and survive.[38] Such arrangements were not dissimilar to that of the poor in other large cities in faraway countries. In Mexico City, for example, the *casas de vecindad* showed the same general characteristics as the *conventillos*: a repurposing of old buildings or the building of new apartment compounds, tremendous crowding, and cheap rent.[39] We might even go as far as to say that there was a kind of universality or sameness to the living arrangements that the urban poor were subjected to throughout the Western world in the nineteenth century: European and North American slums did not look that different from what we find in Spanish America.

Late nineteenth-century scientists viewed *callejones* and *conventillos* as breeding grounds for disease, alcoholism, and criminality, and as the expression of the biological inferiority of entire classes of people, such as Indians, Afro-descendants, and immigrants (including the Chinese in Lima and the Italians in Buenos Aires). The scientists and policy makers used infectious diseases to argue for the existence of a deeper moral disease that the poor embodied, and which condemned their fundamental worth as human beings. In the minds of most of the learned, the social evils of disease, crime, gambling, and alcoholism among the poor were all offshoots of the same fundamental problem: a lack of order or structure. The panacea to this disorder was cleanliness, health, and civilized conduct, all of which were bound together into the idea of hygiene, a nineteenth-century ideological construct that authorized certain classes of people (medical doctors, scientists, bureaucrats) to regulate spaces, actors, and social habits in the name of the common good. "Hygiene" was a symbol of containment and of knowing one's place. As one notable Peruvian scientist wrote, the lack of public or private hygiene compromised the vitality and prospects of a people's ability to progress, and indicted its level of civilization and biological vigor.[40]

If the City of Light was one of the most sought-after utopias of nineteenth-century Spanish America, the Dark City represented a frightening descent into chaos. In its filthy bowels, and through its dangerous channels, commentators saw disease, crime, and a breakdown in social norms that contradicted their hopes for national progress. The City of Light was defined by the desire to be like Europe, and was a kind of denial of the self, while the Dark City was the return of the repressed (and the oppressed). You could build as many new buildings and vast avenues as you liked, but the *callejones*, *conventillos*, and *casas de vecindad* reminded you that poverty pulsed underneath the cobblestones, the presidential palaces, and the boastful monuments.

The City of Carnality

The archetype of the prostitute was the most powerful nineteenth-century embodiment of the Dark City. Telling stories about prostitutes was a way of narrating the horrors of urban poverty and disclosing the threatening and backward nature of urban life. The life stories of prostitutes crystallized urban realities that all city dwellers experienced, but to a degree that was extreme. These conditions were the breakdown of traditional family and community networks, the coexistence of extremes of poverty alongside affluence and opulence, the ubiquity of disease, the mortal threat of criminality and, in general, the impersonal hostility of the bustling city toward the individual. Take, for example, the story of M. Eduwigis R., a twenty-year-old woman who was interviewed in 1904 by a famous criminologist in Belen, Mexico City's most notorious prison. Eduwigis was the daughter of a Mexico City day laborer who died of typhus when she was a little girl. Her alcoholic mother was a tortilla maker who spent her days in a city plaza, leaving Eduwigis and her sister alone for most of the day. At age ten, Eduwigis lost her virginity to a thirteen-year-old boy and soon afterwards began drinking alcohol with a prostitute who lived in her neighborhood, as well as wandering around the city as a beggar. One night, the police arrested Eduwigis, her sister, and an eleven-year-old girl for having sex in a dark alleyway with two "gentlemen" who had been out to the theater. When the authorities examined Eduwigis, they discovered that she was suffering from gonorrhea and sent her to a hospital that specialized in treating prostitutes. After her release, she worked menial jobs, fell back into prostitution, and was arrested repeatedly for disorderly conduct. In 1904, she sat in a room at Belen in front of Carlos Roumagnac, a Spanish criminologist, who patiently wrote down all of these details on paper.[41] When he was done, he measured the dimensions of her body and her face and ordered a policeman to take her to the prison photographer. Eduwigis was a victim, but now she entered history as a case study about the horrors of modern city life. There were an astonishing number of women with stories like hers. One of Dr. Roumagnac's colleagues argued that there were ten thousand registered prostitutes among the nearly four hundred thousand inhabitants of the city.[42] That number did not include clandestine prostitutes (like Eduwigis), so the actual number must have been significantly larger.

Late nineteenth-century debates about city life, hygiene, and progress were dominated by the topics of criminality and prostitution. Across Spanish America, policy makers, doctors, and writers wrung their hands about how common prostitution had become, and how the unchecked spread of syphilis and venereal diseases posed a threat to society as a whole. In his 1887 application to join the faculty of Lima's most important body of medical doctors, the hygienist Manuel Muñiz wrote that venereal diseases were more frightening than cholera, typhus, and smallpox because they originated in the passions of men and were nourished by society. "It is a duty," he wrote, "and a sacred one, for the authorities to monitor and impede the development of such an evil."[43] Following the lead of a voluminous body of European medicine and social policy, Muñiz argued that doctors and policy makers should recognize the impossibility of eradicating prostitution, and work toward bringing it out into the light so that it could be hygienically regulated and controlled. In Argentina, Uruguay, Mexico, Costa Rica, and Cuba, authorities instituted systems for regulating prostitution and controlling the spread of venereal disease—especially syphilis, which was the most fearsome affliction of all.[44] Everywhere else, men of learning and science lobbied their governments to institute similar systems in the name of public health.

We can illustrate the ideology behind the regulation of prostitution by considering Argentina's Law of 1875 as a representative example. Prostitution is never a neutral subject, but in Argentina it was particularly explosive because it was intertwined with immigration and international relations in ways that did not apply to other countries. More Europeans emigrated to Argentina in the last quarter century than to any other country in Spanish America, with most immigrants settling in Buenos

Figure 1.2. M. Eduwigis R., inmate of Belen Prison, Mexico City, from *Los criminales en México* (1904) by Carlos Roumagnac. Nettie Lee Benson Latin American Collection, University of Texas Libraries, The University of Texas at Austin.

Aires. The dizzying internationalization of the city, the fact that most immigrants were men, and the growth of urban poverty made prostitution not only the focus of issues of public health but also anxieties about race and class.[45] In Europe, rumors about the kidnapping of unsuspecting European girls and women for transport to bordellos in Buenos Aires became an international cause célèbre. Prostitution was thus an inescapable, prominent policy problem for the Argentine government. The Law of 1875 stipulated the following regulations, which were typical of policy on both sides of the Atlantic: bordellos were prohibited from being located near churches, theaters, or schools; prostitutes employed at bordellos should be eighteen years of age or older (in other countries, girls as young as fourteen were permitted to practice); prostitutes were not permitted to traffic their services outside of the bordello; prostitutes were required to subject themselves to frequent medical inspection by doctors affiliated with the city's department of public hygiene; prostitutes must carry a special passport at all times indicating the bordello where they were employed; and minors, drunks, and men infected with venereal disease were not allowed to enter bordellos.[46] Besides these kinds of rules, the regulation of prostitution was also defined by its bureaucratiza-tion, meaning that lawmakers sought to systematically classify different kinds of bordellos and prostitutes (such as differentiating between high-class and low-class prostitutes and bordellos), to enforce a strict regime of record-keeping and registration, and even to collect fees, taxes, and penalties. The will to regulate prostitution, however well-intended and pragmatic, was ultimately an exercise in futility, because clandestine pros-titution was widespread and uncontrollable. Only the most enterprising agents—those who wanted to publicly attract the best clientele—or those whose bordellos were large enough to be conspicuous were likely to play by the rules of the sex industry bureaucracy.

The ways that men of learning understood prostitution and its causes provide us with valuable insights into the mindset of the period. Their writings demonstrate, again and again, the influence of European science, and the prevalence of racist, classist, and sexist beliefs about working-class women. The most influential stream of thought was that of positiv-ist criminology, especially the theories of the Italians Cesare Lombroso and Enrico Ferri. In several works, Lombroso advocated for biological causation, explaining that criminality was a function of the size of the head, or of the relative proportions of the human body. (This explains why Carlos Roumagnac so diligently measured the features and body of Eduwigis at Belen Prison.) Lombroso also theorized that certain kinds of people were more atavistic or primitive than others, and as such more prone to uncontrolled passions and violent behavior. Ferri was Lombro-so's pupil, and acknowledged the validity of biological causation, but he also emphasized environmental and social factors in the making of some types of criminals. Policy makers and observers also drew from gender to explain prostitution. They argued that women were prone to prostitu-tion because of innate tendencies that were more pronounced in them than in men. These tendencies were vanity, materialism, and naïveté. Women's tendency to fetishize their own beauty and to want to display it publicly with expensive fashion accessories was a form of lust and ad-diction that, if left unchecked, could lead to prostitution. Dr. Benjamín de Céspedes y Santa Cruz, a Cuban reformer, wrote that love of luxury and envy were powerful causes of prostitution.[47] Similarly, his Mexican colleague Dr. Luis Lara y Pardo wrote that the will to imitate (a tendency commonly associated with women's vanity and love of luxury) was sec-ond only to the social and psychological inferiority of certain classes of women as a cause of prostitution.[48] A more nuanced and sympathetic explanation was put forward by Mercedes Cabello de Carbonera, a Peruvian writer and early feminist, who in her novel *Blanca Sol* (1889) argued that prostitution was caused by miseducation. The novel tells the story of an upper-class woman who descends into prostitution in part because she had not been taught the kinds of values that would have stopped her from becoming obsessed with luxury and status. At the end of the novel, the protagonist reflects, "How was it her fault, if since childhood, since her school days, they had taught her to love money and consider the glow of gold as the most important feature of her social position?"[49] This argument about education seems to trace causation to the environment, but the identification of women with social climbing and love of luxury was a well-established cultural stereotype that the novel reinforced. Tragically, Cabello de Carbonera became another victim of prostitution when she contracted syphilis from her husband, a well-known medical doctor who consorted with prostitutes.[50]

As dangerous as prostitution was, it remained a thrill for johns. Of the novels published in Spanish America about prostitution, none was more successful than *Santa* (1903) by Federico Gamboa, which became a runaway best seller in Mexico and a major cultural landmark that inspired a classic bolero song, four movie adaptations, and some comic book adaptations. Gamboa was uniquely qualified to write a titillating novel about prostitution because, at least until his marriage at age thirty-four, and possibly beyond, he was incorrigibly addicted to and fascinated by prostitutes, having frequented them in New York, Paris, and Mexico, and probably in Buenos Aires as well. During his rabble-rousing days, his Mexican friends called him El Pajarito (the birdie) because of his penchant for singing a song that went: "A birdie that I had got away from me / and a girl that I loved died on me. / That's how all who love us are: / some leave, others die / and man says: God help me!"[51] (The nickname Pajarito was moreover in all likelihood a winking reference to Gamboa's obsession with sex, since *pajarito* is also slang for "penis.") What was most remarkable about Gamboa's sensuality was his fascination with disclosing it in his writing. In his published writings and diaries, Gamboa sentimentally evoked his love affairs with prostitutes in Mexico City and Paris, and unabashedly evoked the thrill of their flesh. For him, like for many of his contemporaries, prostitution was a sensual and romantic thing.

In *Santa*, Gamboa tells the story of the innocent fifteen-year-old village girl who loses her virginity to a soldier and who is driven into prostitution in Mexico City by her family's coldhearted rejection of her. After achieving fame at one of the city's elite bordellos, the syphilitic Santa fails in her attempts to leave the profession and eventually dies a gruesome death on an operating table. Gamboa advertised his novel, which was inspired by Leo Tolstoy's novel *Resurrection* (1899) and Émile Zola's *Nana* (1880), as an homage to the voiceless, and as a morality tale, but his leering, pornographic descriptions of Santa and her sexuality go a long way toward explaining why the novel was so popular and controversial. *Santa* reminds us that, despite the consternation caused by prostitution, there was something else at play: desire. Men of all classes were drawn toward prostitutes, seeking out pleasure and, sometimes, even love. The reality of prostitution, however, was something darker, colored by violence, abandonment, and victimization. If nothing else, that is the legacy of the stories of young women like Eduwigis R.

The City of Exclusivity

Nineteenth-century cities were supposed to be rationally organized and smooth-functioning communities of people dedicated to the advancement of society and the betterment of the individual. However, as we have seen, the realities of the Dark City told a very different story, one in which exploitation, poverty, and violence denied the utopian aspirations of the City of Light. For a person of privilege, the city was a hostile space that was tenaciously resistant to control. The dress, manner, and speech of the poor assaulted the sensibilities of *la gente decente* (decent people), whose primary concern about the poor was keeping them at work and out of their way. In this context, it's not surprising that people of privilege joined exclusive clubs to associate with people of a similar background. The most ambitious of these clubs were designed to be miniature utopias in which *la gente decente* could broker deals and form a consensus about a variety of cultural and social problems. The club was also a space of leisure where its men and women (if women were permitted to join) could procure meals and attend social events like dances and lectures. Another important function of club life was to serve as a gateway for introducing travelers of distinction to high society. For a foreign diplomat or an enterprising capitalist from abroad, joining a club or simply being invited to a club function was the quickest way to tap into a community of influence.

The Liceo Artístico y Literario of Havana (1844–1870), an organization that inspired similar clubs in other Cuban cities, was an association of affluent people who paid a monthly fee to attend balls, concerts, art exhibits, and educational lectures.[52] The Liceo building included a library of books, newspapers, and magazines for its members to peruse, as well as art and science supplies for its numerous classes. With eight hundred subscribers on its rolls, the club could also afford to donate some of its revenue to charity. A Cuban admirer of the Liceo wrote that besides educating its members, and drying the tears of the poor who had received its support, the club "was the rendezvous of educated Havana, a place where everything was moved by selfless enthusiasm, by true love for progress, by the love and enthusiasm of those who never intervened in political disturbances or in the resentments and schemes of narrow factions."[53] Originally, the founder of the Liceo had dreamed of building a massive clubhouse that would contain classrooms, a dance hall, a hotel, and a theater, as well as a complex of gardens, pathways, and streets surrounding it. As these unrealized plans indicate, the Liceo represented a fantasy of a self-contained, perfect city of *gente decente* within Havana.

Exclusive clubs that members paid to join, and which provided them with an assortment of perks and entertainments, were common to all of Spanish America's major cities, as they were in Europe and the United States. Buenos Aires arguably had the largest variety and most luxurious clubs of all. Some of its clubs included the Naval and Military Club, the Club for Foreigners Residing in the Country, and the Exercise and Fencing Club. There were also clubs specifically designated for residents and visitors of a specific nationality, such as the German Club, the French Club, the Spanish Club, and the Oriental Club, which was for Uruguayans, whose homeland was known as the Banda Oriental.[54] The two most important clubs, however, were the Club del Progreso, founded in 1852, and the Jockey Club, founded in 1882.

The Club del Progreso was founded after the fall of the caudillo Juan Manuel de Rosas to foster community among the best and brightest men of the city and to promote a peaceful politics rather than continued sectarianism and violence. The club's bylaws stated that its mission was to develop a spirit of association for locals of distinctions and foreigners, to channel everyone's efforts toward the moral and material progress of the country, and to create a shared political consensus through conversation.[55] These grandiose objectives notwithstanding, the Progreso was primarily a social club in which its paying members could take drinks, meals, read newspapers, and socialize at banquets and masked balls. After the club began to admit women in 1854, its premises soon became the preferred playground for young men to court women. In his classic novel *La gran aldea* (The big village; 1884), the Uruguayan-born Argentine writer Lucio V. López immortalized the excitement and thrill of attending one of the club's balls. He wrote that the club was an awe-inspiring destination for men and women who had never been to Europe. It was "something like a dreamed-of mansion, the annals of which are full of prestigious love stories, and to which few mortals are allowed access." Only the "whipped cream" of the bourgeoisie could set foot on the cushiony rugs of its halls. López guides us into the bustling premises and into the dance hall, which is packed with men and women in their finest clothes dancing to the sounds of the Toreador Song from Georges Bizet's opera *Carmen*. There are sculptures, chandeliers, a gallery of somber portraits of Argentine heroes, heavy curtains, and the smoke-filled reading and game rooms. In the dining room, a visitor could see tabletops with whole hams on beds of red gelatin surrounded by floral arrangements, and waiters ceremoniously filling glasses with champagne while club members decided whether or not to order the bisque.[56]

By the end of the century, the Jockey Club replaced the Club del Progreso as the most popular club in the crowded Buenos Aires club scene. The Jockey Club had at first been primarily dedicated to the promotion of horse racing in the city, but beginning in 1897 it emerged as the city's most desirable club.[57] The Progreso paled in comparison to the luxuries of the newcomer, and could not compete with its ability to raise astronomical profits for itself from the sponsorship of the horse races held at the Hippodrome in the park of Palermo. The cost of joining both clubs in 1890s was comparable ($1,000–$1,500 for registration, plus a monthly or bimonthly fee), but membership in the Progreso remained stuck at 1,500 members while the Jockey Club quickly overtook it in the first decade of the twentieth century.[58] By 1908, the Jockey Club had 2,000 members and an annual budget of 360,000 pesos. This excluded the cut that the club took from the millions of pesos that were wagered on the horse races held at the Hippodrome every year.[59] At its palatial home on posh Florida Street, members of the club enjoyed the ornate elevators, electric lighting, overstuffed furniture, numerous sculptures, and luxurious decorations, including sumptuous arrangements of orchids and lace on white embroidered tablecloths. One traveler wrote about how strict the club's traditions were, as exemplified by the rule that no gentleman was allowed to remove his coat while playing billiards. "Laxity elsewhere, if you like," he wrote, "but in the Jockey Club, no!"[60]

In other Spanish American countries, there were organizations like

Figure 1.3. Club life, Caracas, Venezuela, circa 1900.
Courtesy of the Library of Congress, LC-D4-9248.

the Club del Progreso and the Jockey Club of Buenos Aires, often with identical names. For example, there were Jockey Clubs in Bogotá, Lima, Caracas, and Mexico City. Santiago, Caracas, and Quito all had influential clubs named Club de la Unión, underscoring the idea that club life was defined by unity and association. In sum, club life was an essential component of the social life of people of affluence and distinction in the second half of the nineteenth century and beyond. Such organizations segregated the social life and leisure activities of the upper classes from everything that was undistinguished or ugly in the city environment, providing both an escape and a visible symbol of power and status. At the beginning, most clubs declared grandiloquent plans to reform society and to promote education, but by the end of the century most were nothing more than a staging ground for the building and maintenance of a new aristocracy.

But what about the less affluent? The working poor and the artisan

Figure 1.4. Store in Caracas, Venezuela, circa 1900. Courtesy of the Library of Congress, LC-D4-9247.

classes had their own thriving associations. The most traditional and ancient of them was the *cofradía* (religious brotherhood), in which members of a given confraternity supported the church on its feast days, celebrated a particular patron saint, and worked together on behalf of each other and the less fortunate. A more recent, nineteenth-century invention was the mutual aid society, which catered to the needs of artisans and tradespeople such as bakers, printers, carpenters, and others. In a mutual aid society, members paid dues into a common pot that was used to fund entertainment and educational activities, and to help members suffering through hardship. As with elite clubs, promoters of mutual aid societies believed that community life was a way of promoting civilization, morality, and progress. A hardworking carpenter and his family might not be rich, but they too were capable of believing in their own nobility and in the nobility of their class, and the mutual aid society system bolstered that confidence through club life.[61] However, by the beginning of the twentieth century, the rise in worker's unions and the spread of socialist ideas diminished the influence of mutualism and replaced it with more political and revolutionary forms of communal identity.

City Cafés

People who lived in cities and who had change in their pockets could pick from a wide array of eateries to have a drink, eat a meal and, most importantly, be in the company of others for a conversation. There were different establishments available to passersby for these purposes, but distinguishing between cafés, *cafecitos* (little cafés), restaurants, bars, ice cream shops, and *confiterías* (pastry shops) is difficult. The Chilean *chingana* is a case in point about the dangers of generalizing about places where people drank, listened to music, and talked. Like many cafés and bars from other parts of Spanish America, the *chingana* was a tavern that hosted live music, local dances, billiards, drinking, and other entertainments. A *chingana* could be high-class or low-class; it could be fixed in a reputable establishment or be an outdoor, ambulatory affair patronized by country people. Andrés Bello, the famous Venezuelan grammarian who lived most of his life in Chile, called *chinganas* sites of immoderation that schooled the working class in laziness and licentious behavior.[62] Yet, an expensive *chingana* in the capital of Santiago could take on many of the characteristics of an elite club, in contrast to *ramadas*, which were rural establishments patronized by the poor.[63]

Here I use "café" as a catch-all for establishments where city inhabitants snacked and drank and socialized with each other. On the one hand, there were places that evoke our contemporary definition of a coffee shop (hot chocolate, coffee, snacks) and those closer to our current definition of a bar. Still, the distinction between the two does not always hold up because in each category there could be big differences, depending on the clientele being served.[64] Also, cafés could be hybrids of coffee shops and bars, even to the extent of serving hot coffee with shots of alcohol in them, as in the case of the popular drink called *fósforo* served in modest establishments in Mexico City.[65] Sometimes cafés were also dance halls, complicating narrow definitions of their function. The most important thing for our purposes is that all these businesses were hubs for discussing the news, for social networking, and for leisure activities like people-watching, reading, and gambling. While cities are undoubtedly defined by commerce, bureaucracy, and everyday survival, they are also places where opinions aggregate and communities are formed. Cafés and related establishments are vital places for togetherness and consensus, and for facilitating social interactions between classes of people that might not otherwise mingle.

In the nineteenth century, the Uruguayan city of Montevideo had a particularly well-developed café culture. One of the most popular cafés in the first half of the century was the Café de San Juan, which was run out of a squat, one-story house with a red tile roof, located near the city center. In the café, which belonged to a talkative Spaniard from Andalucía called One-Eyed Adrian, there were a few unfinished wooden tables and benches underneath two oil lamps that cast a dim light. One-Eyed Adrian was famous for serving coffee and steaming hot chocolate in huge, bowl-like cups, and for outstanding buttered toast sprinkled with sugar and cinnamon. The coffee and the toast were considered by his patrons to be a *tente en pie*—a "get you on your feet" to start the day or to boost your energy in the afternoon. Customers could also order home-cooked meals for lunch and dinner while listening to One-Eyed Adrian's nonstop

Figure 1.5. A Chilean *chingana* with a couple dancing a *zamacueca*, from *Atlas de la historia física y política de Chile* (1854) by Claudio Gay. Courtesy of the Peter H. Raven Library, Missouri Botanical Garden.

chatter. Another popular café in town was the Café del Agua Sucia (Dirty Water Café), also owned by a talkative Andalucian and famous for its flavorful coffee, which was rumored to be made out of dirty water. It was where the political class gathered to conspire or to hide from the police, and where men crowded around tables to gamble as tobacco smoke hung in the air.[66]

One of the most important cafés in nineteenth-century Mexico City was the Café del Progreso, which combined the functions of bar and coffee shop, and adjoined a hotel and restaurant also called Progreso. Located on the Calle del Coliseo, these overlapping establishments were housed in a building that was next to one of the city's most important theaters, the Teatro Principal. The heart of the café/bar was a spacious indoor patio ringed by thick wooden columns. On any given day at mid-century, a visitor could find different kinds of people sitting around small marble tables drinking coffee, hot chocolate, or spirits, and eating ice cream or long, narrow slices of buttered toast. There were gentlemen playing chess while people who had placed bets on the game crowded around. A group of loud men in top hats sat with folded newspapers in hand and argued about politics. Near them sat a family of country people: a sunbaked man in a rough cotton tunic and a large straw sombrero, his silent wife with her head covered in her *rebozo* shawl, and their two wide-eyed boys, their sandaled feet dangling over the floor. Their refreshments were cups of shaved ice flavored with lemon, which they earnestly blew on before gingerly taking sip-like mouthfuls. The writer Manuel Payno, who described the Café del Progreso in his novel *El fistol del diablo* (The devil's tiepin; 1845–1846), wrote that conspiracies, financial deals, boasting, and cruel rumor swirled about uncontrollably in that famous patio.[67]

In Havana, the most important café was the Café Escauriza, which primarily served flavored soda water and spirits to the crème de la crème of the city's elite. It was a well-known dance hall and critics never tired of complaining about how it was the main stomping ground for young men of leisure who had nothing better to do with their free time than showing off their pretty clothes and striking poses.[68] We see similar sights in other parts of Spanish America, as in the Confitería del Aguila in Buenos Aires, a posh bakery that was as famous for its opulent, shiny wood-paneled interior as it was for the crew of elegantly dressed, mustachioed young men who loitered at its entrance on Florida Street, staring at women passersby and flirting with them.[69] The working poor had their own establishments, where they mingled late into the night with drinks, cards, and music, and violence occasionally broke out between drunken men armed with knives.[70] All these locales were alive with activity, with the elbows of café patrons sharing table and counter space with hands holding cards, dominoes, saucers, and cups, all enveloped by a din of voices.

For all of its diversity, café culture was ultimately about people exchanging impressions and information. It was a space defined by contact and interaction, where members of the upper class could mingle with each other, or different classes of people could come together on common ground. Here they could size each other up, measuring their distance from and their proximity to others. When someone got heated and stood up from a crowded table to loudly make a point about the present state of affairs, others at a nearby table might pause, and even come forward to listen, and maybe speak up as well. Amid the foaming cup of hot chocolate, the mug of coffee, the narrow glass of flavored soda water, and the paper cone of lemon ice, café culture was a concert of voices and a theater of laughter and music.

The Modern City

The nineteenth-century city in Western culture was modern not because it had left the past behind but because it strove to make something new. My sketch of key aspects of the city—its utopianism, monumentalism, poverty, and habits of association—underlines that it was a contradictory symbol of modern life. On the one hand, the city was a laboratory for urban planners to implement proposals for making it more sanitary, industrious, comfortable, and inspiring. The city was an idea tied to the keywords of "progress" and "civilization." Yet, the city was also a showcase for the most intractable and alarming characteristics of modern life: alienation, crime, exploitation, and chaos. This facet of the urban experience challenged the idea that the city—and, by extension, the modernity it was supposed to embody—could promote positive social change and progress.

This duality of the city is a cultural phenomenon because it is bound up with the values, social habits, and inner lives of its inhabitants.[71] For the purposes of our story of Spanish American culture, the city is key because it was the place where new ideas from abroad encountered different classes of people and the traditions of the past. The city was where European ideas and fashions mingled with Indians and Afro-descendant shoemakers who never saw the insides of theaters or elite clubs. We be-

Figure 1.6. El Recreo Pulque Saloon, by Antioco Cruces y Luis Campa Photographers, Mexico City, circa 1870. Photograph courtesy of the Collection of Wolfgang Wiggers.

gan here, in the place of encounters *par excellence*, because the following chapters will show how the city was the preferred place to stage new ideas about culture, as well as being a place of resistance and unexpected combinations between the old and the new. Change and cultural dialogue also occurred in the countryside, but at a slower pace and with less intensity. It was on the stage of the city that modern ideas gained the most immediate and visible traction, giving rise to a wide array of revealing phenomena and artifacts that help us understand the story of culture. This is not to say that traditional ways and country life were absent from the cultural life of the city or that they were unimportant to the history of the period; as we will see in the pages that follow, the city interpreted, adapted, and edited rural life. On the one hand, rurality was a conceptual opposite that the city needed to define itself as a symbol of progress, while on the other it was a key ingredient in the manufacture of modern cultural expressions rooted in urban life, such as the vogue in certain kinds of literature, entertainment, and dance.

CHAPTER 2

Print

THE WIDELY DISSEMINATED lecture "Las letras lo son todo" (Letters are everything, 1869) by the Venezuelan Cecilio Acosta eloquently summarizes the core beliefs of nineteenth-century Spanish American writers and educators about the social and spiritual value of writing and learning. Acosta argued that letters were the body of memory and the stuff of glory; they were the light of civilization in the darkness of barbarism. In one impassioned flight of rhetoric, he proclaimed, "Letters are everything. Letters travel—they are the light that instantly floods and colors space, the chaff that carries the seed of an idea, swept away by the winds of time to carry everywhere the germ, the tree, the flower, and the fruits." To allow letters to flourish, Acosta argued, was to create an "atmosphere of civilization" that citizens could breathe and use to build peace, prosperity, and glory.[1]

Acosta's magical conception of letters echoes throughout nineteenth-century literature and journalism. In 1833, the Lima newspaper *Mercurio Peruano* celebrated the literary culture of Iceland, observing that despite the destruction wrought by continuously exploding volcanoes and the fact that her shivering inhabitants were forced to live in subterranean caves, the country was exceptionally rich in printed matter and enlightened literary societies.[2] The subtext of this article was clear: if Iceland can do it, so can Peru. The Mexican nationalist Ignacio Manuel Altamirano argued that there could not be any meaningful material and social progress without the inspiration provided by the written word. He wrote that novels could spread national pride and civic duty among the masses, in the same way that Spanish missionaries had used the Bible to spread the word of God among the Indians.[3] This kind of faith in the civilizing power of the word was a fundamental cornerstone of nineteenth-century Spanish American intellectual and cultural history.

Yet, the promoters of reading and writing faced a major obstacle in their quest to civilize Spanish America: dismal literacy rates. In Mexico, at the start of the century, 90 percent or more of the population was illiterate, and by the end of the century, that number was reduced only by 5 percent. The Peruvian census of 1876 indicated that at least 80 percent of its citizens were illiterate, while estimates for Colombia show that nearly 90 percent of its population was illiterate by the turn of the twentieth century. Notable exceptions to these general trends were Argentina and Uruguay, where nearly 70 percent of the population was literate by the end of the nineteenth century.[4] Despite these barriers, the printing of letters was key for defining political and cultural programs, shaping ideologies, and even appropriating elements of popular culture into elite forms of writing. Letters, however unequally distributed among different classes, succeeded in establishing themselves as prominent arbiters of what culture could and should be.

In the pages that follow we explore the materiality and ideology of letters through questions of access and distribution, reading habits, popular writing, and the ways in which people used print to create community. We trace two competing and intertwining patterns: the use of letters from above to shape and define culture, and letters as resistance to those designs. Most important, we'll explore the elusive yet omnipresent quality of letters that Acosta described as an "atmosphere of civilization." This colorful expression is a metaphor for what scholars call "print culture," which refers to any and all kinds of printing as well as to its themes, status, distribution, institutionalization, and reception. Ultimately, print culture binds together reading and writing practices with economics, values, and ideologies; it transforms words and pictures into the stuff of conversation, relationships, and action.[5]

The Secularization of Reading

With the exception of Mexico City and Lima, which acquired printing presses in the sixteenth century, most of the Spanish New World did not start printing until the eighteenth century, and sometimes not until the start of the nineteenth century, as in the case of Venezuela (1808) and Costa Rica (1830).[6] Before Independence, church and political authorities regulated printing, limiting the kinds of subject matter and opinions that could be expressed in print.[7] The colonial printing press published books of Christian doctrine, linguistic studies about indigenous languages, histories, catechisms, medical treatises, and official gazettes. Printing was also for edicts and official announcements on broadsides that were circulated as loose leaves among government bureaucrats, posted in public places, and read out loud by *voceadores* (town criers). The official and religious bent of print culture was also reflected in the censorship of certain kinds of imaginative literature, Protestant books, and publications related to the Enlightenment. Although such bans did not stop enterprising and determined readers from acquiring prohibited items, they drove underground the discussion of the ideas those publications contained.[8] It was not until after Independence that print culture became a vehicle for the freer expression of ideas, and for the exploration of secular topics.

If colonial print culture was predicated on the strengthening of royal and religious values in the New World, postcolonial print culture was characterized by intense competition between conservatives and liberals, albeit with a shared commitment to promote civic values. Among the intelligentsia, the idea of blind obedience to God and king was replaced by Republican sociability, a set of values and practices designed to foster community, intellectual exchange, and the peaceful advancement of the greater Republican good. In an essay titled "Sociabilidad y progreso" (Sociability and progress), published in a Chilean newspaper in 1859, Justo Arteaga y Alemparte defined "sociability" as the coming together of citizens to ensure that every idea, thought, and truth exists for the benefit of all, like a light illuminating the largest possible number of minds. The push and pull between political parties, often leading to violence and civil war, represented the failure of sociability because the persuasive power of ideas had not been permitted to promote the reconciliation of opposites and the revelation of truths. "If we want to break with underdevelopment and enter onto the stage of progress with the expectation of success," Arteaga y Alemparte wrote, "let us ensure, before anything else, that our sociability be strong and effective, that it be free to grow in every way, that it be as energized as possible."[9] Republican sociability could only work, however, in a society composed of educated and well-informed citizens who could be trusted to act in the name of society's best interests. Forward-thinking intellectuals like the Venezuelan Simón Rodríguez wrote that the state should take a direct role in promoting this consensual and deliberative form of civilization by educating citizens to understand their rights and responsibilities. The educated citizen is not ruled by the fear of punishment, he wrote, but by the morality of civilization and its precepts, which teach respect for institutions and nonviolence.[10] Freedom was thus not only about political systems and economics, it was a kind of subjectivity that different kinds of governments could limit or expand. Print, in theory at least, held the promise of being able to realize the full potential of Republicanism by building consensus about the most important and controversial questions of the day.

The writings of the Mexican printer and novelist José Joaquín Fernández de Lizardi provide a revealing case study about how journalists, printers, and writers redefined the meaning of print in the nineteenth century. Lizardi was a *criollo* (a Spaniard born in the New World) from a respectable family of limited means. Although he did not complete his formal education, Lizardi was a voracious autodidact who fell in love with reading, writing, and printing. Beginning in 1811, he published a large number of pamphlets and broadsides, as well as numerous newspapers, among them *El Pensador Mexicano* (The Mexican Thinker), the title of which he took as his pseudonym.[11] Early in the War of Independence, in 1812, he had the temerity to criticize the viceroy in print and to blame the outbreak of revolution in Mexico on Spanish corruption, an argument that landed him in jail. In 1821, before the military consolidation of Mexican independence, the authorities imprisoned him again for defending the ideal of political liberty. The rabble-rousing didn't stop there. Lizardi called for greater political and religious freedom, defended freemasonry, attacked the corruption of parish priests, and even questioned the infallibility of the pope, all of which cut against the conservative grain of the political culture of early Republican Mexico.

In 1816–1819, while freedom of the press was restricted, Lizardi serialized three satirical novels, the most popular and influential of which was *The Mangy Parrot* (1816). This foundational classic of modern Mexican literature tells the story of the misfortunes, adventures, and travels of Periquillo, a young rogue who is always falling in with the wrong people. The novel combines colorful episodes about the misbehavior of Periquillo and his friends with soliloquies and parables about how to lead a moral and productive life. The protagonist's wanderings and his interaction with several strata of urban and rural Mexican society allows Lizardi to skewer many social types: ignorant wet nurses, indulgent mothers, incompetent schoolteachers, lazy priests, corrupt village mayors, inept doctors, sleazy notaries, and deceitful beggars. This inventive representation of Mexican social types underlined that literature could be an entertaining alternative to more pedantic and religious forms of moralizing. Indeed, Lizardi wanted his novel to be attractive to those readers who were most in need of guidance and moral instruction but who would never be drawn to religious and other kinds of preachy writing. "Books such as this," he writes about Periquillo's tale, "are like the pills that are coated with sugar so that the wholesome antidote they contain will go down more easily."[12] By enjoying a story, a reader was likelier to internalize its teachings than the solemn lessons of conventional religious discourse, which fall on deaf ears more often than not. In his posthumously published novel *Don Catrín de la Fachenda* (1832), Lizardi stressed the point more emphatically by singling out the sermons of friars and "gloomy" books as the worst kinds of instruments for changing the behavior of rogues.[13] To improve society, and to correct conduct, reading should be fun; it should be imaginative, humorous, and defined by the needs of its audience, not by rigid moral formulas or institutions.

My argument here is not that Christian print faded away in the nineteenth century but that print diversified and expanded to include new subjects and styles that were not framed by religious discourse. Print acquired new forms of authority and truth that did not spring from God or the church, but from the interrelated concepts of republic, citizen, modernity, progress, civilization, and beauty. Readers were expected to use these authoritative concepts to deliberate with each other about how to steer society toward civilization and away from barbarism. Like Lizardi's brilliant experiments in fiction, nineteenth-century print tried to reflect and to transform reality, and to become an arbiter of right and wrong and a guide for making a better tomorrow.

Reading, Progress, and the *Cuadro de Costumbres*

In the Republican era, novelists and literary critics (they were often one and the same) tirelessly celebrated the social utility of writing, linking it to the development of good citizens and to national progress. One of the dominant forms of nationalist writing was the genre of the *cuadro de costumbres*, or sketch of customs and social life. The *cuadro de costumbres* was a short prose narrative form that sought to depict, with varying degrees of irony, criticism, or detail, a given social reality or social type. One of the founts of inspiration for the Spanish American *cuadro de costumbres* was the widely read and praised Spanish *costumbrista* writer José Mariano de Larra. Another source of inspiration were popular illustrated books from Europe like *Les Français peints par eux-mêmes* (The French painted by their own hand; 1839–1842), *The Heads of the People; or, Portraits of the English* (1841), and *Los españoles pintados por sí mismos* (The Spanish painted by their own hand; 1843).[14] These books, imitated in Cuba and Mexico, married word and image to provide focused portraits of people associated with certain trades, such as coachmen, cockfighters, seamstresses, musicians, store clerks, and even typesetters at a printing office. The rise of *costumbrismo* was also a function of the anxiety about who should define Spanish America: foreigners or nationals? The late eighteenth and early nineteenth century saw the publication of several European travel books about Spanish America, some profusely illustrated, which inspired local writers to undertake similar projects.[15] Whatever its origins, the *cuadro de costumbres* was an excellent vehicle for nationalist writers because of its brevity, which allowed it to circulate nationally and internationally in periodicals.

It's difficult to narrowly define the *cuadro de costumbres* because of its great tonal and thematic variety. One of the social types featured in the *costumbrista* work *Los mexicanos pintados por sí mismos* (The Mexicans painted by their own hand; 1854) is the *aguador* (water carrier). This figure, universal to every Spanish American city in the nineteenth century (and throughout much of the twentieth in many areas), is not the object of censure or derision. He is appreciatively described with a wealth of journalistic detail.[16] In contrast, the Cuban *costumbrista* José María y Cárdenas takes a more humorous tone in a sketch titled "Educated Out of Country!," which mocks adolescents who return home from studying abroad with impertinent attitudes, broken Spanish, and ignorant notions:

> "Eh bien!" Esteban said after we sat down again: "As I was saying, the governation of those countries is . . . is . . . Jeremias, how do you say in Spanish when a thing is like . . . like . . . ?"
>
> "He's a bit slow in expressing himself," Doña Mamerta volunteered. "As you can see! Five years without speaking his own language."
>
> "Oh! In Germany everybody always speech German. . . . And later I went on London, and I told a friend how many carriages crossed the London Bridge; and he not me believe."[17]

Figure 2.1. *El alacenero* (The storekeep), from *Los mexicanos pintados por sí mismos* (1855). Nettie Lee Benson Latin American Collection, University of Texas Libraries, The University of Texas at Austin.

Figure 2.2. *El aguador* (The water carrier), from *Los mexicanos pintados por sí mismos* (1855). Nettie Lee Benson Latin American Collection, University of Texas Libraries, The University of Texas at Austin.

This lighthearted style was common, but it was not the only register. "The Slaughterhouse" (1838) by the Argentinian Esteban Echeverría is a hybrid of political allegory, short story, and *costumbrista* sketch that presents a blood-soaked description of the main slaughterhouse of Buenos Aires under the reign of Juan Manuel de Rosas. In the story, butchers, proletarians, and beggars swagger through and roll around the bloody offal, excrement, and mud of the slaughterhouse, drunk on their own debasement, while an unsuspecting liberal gentleman strolls toward the mob and a humiliating, violent end.

The inherent variety of the *cuadro de costumbres* aligned it with other kinds of historical and folkloric writing. One variant was the *tradición*, a cross between historical miscellany and the *cuadro de costumbres*, popularized throughout the Spanish American world by the Peruvian bibliophile Ricardo Palma. His *Peruvian Traditions* (1872–1910) were historical, linguistic, and sociological anecdotes that the author culled from oral traditions and dusty books of history. Witty, conversational, and ironic, some of Palma's subjects included the Inca Atahualpa's penchant for chess, the conflicts between church and viceregal authorities during the colonial period, Simón Bolívar's sex life, the origin of the sayings of Lima, urban legends, and any imaginable subject related to the life and culture of Peru. His *tradiciones* made him a continental and international celebrity and spawned numerous imitators, whose pale attempts to capture the charming spirit of Palma's originals have been largely forgotten.[18]

The *cuadro de costumbres* was also important to the development of nineteenth-century novels (as well as of the theater, which we will discuss in the next chapter). For novels to teach readers Republican values, writers believed they should incorporate local settings and characters. In a way, the *cuadro de costumbres* was an embryonic form of literary realism that, when blended together with plots about love, heroism, and sacrifice, could both teach and inspire. Chile's greatest nineteenth-century novelist, Alberto Blest Gana, celebrated the *costumbrista* novel because of its immediacy and vivid nature, which made it impactful and educational. He argued that it could chart a path forward for nations stuck between the old colonial ways and modern, European influences. Other novelists agreed. The Argentinian Bartolomé Mitre, one of his country's most influential liberal presidents, authored a romantic novel called *Soledad* (1847) that featured a preface in which he too complained about the flood of foreign and corrupting novels and celebrated the nationalist potential of depicting local customs in literature. In Mexico, Ignacio Manuel

Altamirano made the same argument in a landmark essay reviewing the progress of Mexican literature up to 1868, after which he wrote two classic novels that featured *costumbrista* themes and techniques: *Clemencia* (1869) and *El Zarco the Blue-Eyed Bandit* (1901).

It's not surprising that the citizens of newly independent nations turned their eyes, pens, and printing presses inward. Now that these societies were *not* Spanish, how would they define, catalog, and celebrate their newfound identity? The printing press could play a key role in building a gallery of characters, places, events, and aspirations that writers could claim as belonging to their nations. Nationalist writing provided a way to symbolically reconstruct culture after the destruction of the Wars of Independence. For that purpose, the *cuadro de costumbres* proved to be the most important kind of writing for visualizing who a nation's inhabitants were, and which forms of culture should be preserved or eliminated in the name of progress.

Print Matters

Literary taxonomies and questions of style and ideology are only one part of the story of the printed word. The materiality and availability of print shaped and sustained most conversations about knowledge, politics, and the arts, as well as promoting different kinds of reading and writing practices. One of the most important lessons about print culture in nineteenth-century Spanish America is the ubiquity and easy availability of newspapers and printed ephemera and the difficulties surrounding the printing and circulation of books, which were often prohibitively expensive.

Unless money was no object, an educated reader of reasonable means received most of his or her reading content by way of newspapers and literary magazines. From the middle of the century onward, our reader could choose from a wide array of such print: newspapers that dealt with politics, literary magazines, women's magazines, trade-specific publications, and satirical newspapers. Longer works, especially novels, were serialized in pamphlet form or embedded in the bottom half of daily newspapers, in one- or two-page installments per issue. These novels-by-installments were called *folletines* and were the primary mechanism for readers to experience fiction. For example, the first Mexican edition of *The Three Musketeers* by Alexandre Dumas was not in book form, but a *folletín* serialized on the front page of the newspaper *El Republicano* in

1847. One of the most celebrated and popular Spanish American novels of the nineteenth century, *María* (1867), by the Colombian Jorge Isaacs, was an early transnational bestseller because it was serialized in newspapers in both Argentina and Mexico. A copy of the novel's second edition landed in the offices of the Buenos Aires periodical *Revista Argentina* in 1870 by way of the Colombian consul in Chile, Don Jerónimo de la Ossa, who claimed that it was the last available copy in Chile. The magazine serialized the novel to immediate acclaim, leading to the first Argentine book edition in 1870. In the same year, Mexico saw the serialization of the novel in the newspaper *El Monitor Republicano* and the publication of the first of several Mexican editions in book form.[19]

Although the word *folletín* came to be used generically to designate serialization, whether as a loose "insert" separate from a newspaper or as a text embedded in the page of a newspaper, its original definition had the connotation of a guilty reading pleasure: it was sensationalist, sentimental, or melodramatic. Domingo Faustino Sarmiento described *folletines* as a dessert that cleanses the palate after a meal—a remedy for the tedium of political and philosophical subjects.[20] Often, as in the example of Dumas and other popular European novelists, Spanish American newspaper editors translated their serials straight out of European newspapers or books to make them available to local readers. This is how most of the giants of nineteenth-century European fiction—Dumas, Balzac, Dickens, et al.—found their way to Spanish American readers.[21]

The publication of books did occur, but it presented challenges. Printers were hesitant to publish books because of the high cost involved and because of the lack of any guarantee that readers would buy them. To address this problem, printers and booksellers made announcements in newspapers and book catalogs, seeking subscribers to commit to titles in advance. For a discounted price, a subscriber could reserve his or her copy of a book and, if enough funds were collected, ensure its printing and a modest profit for the bookseller.[22] For local authors, books were privileged objects of esteem and powerful symbols of writerly achievement, but it was notoriously difficult to finance them and to find an audience. Ignacio Manuel Altamirano bitterly complained in 1887 that it was almost impossible for an author to get a book published in Mexico. Unless a book was assured of becoming a best seller, printers would not front the money to print it. The cost to the author was prohibitive because of the cost of quality paper from Europe, which the Mexican state taxed heavily in order to protect local paper makers. In addition to the cost of quality paper and printing, prospective authors had to pay out of pocket for additional features, such as illustrations. The troubles didn't end there, Altamirano complained, because there weren't enough readers willing to buy the book after publication. After the author sent out two hundred copies of a print run of one thousand to newspapers and magazines for review, the already tiny pool of prospective readers was reduced further by the social pressure to gift copies to friends and acquaintances. Then there was the problem of literary societies, libraries, and clubs formally requesting that the author donate copies to their organizations. At the end of the day, the author was left with few readers who were actually willing to buy copies, and ended up selling the rest of his stock to a used bookseller, at a slashed price.[23]

Despite all these challenges, books were both imported from abroad and printed locally for readers. Where could readers browse and buy them? In the first half of the nineteenth century, dedicated bookstores were few, even in major metropolitan centers like Mexico City and Buenos Aires. Readers could locate books for sale in convenience stores and haberdasheries, and in popular market stalls in city plazas. Mexico City had a thriving commerce in books in the first half of the century, with well-stocked bookstores and movable book stalls, kiosks, and knickknack stores around the Plaza Mayor. On the corner of Mercaderes and Agustinos, a reader could stop at a shop run by a Don Antonio, a well-spoken gentleman with impeccably clean hands who wore a white vest and a long yellow calico jacket. The store was crowded with print matter: portraits of saints, catechisms, grammars, novels, recently printed newspapers, and pamphlets of every kind. It was a nerve center, where people congregated to discuss the news and to conduct all kinds of business.[24] For all except the most affluent, it was probably more tempting to buy several newspapers and pamphlets at Don Antonio's store rather than books, which were expensive. One volume could range from four to eight pesos, and a multivolume work could sell for upward of twenty pesos. A university professor made around six hundred pesos a year, meaning that the four volumes of the plays of the Golden Age Spanish playwright Pedro Calderón de la Barca would be equivalent to 5 percent of his yearly salary. For a schoolteacher making one hundred to two hundred pesos a year, the purchase of the same volumes would have been impossible.[25] In contrast, dailies and weeklies cost anywhere from ten to fifty cents per issue, and a peso or less for a monthly subscription.[26] As a point of comparison we go south to Argentina. The monthly salary of a rural worker in the 1870s ranged between 150 and 300 *pesos corrientes*, out of which that worker would have had to spend 3 pesos for a cheap broadside or periodical from Buenos Aires, and 20 pesos or more for an actual book.[27]

Most of the books for sale in Spanish American bookstores in the first half of the century were not by local authors. The 1829 catalog for a Buenos Aires bookseller listed only European titles and authors, with most hailing from France (144 titles) and Spain (94).[28] The Chilean writer José Victorino Lastarria remembered that at mid-century his country's printers published only around one hundred titles a year, of which only 10 percent were by local authors.[29] Most of the books printed were translations of European authors such as Charles Dickens, Jules Verne, Alexandre Dumas, and state- and church-funded translations of titles relating to education and theology.

If the Spanish American book trade and printing scene was relatively poor and dependent in the first half of the nineteenth century, the second half saw a veritable flood of titles published in Europe for readers of Spanish in the Americas. The case of *María*, which had over forty editions between 1867 and 1900, underscores this phenomenon. In the 1870s, Argentinian and Mexican publishers disseminated the novel, with four editions apiece, while the period of 1880–1900 saw the globalization of *María*, with at least a dozen editions printed out of Barcelona, eight editions out of Paris, and two editions of an English translation of the novel. Although Argentina, Mexico, Peru, and Chile continued to publish the novel locally, the flood of European editions depressed the market for local editions. Scholarship on early nineteenth-century publishing in Europe and the United States tells us that average print runs were at least one thousand copies per title, which tracks with the print run of *María*'s first edition, and Isaacs's target for the second.[30] That said, Spanish and French publishers who capitalized on the transnational market for books in Spain and Spanish America published titles with print runs that could run from five thousand to ten thousand. This means that anywhere between sixty thousand and one hundred thousand copies of *María* circulated between 1867 and 1900, excluding serializations in newspapers and literary magazines.[31]

Such isolated successes notwithstanding, the most important and successful form of print matter in Spanish America was simply the newspaper. In the first half of the century, while civil wars raged, it was common for newspapers to be partisan publications drenched in political propaganda. The papers were also organized in irregular ways, mixing *folletines* with *costumbrista* sketches and news stories. Later on, the daily newspaper began to redefine itself as a commercial, independent venture with a structure that subordinated literary and cultural miscellanies to the news. When former Argentina president Bartolomé Mitre founded the newspaper *La Nación* in 1870, he declared that its mission was "to propagate and defend the principles" of the Liberal Party and the Argentine state.[32] Beginning in 1875, however, the newspaper began to push in a different direction, as indicated by the journalist who wrote that the paper was now moving "into a more solid terrain . . . into the current of information from which it had been separated, and which is the principal source on which journalism feeds."[33]

Another change was at work as well. Until the last quarter of the century, the boundaries between different kinds of writing (political, pedagogical, literary, news, etc.) were blurred, empowering journalists to conceive of themselves as architects of opinion and social change. This changed at the end of the century, when newspaper editors pigeonholed journalistic writing as a form of technical writing.[34] In other words, authors who had conceived of their newspaper writing in a broad, loose sense had to adjust to becoming a very specific kind of writer: a reporter. Some of the greatest writers of the turn of the century, such as Rubén Darío, José Martí, and Manuel Gutiérrez Nájera, chafed under the pressure of writing short articles to order for newspapers. They aspired to be *writers*, not simply reporters. In his classic 1888 tale "The Bourgeois King," Darío wrote about the inhospitable climate in which literary artists were working at the end of the century. The story describes a lush, fairy-tale-like land inhabited by a rich, bourgeois king who collects objects without appreciating their intrinsic or spiritual value. One day the king discovers a writer on his castle grounds and adds him to his collection of entertainments. Although the writer claims to have access to deep, transcendental truths, the king relegates him to turning the handle of a music box in a garden where, covered in snow, he dies of exposure. As this melancholy fantasy shows, the technology of printing and the utilitarian redefinition of writing were a kind of mechanization that threatened more outdated romantic ideas about what it meant to be a writer in society.

In response to these changes, a diverse array of specialized publications in which readers and writers could indulge in literary explorations or partisan politics emerged. Literary and cultural magazines catered to the leisure class and featured the writings of poets and literary essayists. Advances in photographic reproduction, and the dramatic rise of advertising for consumer goods directed to middle- and upper-class readers, gave rise to fancy, illustrated glossies like *Caras y Caretas* in Argentina, *Paginas Ilustradas* in Costa Rica, and *Musa Americana* in Chile. These attractive magazines, close relatives of twentieth-century magazines, featured sharp photographs of important personages, socialites, and landscapes, as well as lush illustrations and artistic graphic design. The magazine, freed from the burden of politics, emerged as a luxurious commodity that was more than the sum of its articles. In contrast, cheaply produced newspapers—catering to different interest groups, clubs, or tradespeople—attacked their political rivals through vehement opinion pieces and risqué political caricatures. For example, Mexican, Argentinian, and Peruvian socialists and anarchists published newspapers at the end of the century that attacked middle-class people, factory owners, and politicians, often with violent language and sexual innuendo. One Buenos Aires anarchist commentator attacked bourgeois reporters for being active and passive sodomites of the pen who were paid to print lies.[35] The title page of the working-class Mexican newspaper *Don Cucufate* shows the publication's titular don with a threatening, phallic pen looming over a ballerina, a bourgeois matron, a gentleman, a policeman, and the dictator Porfirio Díaz.[36] In short, by the dawn of the twentieth century, there was a broadening of print offerings for different kinds of urban readers, as well as continued specialization among those offerings.

Reading and Association

One of the most widely read and respected authors in nineteenth-century Spanish America was the French writer Anne Louise Germaine de Staël-Holstein, known as Madame de Staël (1766–1817). Besides publishing numerous popular novels, Madame de Staël published an influential treatise on the social, historical, and moral implications of literature titled *Literature Considered in Its Relations with Social Institutions* (1800).[37] Staël argued that great literature triggered "a kind of moral and physical emotion, an agitating transport of admiration" that infuses the very blood and organs with revelations and incentives for virtuous action. For Madame de Staël, the spiritual and physical chemistry of this kind of inspiration was best acquired through recitation and association, rather than solitary reading.[38] To enact this kind of literary sociability, Madame de Staël hosted a literary salon out of her home in Paris beginning in 1776 at which men and women recited and conversed about literature.[39] This kind of association, predicated on the belief that words had to be performed in community to activate their civilizing power, was an important component of nineteenth-century Spanish American intellectual and social life.

At the outset, it's important to underline that Spanish American reading clubs took a variety of overlapping forms. Sometimes, printers and bookstores provided space for writers to come together to read and discuss literature, as in the case of the bookstore of Marcos Sastre in Buenos Aires in 1837, the bookstore of Mariano Gálvez in Mexico City in the 1840s, and Bogotá's Mosaico Club. Another space for reading and association was the *gabinete de lectura* (reading room), a kind of pay-by-subscription library in which patrons could sample, on site, an array of newspapers, magazines, and books. These reading rooms could be modest or more upscale, but they all provided their patrons with a place to socialize and discuss the ideas of the day. Clubs and private societies (of tradespeople or of gentlemen who shared a particular interest) might set up reading rooms for their members, and governments sometimes provided support for the establishment of reading rooms for the working class.[40] In the words of one Mexican commentator, "On the day in which our artisans, upon leaving their workshops, go to the reading room instead of making their way to a tavern, society can rest easy because it is not possible to think about crime when the mind is occupied and the soul moved . . . by the feelings inspired by reading good books."[41] One of the more structured and ambitious forms of reading association were elite clubs, which I already touched on in Chapter 1. Such clubs contained libraries, and sometimes hosted events and instruction related to academic subjects.

The purest form of literary association, however, was the literary salon as practiced by Madame de Staël and others in eighteenth-century France: a ritualized social gathering, held at a private residence, that celebrated community, refinement, elevated feeling, and intellectual curiosity. The most fascinating literary salon of nineteenth-century Spanish America belonged to an extraordinary woman who might be deserving of the title of the "Spanish American Madame de Staël." I am referring to the literary salon of the exiled Argentinian writer Juana Manuela Gorriti, which was held in the summer of 1876 at her lodgings at 188 Cumaná Street in Lima, Peru. Gorriti hailed from an elite family from northern Argentina that fled to Bolivia when she was thirteen because of the rise of the Federalist caudillos Facundo Quiroga and Juan Manuel de Rosas. In Bolivia, the fifteen-year-old Gorriti married a soldier called Manuel Isidoro Belzú who eventually became president of Bolivia, and had two daughters with him. Belzú's military and political career resulted in Gorriti settling in Lima with their daughters, where she ran a school for girls, and where she gave birth to two children fathered by a businessman called Julio Sandoval. (In spite of these developments, she maintained a close friendship with Belzú until he was assassinated in 1865). Gorriti spent the rest of her life distinguishing herself as a cultural and political ambassador, gaining recognition for her work as a nurse during the War of the Pacific, returning to Argentina to negotiate pensions for veterans of the Wars of Independence and tirelessly living the literary life in Lima and Buenos Aires until her death in 1892. Indeed, Gorriti was arguably one of the most recognized and respected women writers in nineteenth-century Spanish America.[42]

Gorriti was a powerful and charismatic person whose intelligence, erudition, and energy commanded the respect and loyalty of members of Lima's cultural elite, who respected her as a paragon of virtue and enlightened learning. Her literary salon meetings, which were held on Wednesday nights, starting at 8 or 9 p.m. and ending well past midnight, illustrate the confidence that readers and writers had in the civilizing power of literature as a communal experience. On more than one occasion, in their lectures and recitations, members of the salon extolled the virtues of the salon experience. In one of her lectures, Doña Rosa Orbegoso, a well-known member of the city's elite, declared that unity is strength, especially when it came to using the regenerative powers of literature "like a searchlight."[43] Mercedes Cabello de Carbonera, one of nineteenth-century Peru's most important woman writers, echoed these sentiments in an essay she read at the first meeting of Gorriti's gatherings: "When it is cultivated by clear intelligences and well-intentioned hearts, Literature is the purest and most beneficent light that can reach the conscience of a people; it is best at scrubbing out bad customs and the vicious habits of a society."[44] The major newspapers of Lima—*El Nacional, La Opinión Nacional,* and *El Comercio*—wrote glowing reviews of the activities held at each salon, exulting in how the meetings inspired the soul and elevated the mind to great heights.

What transpired at these meetings? Gorriti opened each gathering with brief words of gratitude and encouragement, after which writers and members of Lima's elite proceeded to read poems (sentimental or patriotic), educational tracts (on the value of literature and the education of women), historical miscellanies (such as Palma's historical traditions), and short stories. The act of recitation was not necessarily passive; one of the entertainments of the salon was for a poet to read a poem in the form of a charade that audience members would compete to decipher. Literary contests and bets were held that required winners and losers to write compositions on particular topics, which they would recite publicly at subsequent meetings. Interspersed throughout were music performances on the piano, including European compositions (such as the overture to *William Tell* on piano, for four hands) and the singing of *yaravíes*, an indigenous Peruvian lament usually accompanied by a flute. This kind of nationalist appreciation of Peruvian and Spanish American culture also extended to the exhibition of an oil painting of an Inca mummy during one meeting, and the raffling of a terra-cotta sculpture of a *payador* (gaucho singer) at another.

One of the striking features of Gorriti's salon was the way it included—even emphasized—women in the conversation about literature and culture. Many women writers read compositions at the salon, and its members listened to more than one presentation exalting the ways in which enlightened womanhood was central to the building of modern societies. One male attendee reminisced about how Clorinda Matto de Turner, who later became one of Peru's most successful and controversial novelists, was first introduced and received at the salon:

> With her own hands, Señora Gorriti rested a rich filigree crown on the head of the young and beautiful author . . . and put in her hands a valuable pen and a gold notecard, while at the same time giving her a magnificent set of expensive buttons—a token from her woman friends and an homage from her sisters in letters. That party was one of the most splendid. . . . Poets sang the virtues of the young author and we all rushed to put a flower at her feet, as a humble tribute of affection and admiration.[45]

The association of literary salons with women was strong in Western culture thanks to eighteenth-century French women like Madame de Lambert, Madame du Deffand, and Madame de Staël. Juana Manuela Gorriti capitalized on that distinguished history, not only to take upon herself the role of hostess, but in recruiting writers and gentlemen and gentlewomen to agree that a woman-driven conversation was a valuable and even admirable enterprise.

Gorriti's neighbors included Mariano Ulloa (a blacksmith), José Sebastián Heredia and Agustín Reller (both carpenters), Ana Quesnel (a seamstress), and Valentín Chávez (a tailor).[46] These artisans and service providers did not move in the same social circle as most of the attendees of their distinguished neighbor's salon, and were probably not on the guest list of this or any other literary salon as we have described it. This begs the question of what kinds of associations were available to readers and consumers of texts who did not belong to the elite. The answer may be found in a *costumbrista* painting by the Mexican José Agustín Arrieta called *Tertulia de pulquería* (Pulquería gathering; 1851). The painting shows a gathering of rough-looking working men drinking pulque, a white spirit made from fermented agave, as they congregate around a table, handling newspapers titled *El Maquinista* (The machinist), *El Mite* (The mite), and *La Mojiganga* (The Farce). A woman in a white blouse and a red skirt leans over the table with her mouth agape in merriment, surprise, or drunkenness. Across from her, a man in a dark top hat and a dark overcoat has his finger on the sheet of *El Mite*. Thus, while intellectuals held literary salons in private homes, commoners like those depicted in this painting met in saloons to recite and to circulate the printed word. Since colonial times, official and unofficial town criers, night watchmen, and traveling troubadours (like the accordion-playing newscaster Francisco el Hombre in *One Hundred Years of Solitude*), had spoken, sung, and declaimed the news while those who did not know how to read crowded nearby.[47]

The story of how print could be a part of communities that were largely illiterate takes us to the Southern Cone, to the territories that are now the countries of Uruguay and Argentina, where a culture of unlettered plainsmen called *gauchos* emerged in colonial times and survived until the middle of the nineteenth century. During the era of Independence and the civil wars that followed, gauchos were continuously conscripted into battle, giving rise to a genre of poetry called "the gauchesque" that was based on their speech and culture. In this literature, non-gaucho poets sought to imitate the gaucho and write poetry about society and politics in his distinctive voice and with his vocabulary. This kind of minstrelsy could either consist of insubstantial parodies for elite readers with prejudiced views of the gaucho or more populist statements directed to the gauchos themselves.[48] The first poet of the gauchesque, Bartolomé Hidalgo, adopted the style of *cielitos* (rural ballads) to print populist verses on broadsides intended for rural readers. In his poems, published in the first two decades of the nineteenth century, he attacked elites for discriminating against the rural poor and the valiant gaucho veterans of the civil wars that followed Independence.[49]

Because the gauchesque straddled print and oral culture, populist forms of the gauchesque lent themselves to public performance and dissemination as mass literature. Poems of the populist gauchesque were printed and circulated as broadsides or in cheaply produced newspapers for the purpose of being read aloud in public places. In fact, the character of a town crier or broadside reader appears in the poetry of Bartolomé Hidalgo and others, reading or singing the news to crowds of rough country people in *pulperías*, establishments that functioned both as saloons and general stores.[50] The fact that gauchesque poetry was modeled on song facilitated its reentry into the oral culture that inspired it in the first place. All it took was one *payador* to put a gauchesque poem to music for it to take on a life of its own as singers passed it on to others, making improvisations along the way and changing the original. Indeed, there was a thriving market for gauchesque poems and writings in mid-nineteenth-century Argentina and an increasing recognition by journalists and politicians that print culture could be used as political propaganda to reach both cosmopolitans and underdogs. For example, in the 1830s, a Federalist newspaperman called Luis Pérez produced an astonishing number of newspapers and printed material themed around gaucho and cattle culture, all keyed to an oral register and elements of gaucho life and experience. The popular success of Pérez's poems among the poor was such that Argentina's ruler, Juan Manuel de Rosas, marveled at how Pérez could draw crowds of peasants to "gather in throngs . . . fighting for a space" to listen to his gauchesque verses.[51]

The cliché "knowledge is power" helps to explain why elites and political authorities were wary of printing that could reach illiterate people, and writers and readers who might help the illiterate consume forms of print that were rebellious or at least critical of existing social hierarchies. Perhaps the novelist and printer José Joaquín Fernández de Lizardi was such a facilitator; he joked that his readers were "plebeians, Indians, mulattos, blacks, criminals, fools, and idiots."[52] Although today he is commonly read as an author of classic novels, in his lifetime most of his print was deeply invested in rabble-rousing and mocking authority. Less remembered are the *evangelistas* (letter writers) and *tinterillos* (copyists) who gathered in the Portal de los Agustinos near Mexico City's Plaza Mayor, eking out a modest living helping illiterate people understand

Figure 2.3. Gaucho of the Argentine Republic, circa 1870. Courtesy
of the Library of Congress, LC-DIG-ppmsca-19409.

written communications, and writing letters and documents for them. Authorities and respectable journalists complained about how these low-class scribblers sometimes fomented unrest among the masses with their speeches and their cheap pamphlets and flyers.[53] Such men were advocates for the disenfranchised and potential leaders of their cause. On the border between Brazil and Uruguay, an Afro-descendant named Jacinto Ventura de Molina was precisely such a defender of the people. His love of reading and writing and his dedication to using letters to promote equality and justice provoked bitter recriminations by white men of letters, who called him a mad Ethiopian savage. The son of slaves, Ventura de Molina was raised and educated under the protection of his family's former master, Josef de Molina. His uneducated parents and his beloved wife nurtured his love of learning and encouraged him on the path of letters. While Portugal occupied Uruguay in 1817, Emperor Pedro I conferred on him the title of defender of the poor and blacks, which allowed Ventura de Molina to use his pen to argue for the rights of the powerless. After the removal of Portuguese forces from Uruguay, Ventura de Molina continued to use his pen to defend the interests of Afro-descendant groups and individuals, as well as those of poor whites. He saw himself as a reformer and an educator of his people, working assiduously to gather funds to start a school where they could improve their standing in society through learning. Yet, throughout his career, Ventura de Molina was embattled by racist critics who mocked his claims to knowledge and the written word.[54]

Another kind of disquieting, mediating figure who straddled the worlds of orality and print was the *lector* or reader, who read newspapers and books out loud to workers in cigar factories in the Caribbean and the United States. Political authorities banned the practice on and off during the last quarter of the century because they discovered that through the recitation of words from the printed page, new ideas had a way of breeding class consciousness and resistance to power.[55] In cigar factories in Puerto Rico, Cuba, the Dominican Republic, Mexico, Florida, and New York, the *lectores* sat or stood at special prosceniums or balconies and read newspapers, popular novels by authors like Dumas, Tolstoy, Hugo, and Verne, or political writings by socialists like Mikhail Bakunin and even Karl Marx. One famous reader was the Puerto Rican essayist and labor organizer Luisa Capetillo, who was fond of dressing like a man (in trousers and a hat), and who made it her life's mission to defend workers and their interests in Puerto Rico, Cuba, and Florida.[56] Jesús Colón, who published a memoir titled *A Puerto Rican in New York and Other Sketches* in 1961, remembered hearing in turn-of-the-century Puerto Rico the voice of the *lector* drifting out from a nearby factory through his bedroom window. Colón remembered that some *lectores* were so adept that they could close the book and recite from memory while a fellow worker read along in the book to see if they could catch any mistakes.[57]

Words were powerful in nineteenth-century Spanish America because they had the power to convene people, cement relationships, and promote values and interests for different ends. Whether a person was a reader or a listener of words, the words consolidated the beliefs of the community to which that person belonged. The collective reading of words was a kind of cultural glue that defined a group's identity. The men and women who stepped down from their carriages on Cumaná Street to enter Juana Manuela Gorriti's house represented the viewpoint that reading and association represented national progress and the refinement of their social rank. The lovers of print who gathered in Mexican *pulquerías* or Argentine *pulperías* to listen to the reading of a broadside or a newspaper article, holding drinks and stringed instruments in their rough, calloused hands, laughed louder and moved more freely; they talked back to power, and cheered when the letters took the shape of their own speech and worldview.

María and the Weeping Continent

What did nineteenth-century Spanish American readers *enjoy* reading? What kinds of reading and writing meant the most to them? The answers to these questions lead us into different directions, depending on what kinds of readers we focus on. Within the constituency of educated readers of novels, the most popular novel of the century was *María* (1867), by Jorge Isaacs. It was the most widely reprinted and praised novel throughout Spanish America, with at least forty editions between 1867 and 1900, several serializations, and various transatlantic editions published by the French publishers Garnier Brothers (six editions) and Bouret (two editions), and the Spanish publishers Biblioteca Arte y Letras (four editions) and Maucci (one edition). The writer Francisco Sosa claimed that in Mexico alone, over one hundred editions of the novel had been published in twenty years, including cheap serializations and foreign-made editions with luxury bindings.[58] As one contemporary wrote, *María* was the only book written in the Americas that had made readers weep from the Cauca Valley in Colombia to the River Plate in Argentina.[59] It also made readers north of the Cauca cry, all the way to the Río Grande and across the Spanish Caribbean.

Jorge Isaacs was a man of paradoxes and extremes. As the son of an erratic slave owner who held land in the Cauca Valley in northwestern Colombia, he supported the conservative faction in his country's civil wars. When the liberal Federalist general Tomás Cipriano de Mosquera rose up against President Mariano Ospina Rodríguez, Isaacs enlisted to fight against Mosquera. Later, between 1866 and 1869, he served as a high-ranking conservative congressman in Colombia's legislative branch. Yet, in 1869, Isaacs rejected the conservative party and became a liberal, declaring that he had passed from the darkness into the light. As a liberal, he supported the separation of church and state, espoused Federalism, and tirelessly promoted the idea of a free and secular educational system. During a conservative revolt in 1876, he fought to defend the liberal cause, but in 1880 his political career ended in disgrace when he led a failed rebellion in the state of Antioquia. The paradoxes of Isaacs's biography don't end with politics, however. For years he struggled without success to restore his family's lands in the Cauca Valley, while having to make a hardscrabble living as a clerk, a government employee, and a scientific explorer. And despite the fact that he wrote one of the most celebrated and reprinted novels of his time, he did not profit from his literary creation, and was never able to write anything else that appealed to a broad readership. Perhaps the generalization that best applies to his life story and psychology is that loss and a deep yearning were major forces in his life and he expressed both of them admirably well in his iconic novel.

María tells the story of seventeen-year-old Efraín, who returns to his family's hacienda in the Cauca Valley after being schooled in Bogotá. There his parents, his sisters, and his beautiful thirteen-year-old cousin María joyously welcome him home.[60] María has lived with the family since she was three years old, when Efraín's father brought her home from one of his trips to the Caribbean. Efraín's father had spent his youth in Jamaica; he was a European immigrant of Jewish descent, but had become a Christian to marry Efraín's Colombian mother. His cousin Salomón, however, had married another Jew, Sarah, who died when their daughter Esther was an infant. The mournful widower, who admired Christianity for its comforts and consolations, asked Efraín's father to adopt Esther, christen her María, and raise her as a Christian. He does, and Efraín grows up with María until his departure to boarding school. Now that

Efraín has returned from Bogotá, love begins to blossom between the adolescents. They chastely woo each other through timid, oblique glances, through tender acts (exchanging flowers and locks of hair), and through shared experiences like reading Chateaubriand's sentimental novel *Atala*. Tragically, the power of María's feelings for Efraín triggers the life-threatening nervous condition she inherited from her mother. To protect the girl, Efraín's father demands that his son not marry her for a few years, until after Efraín completes his education in Europe. While the young man is in London, María falls ill and dies before he can return to her side. The novel ends with Efraín weeping over María's grave while a crow lands on its iron cross and ominously caws.

This abbreviated summary doesn't do justice to the vivid descriptions, incidents, and inset stories that populate the novel. In true romantic fashion, Isaacs lovingly evokes natural landscapes and scenes to reflect the moods and desires of Efraín. He also offers sketches of hacienda country life, where slaves live, love, and thrive under the benevolent protection of Efraín's father. One of the most vivid episodes of the novel is a jaguar hunt in which Efraín courageously proves his manhood in front of his friends by killing his prey with a single shot to the animal's head. Efraín also recounts the life story of Feliciana, his African governess and the mother of his loyal houseboy, Juan Angel. The inset novel tells the story of Feliciana's youth in Africa, where her name was Nay and she was the beautiful daughter of an Ashanti warrior-chief. In other parts of the novel, Isaacs also introduces other important characters, such as Efraín's Bogotá school friends Carlos and Emigdio who, like him, are trying to reintegrate themselves into country living.

The dominant theme of *María* is the end of Eden, which Isaacs highlights through his treatment of the parallel fates of the three young men who have returned to the Cauca Valley from the city. Efraín, Carlos, and Emigdio are symbols of the fading away of the old hacienda way of life. Carlos is an alienated dandy with little interest in country life, marriage, or procreation. During a hunting excursion, for example, he literally shoots blanks, and he is unable to secure María's hand in marriage. The rougher and undeniably virile Emigdio is also drifting away from the old landed aristocracy by pursuing new commercial interests, and by having an unsanctioned love affair with a mestiza. Finally, Efraín is unable to recreate and perpetuate the old ways of life when the love of his life, María, dies.

What made *María* so popular across Spanish America? No other work by a Spanish American author crossed so many national boundaries and struck such a deep personal chord in readers. Part of the answer lies in literary tastes and nineteenth-century reading habits. *María* was fashioned to please because it was an American version of two French novels that were enormously well known in Europe and the Americas: *Paul and Virginia* (1788) by Henri Bernardin de Saint-Pierre, and *Atala* (1801) by François-René de Chateaubriand. In Isaacs's novel, *Atala* is the book that precipitates María's fateful epileptic attack, and is clearly the inspiration of the plot of the inset story about Feliciana's youth in Africa, among other obvious parallels. By effectively rewriting *Paul and Virginia* and *Atala*, and fusing them together into a unified, Spanish American tale of love and loss, *María* overtook these literary influences and became more impactful. Why dwell on those exotic tales of faraway tropical lands when *María* was set in an equally enchanting Eden situated in South America?[61]

The idea that *María* was superior to its European predecessors because it was American and not European was not only a cultural argument, it was also a personal one. Readers of the novel remarked on how the ambience, the flavor of Efraín's day-to-day life in the Cauca Valley, and the secondary characters reflected a reality that they proudly proclaimed as their own. Unlike foreign fictions, identified with artifice and sensationalism, there was a powerful dose of ordinariness in *María* on which its admiring readers projected their experiences and national types. José María Vergara y Vergara, who helped Isaacs publish *María* and who wrote the preface to the first edition, was the first reader to make this argument, referring to the work as a faithful chronicle of and homage to rural domestic life.[62] The great accomplishment of Isaacs, he argued, was taking a prosaic universal (the home) and making it poetic. Other non-Colombian critics agreed.[63] *María* was thus not only the novel of the continent because of its international dissemination but because it was the first novel interpreted as belonging, by right of experience and verisimilitude, to the entire continent.

The most important factor that drove the popularity of *María*, however, was its emotional power, specifically its ability to make readers, men and women alike, weep. "That book is written in tears," wrote the Colombian poet Silveria Espinosa de Rendón, summing up one of the biggest commonplaces in readers' responses to the novel.[64] This tearful response was not limited to women readers, who were the sensitive audience *par excellence*, but experienced also by men, who made their tears over Efraín and María a metaphor for their spiritual refinement and a corroboration of the novel's deep truths.[65] The pleasures of weeping reflected a culture of sensibility based on eliciting human emotion and celebrating it as an expression of sincerity, spiritual truth, and even superior morality and human connection.[66] Isaacs explicitly sought to stage the tears of sensibility through the dedication of his novel, which called on his readers to weep if the book touched their hearts.

All these tears were not devoid of political content. The tears that propelled the novel into becoming a continental best seller expressed doubt about historical change in Spanish America and its place vis-à-vis Europe's commanding political and cultural influence. The sentimental power of the novel was tied to the fact that, like Efraín mourning the loss of his love in its final pages, readers recognized a parallel loss of innocence in their own lives and culture because of the advances of materialism and European ideas. Commentators from different countries canonized the novel because they saw it as an antidote to the corruptions of foreign influence and unrestrained materialism. María was a refuge from history that encapsulated a universalist and often explicitly religious definition of Spanish American innocence.[67] Maybe it was inevitable because María, through its sentimental power, had a way of linking tears to the alienation provoked by modernization. Readers interiorized the story of Efraín and María as an inner landscape of feeling tied to memories of childhood and sanctified scenes of familial domesticity. Anything foreign to that interiority of feeling, and to those memories of simpler times, became a symbol of decadence and deterioration. Cities, politics, wars, technology, and all the foreign ideas and books stood on the outside of that sacred mansion of feeling inspired by the tear-stained pages of María.

The Printing of the People

Reading María was a safe rite of passage across the Spanish American continent. The novel featured idealized scenes of domesticity in a rural household that observed conservative Catholic traditions and loving family relationships. The love between the star-crossed lovers was chaste and posed no threat to the morality of young readers, male or female. The slaves, peasants, and ranchers who populated the novel's agrarian world idolized young Efraín, resulting in an idealized representation of a well-functioning, peaceful social hierarchy. The novel also appealed to readers who were schooled in the refined literary traditions of sentimentality and romanticism, and who were predisposed to identify with Efraín's privileged family. For these reasons, despite the novel's tremendous reach, it was not popular literature as we will define it here. For cultural elites, writing represented civilization and progress. It negated the body and its instincts, which were associated with sensual pleasure, disorder, and violence, and affirmed the cultivation of the mind and the soul, as well as the improvement of society. Writing was a symbol of order and hierarchy in a social world populated with people of different ethnicities and rank. In contrast, popular writing expressed the realities, pastimes, and mindscapes of commoners in ways that cut against the grain of these elite definitions and value judgments. It affirmed pleasure by encouraging laughter, rage, or sensuality, or preserved traditions and beliefs that members of the elite considered backward or out of step with modern ideas. As we will see below, popular literature was also capable of criticizing the conventions and prejudices of elite culture, or the injustice of the reigning social system.

The distinction between writing and orality is an important one for our conversation because the literature of the people did not primarily spring from lettered learning or books, but from everyday life and everyday speech. When popular literature began to circulate broadly in the nineteenth century, it generally mimicked the speech of everyday people, rather than the refined language of the educated. The source of popular literature, then, is a voice that laughs, pokes fun, and maybe even shocks its listeners. Consider, for example, the streetwise voice of Mexico's Little Black Poet, whose fame was such that he became a populist icon in the nineteenth century. In *The Mangy Parrot*, José Joaquín Fernández de Lizardi mentions José Vasconcelos (1700–1760?), an illiterate man of Congolese descent from the Mexican village of Almolonga. According to legend, Vasconcelos was so good at improvising verses that people gave him the honorific *El Negrito Poeta.* Little is known about who he really was and which of the poems attributed to him were really his, but his reputation lived on long after his death. In Lizardi's novel, an erudite parish priest relates incidents about the Little Black Poet, such as the story that on his deathbed he greeted the friar who was going to take his final confession with an improvisation that goes like this:

Now I know, for sure and of course,
That death is fast on my heels,
Because wherever the vulture reels,
There's bound to be a dying horse.[68]

The Little Black Poet became a popular character in the Mexican puppet theater, as well as the protagonist of a series of cheaply produced calendars and almanacs published between 1855 and 1872. These almanacs were primarily consumed by a humbler class of readers that included farmers, artisans, housewives, and schoolteachers, and contained information about religious holidays, feast days, and the lives of the saints, as well as astronomical data, patriotic miscellany, and even recipes. In the almanacs named after the Little Black Poet, printers included pages of anecdotes about the clever jokester improvising poems and interacting with different kinds of people.[69]

Another important dimension of popular literature was that it was difficult to separate from other forms of cultural expression. The composition of stories and poems for commoners began on the street and in the countryside as musical or oral traditions that were later converted into print. The association of popular poetry with music makes sense; music was the primary mode of transmission of verse among the masses, so the distribution of song lyrics in print functioned as a kind of poetry of the people, regardless of whether or not these lyrics were originally written to music or later put to music. One notable example of popular literature in relation to music is illustrated by our previous discussion of gauchesque literature, in which gaucho song is mimicked in print. Another example may be found in late nineteenth-century Mexico's most important printer, Antonio Vanegas Arroyo, whose print matter was cheaply produced at his crowded Mexico City workshop and on the cheapest Mexican paper available.[70] Vanegas Arroyo oversaw the publication of sensational crime stories, satirical flyers, children's literature, courtship handbooks, puppet theater scripts, magic books, and news reports, most of which were sold at the price of one or two cents and distributed throughout the country.[71] Among the most notable offerings of his print shop were songs that celebrated local heroes and events. By publishing a news item in verse form, Vanegas Arroyo implied that his papers came from the people and were directed to the people. After all, people used songs to tell stories about the world around them, which meant that to publish news in the form of songs was a way of honoring and furthering the populist tradition of singing the news, rather than merely printing it.

A revealing example of how popular literature was linked to other forms of expression is the *listín* (bullfighting advertisement) of Lima. Afro-descendant children sold the *listines* on the streets, loudly calling on the city's inhabitants to attend a *corrida* (bullfight) with their signature street cry of "*Y á claaa ri táaa!* Who wants to see this dirty bull break this afternoon? *Y á claaa ri táaa!*"[72] The *listínes* had been put to political use during the Wars of Independence to disseminate royalist propaganda against the patriots, but in the post-Independence era they were primarily playbills that combined the listing of bulls and horses with poems that celebrated the spectacle of bullfighting, or with risqué verses about love, sex, and class conflict.[73] One *listín*, for example, is a dialogue between two women of limited means, Catalina and Miquita. The dialogue begins with Miquita complaining that she really wants to go to the bullfight but she does not have money because her husband is a no-good lazybones. She tells Catalina that she plans on using her feminine wiles to seduce an ugly humpback in her neighborhood to procure money for her and her friend to attend the bullfight, which she ultimately does. At the bottom of the *listín*, the printers have placed two columns, one decorated with a male bust, and the other with a woman's image. Under the image of the man we read: "Damned be the man who trusts in the words of women, damned is he who procreates with them; love is a foolish conceit to gain a want; it is a fruit of the mind that, when realized, provokes suffering and irritation, hurt and remorse." To the right, under the image of the woman, we read: "Unfortunate is the woman who trusts in man, the day of her ruin and suffering is not far off: they know how to make promises when they are in love, fields tinted in gold, delights, love, all that is fine but in the end just sorrow, all of them are wicked men."[74] The printer knows that there are two points of view to present underneath the telling of Miquita's adultery, one corresponding to men, and another to women. In either case, the substance of the *listín*'s story is not tied to ideas of refinement, patriotism, science, historical memory, or any other concept integral to elite writing and its civilizing designs. This *listín*, like others of its kind, was a call to pleasure: first, an invitation to the lowbrow blood sport of bullfighting, and second, a lighthearted and risqué entertainment that could be debated and enjoyed by men and women alike.

Martín Fierro's Crossover Appeal

Our discussion so far has emphasized the contrast between popular print and elite print and encourages us to think oppositionally about the two. However, there are examples of print that belonged to both camps—to literature with a capital "L" as well as to the reading and cultural habits of commoners. Possibly the most notable example of this intersection may

Figure 2.4. Seller of *listines* (bullfight notices), from *Lima; or,
Sketches from the Capital of Peru* (1866) by Manuel Atanasio
Fuentes. Nettie Lee Benson Latin American Collection,
University of Texas Libraries, The University of Texas at Austin.

be found in the genre of the gauchesque, which I introduced above. Two
of the most popular poems of the gauchesque were *The Gaucho Martín Fierro* (1872) and its sequel, *The Return of Martín Fierro* (1879), by
José Hernández. Hernández's contribution to the gauchesque demonstrates how the same printed words could mean different things to different classes of readers and belong to more than one constituency. The
print run of the first edition of *The Gaucho Martín Fierro* is unknown,
but the poem was so popular that it was republished fifteen times in the
next twenty years, in addition to an unknown number of pirated editions, reaching a total print run of at least sixty-four thousand copies by

the turn of the century.[75] Fernán Silva Valdés, who grew up to become a well-known, early twentieth-century Uruguayan writer, reminisced that as a child he visited some peons at his father's landed estate to tell them of his budding interest in literary representations about gauchos. What happened next was an unusual inversion of the patriarchal power relations of the countryside: the rustics told the landowner's son what it was that he should read, not vice versa. They told him to read *The Gaucho Martín Fierro*. Silva Valdés did, and the poem inspired him so deeply that it helped propel him into a successful literary career as a gauchesque writer and poet.[76]

The Gaucho Martín Fierro contains thirteen cantos and is voiced by Fierro, who sings the story of his life as an outlaw. A local judge who is angered by Fierro's political independence forces him into military service on the frontier, holding the line against the Indians. Fierro escapes the fort to make his way back to his wife and children, only to discover his home in ruins and his family gone. Desolate and brokenhearted, Fierro vows to be as "mean as a tiger / whose cubs have been stolen."[77] At a local dance, he drunkenly mocks a black couple and kills the man in a brawl. Later on, he duels with a local troublemaker and kills him as well, leading authorities to form a posse to hunt him. When Fierro valiantly confronts the posse, his bravery inspires one of his foes, a gaucho called Cruz, to switch sides and help him disperse the attackers. Cruz offers Fierro his hand in friendship and proposes that they make a life together as outlaws. Fierro accepts and tells Cruz that his plan is to escape persecution and start a new life by turning his back on civilization and crossing the frontier into Indian territory. Our sad and valiant protagonist breaks his guitar and the two men cross into Indian territory, not to be heard from again. Well, at least not until the sequel.

In the preface to the first edition of the poem, Hernández outlines the purpose of his poem: to faithfully capture the colorful and contradictory essence of the gaucho without mocking his primitive manners and speech. He describes the gaucho as an inherently original and metaphorical being schooled by Nature; he is primitive, superstitious, arrogant, and prone to violence. Most importantly, however, the gaucho is misunderstood and becoming extinct. These prefatory comments are circumspect and polite—why the gaucho is becoming extinct is not spelled out—but Hernández embeds four newspaper quotations after the body of the preface that directly answer the question. Each quote, pulled from the newspaper *La Nación*, damns the excesses of Argentine authorities in

Figure 2.5. Frontispiece of the fifteenth edition of *Martin Fierro* (1894) by José Hernández. Nettie Lee Benson Latin American Collection, University of Texas Libraries, The University of Texas at Austin.

pursuing policies of forced conscription against gauchos on the frontier. One clip despairs over the prejudice with which gauchos have been viewed by elites, and casts them in the role of Indians, who are being destroyed by latter-day conquistadors. Thus, Hernández frames his poem as an elegy for a vanishing race of people brutalized by Argentine liberalism and by Sarmiento's famous dogma of civilization and barbarism.[78]

The powerful, emotional connection readers felt to Martín Fierro's story underscores that they were indulging in nostalgia for a pastoral ideal ruined by civilization. For educated readers the poem was another romantic commonplace that echoed the themes of works like Chateaubriand's *Atala* and Isaacs's *María*. For readers with little or no schooling, the uncompromising nature of Fierro's tale of injustice and his ultimate rejection of civilization affirmed their distrust of modernity and the Argentine state, a fact that made some contemporaneous critics of Hernández uncomfortable. One of the poem's readers, former president Bartolomé Mitre, wrote to Hernández that he disagreed with the social philosophy expressed in the poem because it promoted bitterness without providing a "corrective" dose of social solidarity to counteract it.[79] Indeed, nothing in Fierro's story constituted an apology for the necessity of civilization, or for trusting in liberalism and its representatives. Hernández composed a great poem of protest but did not clearly delineate a new social compact to redress the imbalance caused by injustice. Perhaps it was this very open-endedness, its uncompromising acknowledgement that the poem's two heroes cannot turn to "civilized" life for justice, that contributed to its appeal among commoners as a poem of protest.[80]

For his sequel, Hernández seemed to heed the criticisms of men like Mitre. He knew he had the ear of country people, who had adopted his protagonist as one of their own, so for his sequel he proceeded to craft a conduct manual of sorts to civilize them and integrate them into modern society.[81] *The Return of Martín Fierro* guides these intended readers through Fierro and Cruz's bloody adventures among the Indians, and Fierro's return to civilization after his beloved friend's death. Reunited with his sons, and joined by the son of Cruz, as well as the brother of the black man whom Fierro killed in the first poem, the gauchos sing their stories and moralize about how to lead a good, peaceful life. The popular speech of the gauchos remains, but Hernández recasts his singers into pedantic moralizers who criticize Indians, men who mistreat women, gamblers, ungrateful children, and so on. Gone is the homage to the vanished premodern utopia of the gaucho, and the existential despair of the hero who had smashed his guitar to surrender to a life among the savages. What we have instead is a treatise on how rural people should behave mildly in a hostile and often unjust world.

If *The Return of Martín Fierro* espoused the need for the pacification of the countryside, a contemporaneous novel titled *Juan Moreira* by Eduardo Gutiérrez, which was first serialized in the newspaper *La Patria Argentina* in 1879–1880, represented a truer continuation of the rebellious spirit of *The Gaucho Martín Fierro* by celebrating the gaucho bandit Moreira as the embodiment of violence and rebellion against an unjust Argentinian state.[82] Based on a real bandit, Gutiérrez's sensationalist tale was about a virtuous gaucho who is abused by local authorities to the point of being driven to a life of murder and unremitting violence. After many close scrapes and knife fights, Moreira is killed by a policeman while trying to escape from a brothel. Originally published in the crime section of a newspaper, *Juan Moreira* is an example of both the late gauchesque and the early modern crime narrative.[83] In the twenty years that followed its original publication, an estimated one hundred thousand copies of *Juan Moreira* were sold.[84] Readers read it as a *folletín*, as a book, and then in a series of poetic pastiches and adaptations of the original. People also collected a series of twenty-one illustrated trading cards packaged in cigarette boxes, or attended a popular circus pantomime adaptation, as well as subsequent theatrical and operatic versions.[85] (In the next chapter we will explore the theatrical adaptation of this classic.) In short, readers could not get enough of the rebel Moreira, who, like Fierro before him, became a deeply troubling iconic figure. Elitist intellectuals believed that *moreirismo*, the rage for all things Moreira, promoted crime among the masses. Whereas Fierro had been quickly rehabilitated—by his creator, no less—as an appropriate chaperone and mentor to the Argentine nation, Moreira remained a figure who threatened the civilizing scripts of the political establishment. This bandit and his anarchic energy had not been tamed. Unlike novels like *María*, Gutiérrez's best seller catered to class resentment and distrust of government and indulged in violent fantasies of revenge.

The record that remains of most of nineteenth-century Spanish American popular print culture, especially prior to the end of the century, is thin because much of it was not valued enough to be preserved. Scholars reconstruct its contours by reading secondhand, distorted representations written by elite writers who found it distasteful and unrefined. Yet, exploring popular literature is key because it gives voice to a worldview and sensibility that thrived on the margins of the cultural establishment, teaching us about how commoners saw their culture and the historical moment they were living. Official and elite print culture, which belonged to professional writers, journalists, and statesmen, was generally a narrow conversation among a minority of readers. It was a grandiose and self-important conversation that sought to project itself into public buildings, private clubs, or well-groomed homes, enunciating nationalist and scientific prescriptions for progress. Popular print was an entirely different conversation, one that took place on the street, in bars,

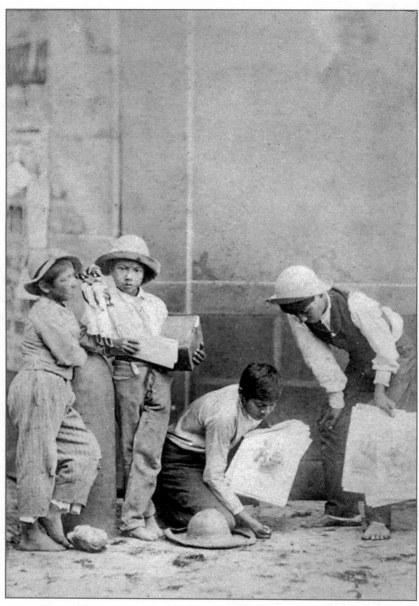

Figure 2.6. Newsboys and street sellers, by Antioco Cruces y Luis
Campa Photographers, Mexico City, circa 1870. Photograph
courtesy of the Collection of Wolfgang Wiggers.

and in country stores, where people of lesser means recited or sang stories and poems. Their heroes included a lowly black poet whose parents were slaves and whose power resided in his wit, and the singing outlaw who smashed his guitar as he turned his back on an unjust society.

The Powers of Print

In this chapter we have explored different types of print. The printing press channeled different kinds of voices, themes, and ideologies. For the learned elites who primarily controlled and consumed print, letters were messengers of civilization and progress, whereas for commoners letters served more pleasurable functions, as well as challenging the values that sustained elite culture. Some kinds of print traveled up and down the social ladder, taking on different meanings for different classes of people. Regardless of its function and location, nineteenth-century print was a vast vessel for gathering up cultural minutiae of every imaginable type— for memorializing everyday life and the dreams and designs of both the educated and the less educated. Even what was not printed found echo in typeset letters, when writers transcribed or adapted the songs of commoners and transferred them into print, or when elements of popular speech entered into novels like Lizardi's *The Mangy Parrot* or Altamirano's *El Zarco the Blue-Eyed Bandit*. Access to letters was undoubtedly limited to a minority, but its reverberations were felt everywhere as a drive to order culture and to define what it meant to be modern, as well as to talk back to power, to laugh, and to weep.

CHAPTER 3

Theatricality

THEATRICALITY IS ANYTHING that pertains to the stage, or to performance, artifice, and spectacle.[1] It is also performative and deliberately physical, hinging on the arrangement and movement of individual and collective bodies. Understood broadly, theatricality is not only about what happens in the theater but also about many other kinds of performances and spectacles. Whether it be the theater of good manners, carnival celebrations, or street theater, theatricality thrives on interactivity and visibility, as well as the literal or implied presence of an audience. It might communicate a high-minded lesson about how to be a better man, woman, or citizen, or a playful challenge to established convention. It is a ritual of order or a challenge to power, and sometimes an ambiguous combination of both. Some forms of theatricality are tied to diversion and leisure; others are tied to power or the choreographies of everyday life. In this chapter, we explore various kinds of theatricality, from elite and commoner entertainments to middle-class manners and popular fiestas. All the performances examined in this chapter have their own symbolic vocabulary and social role; some are hierarchical and reinforce the elite ideal of progress, while others are about pleasure and freedom, like laughter.

Political Theater

One of the most ubiquitous forms of theatricality in nineteenth-century Spanish America was the spectacle of Republican festivals and celebrations. Processionals of political and military leaders, elaborate fireworks,

the staging of nationalist skits, and the erection of allegorical arches, obe-
lisks, and pyramids were key elements of a ritual drama designed to inspire fidelity and pride among the citizenry. Such displays were effective
theater because they were visually alluring and represented a break from
the ordinary routines and rhythms of urban life. During these fiestas, the
city dressed itself in colors, with streamers, banners, and placards hanging from balconies and doorways. It also glowed brighter at night thanks
to a profusion of lights that illuminated the facades of state buildings,
churches, and the cathedral. The city became a mythological and allegorical stage that public dignitaries, cavalry honor guards, and musicians
ceremoniously marched across, carrying symbolic accoutrements and
banners.

Republican fiestas were held on a variety of occasions: to welcome the
arrival of leaders, to inaugurate new governments and elected officials,
to commemorate and swear oaths of fidelity, and to honor important
historical dates and Republican heroes. The new Spanish American nations did not invent these fiestas but rather continued a well-established
tradition from the colonial era that commemorated the arrival of new
viceroys, the ascent of monarchs to the throne, and other notable events
related to the body politic.[2] Although nineteenth-century commentators
believed that Republicanism represented a break from the "dark ages" of
the colonial period, they did not question the effectiveness of using its
official fiesta traditions to legitimize the power of the state among the
masses. They understood that to experience the visually arresting pomp
and circumstance of ritual was to consciously and subconsciously absorb
lessons about power.[3] Public festivals provided symbolic learning on a
mass scale, promoting the willing consent of the people to the authority
of the state and to the more abstract ideals it was supposed to embody
(such as freedom, equality, and progress).

One of the key features of Republican fiestas was their investment in
the sacred.[4] The dignitaries and notables who participated in public processionals usually inaugurated the festivities by marching into Mass and
listening to a Te Deum in a church or the cathedral. Representatives of
church authority, such as priests or bishops, also participated in processionals, and were present at banquets and public gatherings. Sometimes,
the state's representatives inserted themselves in religious celebrations as
a way to establish their preeminence and to not be upstaged by church
officials. Such was the case with President Juan Mora of Costa Rica, who
in 1858 attended the festivities of Corpus Christi with an honor guard of

barefoot soldiers in clean white shirts.[5] Even the most liberal statesmen, such as Venezuela's Antonio Guzmán Blanco, who had challenged the authority of the church in the name of secularism, were eager to use the trappings of religious custom and ceremony in their fiestas. The culture of Catholicism provided a ready-made lingua franca of devotional ritual that governments could easily capitalize on for their public ceremonies and celebrations. What was distinctive about these new celebrations in comparison to their religious predecessors was the way that elements such as arches, monuments, artifacts, and coats of arms sacralized the work and government of Man rather than God or the Church.

The 1849 celebration of Colombian Independence in Bogotá provides one illustration of how intensely theatrical and symbolic Republican fiestas could be.[6] On July 19, a cannon salvo announced the beginning of the festivities. State, municipal, and military dignitaries raised the tricolor flag of Colombia at the capitol and hung it from the turrets of the churches in the city. In the evening, after the pomp and circumstance of a processional of dignitaries on horseback, celebrants carried a decorated float of Saint Librada through the streets. (*La Librada*, who was the patron saint of the politically influential artisan class of Bogotá, had been martyred by her pagan father in the first century because she refused to renounce her chastity and her Christian faith.) The martyr's float was decorated with laurels and the Colombian flag, and was followed by columns of political, military, and religious dignitaries that included President José Hilario López and his cabinet. After placing *La Librada* in the cathedral, officials marched to the town hall to ceremoniously place painted portraits of the heroes of Independence on decorated columns. Outside the building, crowds listened to patriotic speeches and celebrated with fireworks. The most important and dramatic parts of the festivities were yet to come.

On the morning of July 20, Bogotá celebrated with tolling bells, cannon fire, and marching bands. After a Mass at the cathedral, dignitaries and celebrants gathered in the Plaza Bolívar for a dramatic display of Republican generosity. Forty-four slaves wearing red Phrygian caps representing liberty were paraded in front of the dignitaries and made to stand before the guests to receive their freedom.[7] The scroll declaring their manumission was marched through their ranks for each one of them to solemnly kiss. The fiesta's planners had collected funds to buy the freedom of some of these slaves, while others were donated for manumission by their liberal masters. Such practices were not new. The practice began in 1821, when the Congress of Cúcuta decreed that the children of slaves were eligible to be freed at the age of eighteen.[8] From that point onward, until 1851, when slavery was abolished, the ceremonial freeing of slaves was a common ritual during national fiestas.

After the 1849 enactment of this ritual at the Plaza Bolívar, the dignitaries and celebrants proceeded to another plaza to symbolically place the foundation of the new building of the Sociedad Filantrópica, an important mutual aid society and liberal political organization. Still, Bogotá was not done celebrating. For six more days the city saw fireworks, religious processionals, musical concerts, street entertainments, and bullfights.

Some of the most elaborate and symbolically laden Republican fiestas were funerary commemorations for political figures or national heroes. Such events gave voice to necronationalism, a rhetoric and set of symbolic practices that deified the dead or transformed them into exemplary civic morality tales.[9] This wedding of mourning with ornate nationalist celebrations was a way of manufacturing and promoting national unity in the face of turbulent times and political and ethnic divisions. A striking example of necronationalism may be found in the repatriation of Simón Bolívar's remains from Santa Marta, Colombia, to Caracas in 1842. When the Venezuelan-born Liberator died in 1830 in Santa Marta, he had been rejected by both the Bogotá and Caracas wings of the Independence movement he had led. Twelve years later, the enmities of the era of Independence began to be eclipsed by nostalgia for his impressive military achievements and by a desire to establish a unifying, nationalist mythology.[10] In December 1842, the regime of President José Antonio Páez, who had fought at Bolívar's side against the royalists, repatriated the Liberator's remains from Colombia in a week-long ceremony that was marked by great fanfare and mournful rituals. After disembarking the sacred remains from one of the ships that had traveled to Santa Marta to recover them, a solemn processional traveled on foot from the port town of La Guaira to Caracas, which had been decked in elaborate funerary decorations. The processional route in Caracas was decorated with commemorative arches, Doric columns, black streamers, flagpoles wrapped in velvet with gold fringes, a colorful array of Venezuelan and other Spanish American flags, embroidered coats of arms, and pyramid structures painted to simulate marble. In the plaza of San Francisco stood a bust of Bolívar with a laurel-leaf crown, an ancient symbol of victory and glory. The Church of San Francisco, where the funeral ceremony took place before the remains were moved to the cathedral for interment, contained a tall cenotaph behind the altar. This structure, wrapped in black velvet cloth stained with silver tears, was decorated at its base with an allegorical painting that represented the republics liberated by Bolívar as weeping women. It also held the banner of the Spanish conquistador Francisco Pizarro, which the marshal José Antonio de Sucre had won in Bolívar's name after the last great battle of the Wars of Independence at Ayacucho in 1825. As the funeral carriage got ready to travel its route to the Church of San Francisco with Bolívar's festooned coffin, its horses were removed and a group of one hundred men and women who had either served with Bolívar during the Wars of Independence or who were related to him by blood pulled it through the crowded streets as thousands watched in reverential silence. Fermín Toro, one of the observers of this extraordinary funeral procession, marveled at how peaceful and orderly the crowds were. He celebrated the power of Bolívar to bring people together into a harmonious community, a sentiment that was echoed by President José Antonio Páez when he declared, at the end of the ceremonies, that the most valuable monument that the Venezuelan people could erect in honor of their hero was the consolidation of the nation's institutions, a prudent executive, the integrity of magistrates, an educated population, and the unity of all Venezuelans.[11]

As we can see, Republican fiestas were intensely theatrical events designed to instill in spectators a sense of reverence toward state power and its symbolism and mythologies. They were mechanisms for building and maintaining historical memory and making it visible and powerful. As diverse as each one of these celebrations were—no two were identical—they all shared the drive to sacralize a leader or the state and its representatives.

The Theatricality of Good Manners

One of the most ubiquitous forms of theatricality in nineteenth-century Spanish America related to how, on a daily basis, people moved their bodies and interacted with each other in public. Elites and others who aspired to be a part of so-called polite society used *urbanidad* (refinement) as a way of visibly performing education, distinction, and honor. Everyday actions such as greeting someone on the street, knocking on a friend's door, or holding a fork and knife were regulated by complex codes that educated people studied earnestly from childhood onward. These protocols were a kind of interactive theater because they were performed and exchanged with other actors in social gatherings and public places. To perform well was to prove your self-worth and enter into the social circles of power, and to fail was to risk losing your social standing. For middle- and upper-class women, the stakes were even higher because the performance of good manners communicated virtue, chastity, and refinement, qualities that were central to the very definition of virtuous femininity.

To provide a sketch of *urbanidad* or the culture of gentility, we conjure up a hypothetical Spanish American family with impeccable manners. This conceit has some merit in the abstract because the vast majority of educated Spanish Americans had easy access to an enormously influential and widely reprinted conduct manual titled the *Manual de urbanidad y buenas maneras* (1854) by the Venezuelan educator and music teacher Manuel Antonio Carreño. The text was widely taught in schools and endured well into the twentieth century as the most important catalog of rules and regulations for governing conduct in private and public. Up to 1900, Carreño's conduct manual was reprinted at least fourteen times by US and French publishers and distributed throughout Spanish America. Moreover, an abbreviated version for use in primary schools called *Compendio del manual de urbanidad y buenas maneras* was reprinted over a dozen times between 1857 and 1900 by US, Spanish, Venezuelan, Puerto Rican, French, and Colombian printers. Overlooked by literary historians, Carreño's manual was possibly the single most read book in the nineteenth-century Spanish-speaking world. Here, by using this enormously influential book as a guide, we will imagine a family that faithfully follows Carreño's elaborate instructions of good conduct. Our cast of characters includes Señor Bernardo Rodríguez, who is married to Doña Catalina, their daughters Carmen (age sixteen) and Rosa (fifteen), and their sons Roberto (fourteen), Carlos (thirteen), and Ildefonso (six). Don Bernardo is not a member of the old aristocracy, but rather a merchant in a capital city who is now able to afford some of the accoutrements and comforts of the upper class, such as a home in a better neighborhood, nice clothes, and even servants.

The first thing to know about the Rodríguez family is that they are good Catholics.[12] Each member of the family prays upon waking and on going to bed, and gives thanks to the Lord after their meals. On the street, they stop to acknowledge religious processions, and they do not walk past a church without crossing themselves. Piety and religiosity constitute one of the three bedrock obligations of man, the others being man's duties to society and to himself. The humility and nonviolence promoted by Christian piety is reproduced in man's duty to society, meaning that Don Bernardo strives to do no harm to any of his fellows, whether they be above or below him in the social hierarchy. Although he would never consider his Afro-descendant servant Alejo his equal, he avoids scolding the man in public. Instead, he is protective and kindly toward Alejo. When in polite conversation with others of his rank or above, Don Bernardo will not criticize any person, and if an uncouth man speaks harshly to him, he turns the other cheek by not responding in kind. He is a paragon of nonviolence, both in the physical and symbolic realm. Further, the respect he communicates toward the church and its representatives models the respect he performs for the Republican state and its officers, which constitute a kind of secular version of the church. He and his family are also assiduous in honoring their obligations to themselves, meaning that they keep the strictest personal hygiene, a practice that also grows out of the Christian value of taming the body and its passions.

To get more specific about the Rodríguez family and their performance of good manners, we'll take a closer look at a busy day when they have two engagements: the first, a three p.m. *visita* to the home of the Larretas, one of the most distinguished families in the city, and the second, a dinner at the home of the González family. The day begins early because all except the littlest one, Ildefonso, sleep no more than seven or eight hours a night. (It would be slothful to sleep more.)[13] The cool early morning hours are a valuable time for washing, for getting dressed, and for airing out rooms to prevent miasmas and other dangerous, stuffy forms of air. It's important for Don Bernardo to go to work early, after spending some time reading newspapers or a book to cultivate himself, a practice he has inculcated in his sons, who also spend the morning hours before school reading or doing homework.

Cleanliness is key, so upon waking the Rodríguez family does its daily ablutions.[14] The family is lucky to have a bathtub, but it's only used about once a week by each of them. On a daily basis, however, they wash their hands, feet, faces, necks, eyes, and ears with basins of water and towels. It's important to gargle several times and to brush their teeth with care. All this done, they dress in the clothes they will wear throughout the day and in public. Unlike the Larretas, who are much wealthier and have several changes of clothes, each member of our family wears the same clothes for two or three days at a time, which is proper, as long as the clothes are brushed clean and dusted to present a composed appearance.[15] What is not negotiable, however, are the underclothes, which have to be changed every day. Don Bernardo and his sons all carry gloves, and handkerchiefs, which they conscientiously use to wipe their eyes, their noses, and the corners of their mouths to ensure that no bodily excretion is visible when they are in public.[16] No one in the family moves freely or carelessly, not only because erratic and unmethodical movements are uncouth, but because they are conscious of stretching or otherwise wearing out their clothes, which constitute their most visible calling card as *gente decente* or decent people.

To call on the Larretas, who live a few blocks away, the Rodríguez family must negotiate the street.[17] The choreography of their movements is complex. Don Bernardo walks arm in arm with his wife, while his daughters walk in front of them. His sons walk behind him, with the littlest one in tow. Don Bernardo and Doña Catalina have taught their children well about how to behave. If they encounter a woman of distinction walking in their direction, the whole party knows that they need to move to the left, away from the inside of the sidewalk, to allow her to pass. When parties moving in their direction are larger, or include a gentleman of higher standing, the Rodríguezes understand that they must cede the sidewalk. If the Rodríguezes encounter the González family, whose social stature is the same as theirs, the family who holds the sidewalk to their right has the right of way. Strangers are not greeted, unless they are people of distinction who have given the Rodríguezes the right of way.

Fortunately, the route on this day is pretty clear and the Rodríguezes arrive at the Larretas without too many ceremonial sidewalk delays. At the front door, Señor Rodríguez is mindful of the higher stature of the Larretas, which is why he slowly knocks four times instead of three, to let his hosts know that the arriving party is not intimate with them.[18] (In contrast, when going to a *visita* at the home of his friend and fellow merchant Señor González, Señor Rodríguez knocks three times.) Unless socializing with close friends, *visitas* are highly structured and ritualized affairs that must have a specific purpose. There are *visitas* to introduce a person to a family, to offer services, to congratulate, to console a family going through a crisis, to mourn a death, or to bid farewell. Generally, *visitas* take place between noon and four p.m., with the hours of one to three reserved for *visitas* intended to present a stranger to the family. Generally, all *visitas* except those between intimates should take no longer than an hour, and sometimes are as brief as one half hour. If a family is out or otherwise unable to receive company during *visita* hours, the visitors leave a card with their name and address on it, folding one corner if it has been delivered in person by the would-be visitor; an intact card left for a family indicates that a messenger has delivered it on behalf of another party as a substitute for a face-to-face visit. Today's personal *visita* to the Larretas, though planned by the Rodríguezes, is unannounced and uninvited, which is proper at this hour. Their purpose is to let the Larretas know that their oldest child, Carmen, is engaged to marry young Víctor Osorio. For this reason, and because of the higher rank of the Larretas, the Rodríguez family will stay only up to an hour, because it is quite possible that their stay will be interrupted by other guests of a higher social standing, at which point Don Bernardo would politely excuse his family and try to leave, staying a little while longer only if the Larretas explicitly ask them to stay. During the *visita*, conversation is polite, stiff, and repetitive, designed to injure no one and avoid any controversy of any kind.

After returning home, the Rodríguezes have time to freshen up for their dinner with the González family. They are pleased about having satisfied a continual obligation to remain in touch with the Larretas, keeping them abreast of what is happening in their family, and communicating

Figure 3.1. A *tertulia* (social gathering), from *Atlas de la historia física y política de Chile* (1854) by Claudio Gay. Courtesy of the Peter H. Raven Library, Missouri Botanical Garden.

to them the high esteem in which they hold them. Don Bernardo and his wife are proud of knowing the Larretas and are eager to maintain the relationship. Although it would be indecorous for them to dwell on the thought that such a relationship will benefit them socially or even financially, that is the underlying reality of their relationship, since Don Bernardo is a merchant who has done business with the Larretas and their intimates. Most importantly, the Rodríguezes want their daughters and sons to continue to thrive in society as they grow, so there's a powerful parental dimension to keeping up with families of distinction. The Rodríguezes are more at ease about their evening engagement, a dinner with Fermín González; his wife, Laureana; their sons, Juan Carlos and William; and their daughters, Susana, Marta, and Norma. The Gonzálezes are their equals and intimates, and the Domínguez family that will be in attendance is well known to them, and of slightly humbler rank. So they can let their guard down just a little bit this evening.

That night, at the González household, after a hour of leisurely conversation in the living room, Don Fermín approaches Doña Catalina, offers her his arm, and leads her into the dining room. At the same time, he nods to his guest Don Bernardo, who follows, guiding the hostess, Doña Laureana, into the other room.[19] The orderly processional is rounded out by the Domínguezes, and then the children, with girls before the boys. There are two tables set up, one for the men and the other for the women. While dining, all the conversation and every bodily movement is carefully calibrated. Don Pedro Domínguez is mindful of the higher rank of the González and Rodríguez families, so he does not initiate or change the topic of conversation. All the conversation is polite and studiously neutral, without jokes or winking asides; it is straightforward, transparent, and gentle.[20] Controlled yet flowing arm and hand movements, especially of the right arm and hand, accompany the speech of the men. The girls and boys at their tables are mindful about holding utensils and glasses with a prearranged combination of fingers, keeping their elbows down and bodies straight and away from the backs of their seats.[21] Each child uses their left hand to hold the bread while they tear off a slice with their right, at which point they place the slice on the left-hand side of their plate. There is a break between the dinner course and dessert, after which all the diners take coffee in a separate room.

Upon returning home, the Rodríguezes are well informed about what is going on in town among the people of society, thanks to their afternoon visit to the Larretas and the stories shared over dinner. Adolescent

Roberto was a bit taken with one of the Domínguez daughters, twelve-year-old María, and secretly hopes that his parents will undertake a *visita* to the Domínguez household. If he is lucky, maybe the Domínguez family will come for a *visita* to his house so that he can interact with the dark-haired girl again, or maybe he will see her at a party, which will give him an opportunity to ask her out to dance. In the meantime, he un-buttons his jacket, shirt, and trousers, and carefully brushes them before carefully folding them over a chair. He gets into his nightshirt and kneels to pray.

How accurate is this bird's-eye view of a day in the life and the customs of our fictional family? Conduct is always inflected by local culture, so presenting a fictional family as a stand-in for an entire hemisphere will inevitably distort localized practice to some degree. Furthermore, just because a conduct manual says something does not mean that real people in real situations followed it to the letter. The most we can reliably say is that a conduct manual expresses a set of aspirational values and practices—a horizon to strive toward; in this regard, our day in the life of the Rodríguez family gives us a general sense of how people *imagined* they should behave with each other in private and in public. More than any other cultural document of the nineteenth century, the widely read and studied *Manual de urbanidad y buenas maneras* reveals the script and stage directions for the performance of upper- and middle-class identity in Spanish America.

The Release of the Body

As Republican festivals and middle-class manners show, the social ideal promoted by educated cultural elites was primarily structuralist. This meant that elites analyzed society as a structure composed of discrete parts organized in a hierarchical manner; they placed social behaviors, objects, and even spaces on a continuum defined by civilization on one end and barbarism on the other. The ethos of civilization and barbarism blended morality, culture, and politics together and suggested that the intrinsic value of a person and a community was directly tied to refinement and respect for hierarchy. However, yearly Carnival celebrations and other ritual fiestas challenged this structuralist ideal. These events freed the bodies of different classes of people to move in unexpected ways, symbolically breaking down categories, values, and identities.

As in Europe, Carnival in nineteenth-century Spanish America was an exuberant period of excess in the days leading to the start of Lent, when believers repented, prayed, and denied their appetites for several weeks until Easter eve. The traditions of the festival, rooted in medieval European culture, were characterized by excessive drinking and eating and the mockery of social hierarchies and conventions. The attack on the social order was accomplished by reveling in human appetites and by costumes and masks that satirized identity and power relations.[22] Carnival was an explosion of playful, ritual violence and social rebellion that allowed elites and commoners to indulge in the theatrical expressions of freedom that they did not allow themselves during the rest of the year.

One of the key features of Carnival in the Hispanic world was food wars in which combatants threw water and various projectiles at each other. The ammunition used included bags of flour or paint, fruit rinds and rotten fruit, aniseeds and other nuts and seeds, sugar plums stuffed with nuts, and painted eggshells filled with perfumed water or confetti.[23] The intensity of the food fights that took place in public with these items was dramatic. After the Carnival of 1865, a Venezuelan commentator observed that the main streets of Caracas were carpeted with enough tomatoes, oranges, lemons, seeds, and broken eggshells to feed an army for a week.[24] In Lima, bands of men roamed the streets armed with oversized metal syringes that they used to squirt water on passersby and on women who stood on balconies armed with buckets of water of their own. At midcentury, a German traveler in Lima watched as some ladies standing on a balcony went to war with a group of men gathered in the street below. After soaking some of the men with water, the laughing ladies beat a hasty retreat from the balcony as a barrage of nearly three hundred eggshells filled with water crashed into their quarters.[25] Sometimes, parties of revelers stormed homes and businesses, bombing their inhabitants with flour and water. In all the carousing, men broke down the barriers that separated them from women, touching and roughing them up in ways that would have been inconceivable at any other time of the year. For example, a traveler in Tepic, Mexico, described the strangeness of attending a "Flour Ball" in which men and women of society ceremoniously gathered in a hall and broke bags of flour on each other's heads until everybody looked like dusty white ghosts.[26] Such transgressions of the rules of decorum that ruled the interaction of men and women were significant, but not as upsetting as when commoners touched or otherwise disrespected the women and men of the upper classes. For this reason, in Peru and Venezuela, many people of refinement simply barricaded themselves in their homes until Ash Wednesday, or fled to their summer estates, where they would not be subjected to the indignities of Carnival.[27] One Peruvian company even commissioned a cruise ship to remove the genteel from Lima and entertain them with balls and dances in a respectful albeit playful environment.[28]

Carnival also hosted other, more local forms of paganism that served as conduits for values and identities resisting colonial Hispanic culture. In one of the most recognized folk Carnival celebrations in all of Spanish America, the peasants and miners of Oruro, Bolivia, used the celebration to venerate their protector, the Virgin of the Socavón, and to stage ambiguous battles between Saint Michael and the seven sins. Originally, the combat between the saint and the devils was designed to reinforce the Christian evangelization of the inhabitants of Oruro, but celebrants projected the theme of colonial oppression onto the morality play and helped to preserve the memory of the indigenous uprising of Tupac Amaru II against Spanish colonial authorities in 1781. Saint Michael became a pale conquistador who hacked away at large numbers of outlandishly dressed *diablitos* (devils) that were culturally associated with ancient Andean deities. The symbolism of this combat was ambivalent: it had an explicit, intentional meaning (the condemnation of sin by a representative of God) and an implicit, subversive one (a celebration of Indian resistance to Spanish colonialism.)[29] In this way, Carnival ritualized liberation for a few days and invited traditional communities to give voice to ethnic pride and to question authority. Like the inhabitants of Oruro, the Indians of Los Reyes de Culhuacán to the southwest of Mexico City adapted Carnival to their own purposes and injected it with cultural pride and defiance.[30] Originally, the Indians had conducted these celebrations inside the city but moved them outside to the perimeter after authorities banned the celebrations. In the Carnival of Los Reyes de Culhuacán, quadrilles of *huehuenches* (traditional indigenous dancers) paraded down the streets in masks and exaggerated hats, pounding drums and shaking other noisemakers. The master of ceremonies was a mythical effigy known as the *Palegande* who embodied both Carnival and all the injustices perpetrated against the community, for which he was lynched at the end of the festivities. This ritual execution staged the European tradition of burying or killing a figure symbolizing Carnival on Shrove Tuesday, but added the critical dimension of making him the target of the community's indignation over misfortunes or any injustices perpetrated on it.

No discussion of festive celebrations and cultural mixing in Spanish

America can be complete without acknowledging the powerful impact of African culture on the New World. The most extravagant African fiesta of nineteenth-century Cuba was not Carnival per se, but the feast of Epiphany (January 6), which commemorates the revelation of Christ and the visit of the Three Magi: Melchior, Caspar, and Balthazar. Yet, the Cuban Day of the Kings was undoubtedly carnivalesque in form because it was based on extravagant costumes, the suspension of hierarchical conventions, and colorful, syncretic, and parodic performances. To say the celebrants of the Day of the Kings were African or black is to oversimplify complex communities that are resistant to easy generalizations. Nineteenth-century Cuban society was built on slavery and a network of different ethnic identities that sprang from its economy. There were *negros de nación*, who were African-born individuals with strong cultural ties to an African nation or ethnic group, such as the Congo, the Lucumí, the Arará, and the Carabalí, among others.[31] The *negros de nación* who were closer to African rather than Hispanic culture, and who did not speak Spanish, were called *bozales*, whereas the baptized, Spanish-speaking *negros de nación* were called *ladinos*. If most of the *negros de nación* were slaves, the *criollos* (Cuban-born Afro-descendants) were a diverse group that included large numbers of freedmen, most of whom lived in towns and cities like Havana. Taken together, the African peoples of Cuba constituted approximately half of the island's inhabitants in the nineteenth century. To help contain this vast network of subjugated peoples, both enslaved and free, colonial authorities encouraged religious clubs or mutual aid societies called *cabildos*. These urban-based clubs worshipped and celebrated religious holidays, and each club provided communal bonds and services to its members. Since each *cabildo* had a well-defined identity, a distinct banner, and its own leadership structure, they were vital players in festivities like the Day of the Kings.

The Day of the Kings was deeply symbolic to the African peoples of Cuba in part because they venerated the black magus Melchior, whose color made him a powerful iconic figure associated with African belief systems. Another influence on the festivities was the custom of rewarding soldiers for their service with an *aguinaldo* (small coins or candy) on January 6, a tradition that slaves imitated by asking for offerings from their masters and the general public on the same day. A deeper root was in Africa, where dancing masks and the representation of fantastical beings and entities were staples of different tribal African practices that slaves and their descendants preserved in the New World.[32] During the

Figure 3.2. Slaves from Chorillos, Peru, dancing with grotesque masks and jawbone instruments, by Pancho Fierro (circa 1853). Digital image courtesy of the Getty's Open Content Program.

festival of Epiphany, the *cabildos* and their members—each led by a king, queen, and their royal retinues—converged in towns and cities with their drums, costumes, and masks, dancing through the streets in animated, colorful processionals. Onlookers on the streets and the balconies rained *aguinaldos* on the dancers, who scrambled to receive them. The culmination of the processionals was the arrival of *cabildo* royalty and their ceremonial retinues and standard-bearers to the central plaza, where they made demonstrations of loyalty to the colonial officials and received the most generous *aguinaldos* of all: gold coins.[33] Another tradition associated with this encounter with the authorities is reminiscent of the lynching of Palegande in Los Reyes de Culhuacán. The celebrants symbolically killed a very long puppet in the form of a snake that they had carried through the streets as a part of their ritual dances. As the snake died, the dancers sang in Spanish and *bozal criollo*, a hybrid of Spanish and African dialect: "The snake is dead, dead . . . / *Sángala, muleque* [dance, boy]!"[34]

As we can see, the Day of the Kings was an explosion of theatricality and performance. The kings and queens of the *cabildos* were dressed in lush velvet, with sashes, medals, crucifixes, crowns, and big, extravagant hats. *Mandinga* women wore large blue silk turbans and short, tight-fitting jackets. Some of the men parodied the dress of European gentlemen by wearing derby hats, as well as pleated, lacy shirts under their wide-lapelled jackets. Some carried images of the Virgin Mary and other holy objects, while the fearsome *Nañigo* dancers embodied threatening paganism. These fantastically costumed men, viewed by whites as the most malevolent members of a secret African sect, were shrouded head to toe in white and black checkers and stripes, with cowbells attached to their wrists and waists. In contrast, the tom-tom drummers and many of the acrobats and dancers were scantily dressed and barefoot, the sweat gleaming on their skin as they performed all day long. The *gente decente* were fascinated by the spectacle, and participated by throwing *aguinaldos* from their balconies to the Africans below, but (as mentioned above) many were also repulsed and sought to flee their homes or locked themselves in during the festival; they feared being accosted by crowds of Africans wanting to perform for them in exchange for an offering.[35] That kind of proximity to the least powerful in society was just too close for comfort.

Nineteenth-century Spanish American elites and cultural commentators were indeed devoted to the idea of order, which they saw as the key to progress, peace, and stability. Carnival and Carnival-like celebrations violated this agenda by marking the return, symbolic or otherwise, of the repressed and oppressed. Sensuality and aggression, which were condemned not only by religion but also by the idea of good manners, erupted in very visible ways during Carnival. The culture of indigenous and African peoples also returned, using the masks of Carnival and the Day of the Kings to remind society that what lay underneath the surface of a colonialist society was alive and unafraid.

In the Theater

So far we have examined forms of theatricality associated with political power, class identity, and the containment and release of the body. In each case, theatricality made real or imagined identities visible, and defined, maintained, or dismantled socially acceptable conduct. Now we turn to the theater, one of the fine arts and one of the preferred entertainments of the cultural elites. For cultural commentators, the theater was supposed to be more than just entertainment: it was a civilizing experience that worked its transformative magic through pathos, realism, or comedy. This is why the theater was frequently described as a school of good manners—a place where audiences would be able to internalize lessons about how to live in societies that aspired to be modern but which had not outrun tradition, autocracy, and class conflict. Domingo Sarmiento argued that rather than having policemen yell at working people about the evils of drunkenness and gambling, governments should erect theaters to teach people how to lead more productive and meaningful lives. He argued that enlightened governments should recognize that man craves catharsis in his leisure and that the theater was best equipped to provide him with one that would improve his sense of personal dignity and responsibility toward others. These kinds of arguments were common throughout the century, and they influenced the taste of audiences, the favor of governments, the acclaim of nationalist thinkers, and the inspirations of working playwrights.[36]

Most of the plays performed on the Spanish American stage were European and did not always conform to these standards of social utility that critics like Sarmiento dictated. For example, the most popular and spectacular Spanish play of the first half of the century was *La pata de cabra* (The goat's foot; 1829) by Juan de Grimaldi, an insubstantial blend of slapstick comedy and magical effects that delighted audiences throughout Spanish America.[37] Another popular play was *La dame aux camélias* (*The Lady of the Camellias*; 1852) by Alexandre Dumas fils, which told the tearful story of young Armand, who falls in love with a woman of ill repute called Marguerite Gautier.[38] Armand's father, disapproving of Marguerite's past life as a courtesan, shames her into leaving Armand, leading the young man to believe that she has left him for another. The brokenhearted woman dies alone of tuberculosis, a victim of her own past and society's judgment. Audiences loved the tear-jerking play and went in droves to see it performed, as they did Giuseppe Verdi's hit opera *La traviata* (The fallen woman; 1853), which was based on the same story. *The Lady of the Camellias* was not without its controversies, however. Some critics found that it idealized sensuality and overstimulated the audience, specifically women, whose innate love of luxury and melodrama might make them identify with Marguerite and her sensuality. For others, Marguerite's tragic life was a beautiful morality tale about transcending sin and, as such, an edifying entertainment.[39]

Although critics conceded that there were indeed European plays that could teach valuable lessons to Spanish American audiences, they insisted that the best way to teach society was by staging plays that dealt with Spanish American topics. Reflecting national history and portraying local customs and characters were the first steps in shaping society and instilling patriotism and good manners. In this category of drama, there were two kinds of plays: historical dramas and *costumbrista* plays. Ignacio Rodríguez Galván's *Muñoz, visitador de México* (Muñoz, the Mexican colonial inspector; 1838) may serve as a representative example of the historical dramas. The play is loosely based on an incident that took place in sixteenth-century Mexico City, when a small faction of the Creole elite began to question Spanish control of the colony. When officials accused Viceroy Gastón de Peralta of sympathizing with the rebels, King Philip sent three *visitadores* to Mexico to get to the bottom of things. The presiding *visitador*, Alonso de Muñoz, overthrew the viceroy and proceeded to brutally torture and execute members of the Creole elite, among them Martín Cortés, the son of Hernán Cortés and his Indian translator, Malinche. The brothers Baltasar and Diego Sotelo, who hailed from a distinguished family, were among others whom Muñoz beheaded during his purge. Viceroy Peralta was eventually cleared of wrongdoing and the zealous *visitador* was called back to Spain to answer for his deeds. Rodríguez Galván discards everything from these events except the tyrannical *visitador* named Muñoz, who delights in torturing and killing Mexicans, and a nobleman named Baltasar Sotelo who challenges Muñoz and dies in the effort. The dramatic nucleus of the play is the fictional conceit that Muñoz is obsessed with possessing Celestina, Sotelo's beautiful and angelic wife. Twice in the play Muñoz captures the young woman, using cruel threats of violence against her husband to try to make her yield to his volcanic desire. In the end, when Muñoz's men throw Sotelo's dead body onto a chair in front of Celestina, she collapses at his feet and dies. Muñoz, who throughout has been unwavering in his devilish designs, abruptly melts into horror, tearing at his face and hair and gibbering contradictory orders to his fearful henchmen. Obviously, over-the-top plays like this one were designed to pump up audiences to identify with patriotic ideals and with Good in its never-ending battles against Evil. In this case, Celestina symbolized the oppression of Mexican innocents at the hands of a foreign tyrant, and Sotelo represented Mexico's valiant and exemplary resistance against injustice.

A more authentically modern and realistic theater emerged toward the middle of the century: the *comedia costumbrista* (comedy of manners). This kind of comedy, also known as *alta comedia* (high comedy), rejected the histrionic gestures and historical settings of earlier romantic plays like *Muñoz, visitador de México* and replaced them with more contemporary middle-class settings and situations. Rather than promoting grand ideological lessons, these *comedias* moralized about domestic life, exploring the ways in which libertines, liars, and opportunists threatened the fabric of the family. They diagnosed social ills and taught audiences how to avoid them through the representation of local society and culture and the interaction of different classes of people.[40] Typically, the *costumbrista* theater featured a convoluted marriage plot that set parents and their children into conflict, and satirical representations of national or urban character types that were familiar to members of the audience. The resulting combination was often a powerful depiction of how private life intersected with issues of finance, class consciousness, and regional identity.

One of the most brilliant and enduring *costumbrista* plays of the century was the hit *Ña Catita* (1845) by the Peruvian Manuel Ascencio Segura. *Ña Catita* tells the story of a warring husband and wife, Don Jesus and Doña Rufina. Don Jesus wishes to marry their daughter Juliana to young Manuel, the son of a deceased friend of common stock with whom he served in the military. Although Juliana and Manuel are infatuated with each other, Doña Rufina prohibits their courtship and insists on marrying Juliana to Don Alejo, a dandy whose fancy clothes and status promises to elevate the fortunes of the family. The titular character of the play is Ña Catita, a widowed *beata* (old religious lady) who wanders about Lima collecting gossip and sticking her nose in everybody's business. Despite her pious pronouncements, Ña Catita is driven by greed and hypocrisy. She is always ingratiating herself with everybody in order to get money, food, hot chocolate, and even a shot of booze. The old busybody allies herself with Doña Rufina while also meddling and ingratiating herself with both of Juliana's suitors, Don Alejo and Don Manuel. Meanwhile, Don Jesus and Doña Rufina have a knock-down fight over the fate of their daughter. Doña Rufina threatens divorce and schemes with Ña Catita to secretly leave her husband. In the end, after much drama and comedy, Don Alejo is unmasked as a married man, embarrassing Rufina and shaming her into subordinating herself to her husband. Happily, Juliana and Manuel are now free to marry each other.

One of the fundamental themes that *Ña Catita* tackles is how to measure truth in a society defined by lies and ulterior motives. One of the ways that Ascencio Segura explores this theme is through the concept of the *enredo* (entanglement), a series of provocative and overly complicated misunderstandings between characters on the stage. In his widely followed instructions for the well-made play, the French playwright Eugene Scribe decreed that a play's plot should contain many misunderstandings and be based on a secret withheld from the characters on stage but known to the members of the audience. The purpose of the technique is to heighten dramatic tension among characters and intensify audience interest and investment in the play. In *Ña Catita*, the audience knows more than the characters on the stage until the very end, when both audience and characters learn that Don Alejo is a married man. Yet, the *enredo* is also a frame for understanding social relationships. Ironically, the mouthpiece for this point is clownish Don Alejo, who is the very embodiment of falsity. At one point, he says:

> The youngster fools the old man,
> the son fools his own father,
> the little lady her mother,
> and the government the citizen.
> To move up, the soldier fools his superior;
> the artist in his studio
> only thinks of fooling.
> The dumbest tenants fool the landlord,
> and the rascals fleece
> the most upstanding bureaucrat.
> In short, every creature fools,
> little or poor or rich;
> and so it goes the wheel keeps turning;
> it is a well-known thing that to gain an advantage
> in the farce of life no one should fall asleep on the hay.[41]

The idea that the whole world is a stage is an old one, but here Ascencio Segura uses it to argue that *enredos* threaten society with anarchy. The disfiguration of the real, or of truth, is not only the motor of his play, but its moral and its call to arms as well: in order to preserve and protect the family, people need to unmask impostors like Don Alejo and Ña Catita.

Spanish American *costumbrista* plays could be comedic, like *Ña Catita*, or sober and self-important, but all were designed to reflect contemporary middle- and upper-class social realities.[42] These were plays in which marriage plots functioned as dramatic devices for understanding and classifying different kinds of social actors and behaviors, and to moralize about how people should behave and protect themselves from dishonor, degradation, and financial ruin. Although formulaic and trite, and largely blind to the social realities of the urban and rural poor, the *costumbrista* theater represented a turn, however mild, toward realism in the theater.

The People's Theater

We have already explored entertainments and performances associated with the culture of the genteel who prized the exclusivity of their leisure activities and who believed in the civilizing function of their pastimes as symbols of refinement and progress. Now we turn to the public entertainments that were valued by artisans and the working classes, and that embodied a more streetwise sensibility. Such popular pastimes were not exclusive to the commoners, but elite culture often devalued them because of their association with base pleasures and company, and with a violation of the decorum that was generally valued as intrinsic to national progress. For example, the *chinganas* of Chile, which we explored in the "City Cafés" section of Chapter 1 of this book, are a case in point about how certain urban spaces and pastimes could be patronized by different classes of people, and enacted in different social settings to produce different kinds of social situations.

With this caution in mind, we begin our journey through the people's theater on a Sunday afternoon in Mexico City, circa 1850, on the quiet and humble thoroughfare called the Cuarta Calle del Reloj, where Don Soledad Aycardo, known as Don Chole, managed the city's most popular circus and theater.[43] The square wooden edifice, covered with a shingle roof, had rough wooden floors and the interior was cheaply painted. Two or three large oil lamps hung from the ceiling over the arena and the stage, which was covered by a colorful curtain inscribed with the words "With false brilliance and under many names, I give man moral lessons." The afternoon circus featured clowns, acrobats, equestrian shows, and music, and took place in an arena in front of the stage that was later occupied by benches for nighttime theatrical performances. The long-haired Don Chole was ringmaster and head clown; he powdered his face white and wore a gold-rimmed velvet headband or a feathered cap. As master of ceremonies, he not only introduced his performers but also made jokes about mothers-in-law and older ladies, flirted with pretty girls, and sang satirical songs and imparted moral lessons through witty sayings and dialogues. For example, Don Chole sang the following words as he moved around the perimeter of the pit, leering at different girls who sat in the audience:

The Mariquitas are fine girls,
The Juanitas are beautiful girls,
The Catarinas are graceful girls,
And so pretty are the girls called Agustina.
The Tomasas are such flirty girls,
The Pepas are the starry skies . . .
I love them all!
And all shall love me!
And after the circus is over
I shall find them all!
I am a fine-looking fellow
Despite all the paint I am wearing,
Listen, pretty girls:
I would like to see myself married to all of you![44]

After such jocular preambles, the show would continue with acrobats called *maromeros*. The tightrope walker, holding a long crossbeam in his hands, hopped on his wire, alternating between walking it and allowing himself to fall, in a seated position, onto it. All the while, the snack sellers swarmed both the entrance and the interior of the establishment, selling citrus juices, caramel roasted almonds, candied cactus fruits, and egg-yolk sponge cakes called *huevos reales* (royal eggs). A little boy in rags with a single cup sold servings of water to the patrons, who included artisans, functionaries, newspapermen, and even members of the upper class.

At night, Don Chole's establishment became a theater featuring both comedy plays and puppet shows. Once again, Don Chole played a key role in the entertainment as one of the comedic lead actors, along with an older gentleman whose surname, *Cuervo* (crow), eerily mirrored his ugly, long-nosed visage and his screeching voice, both of which he put to great comedic effect when he impersonated older ladies. People of all classes thronged to see plays at Don Chole's not only because of the quality of the performances, but also because the ambiance was a part of the show itself. In elite theaters, audience members were offended and enraged by the impudence of those who interrupted the program by talking during the show. These uneducated rabble-rousers, called *cócoras*, could afford to attend plays in elite theaters, but they refused to abide by the respectful and docile custom of watching the performers in silence. In Don Chole's theater, *cócoras* were an integral part of the attraction. One infamous gang of *cócoras*, led by a man called One-Eyed Suárez, was known to frequent the theater, delighting the audience by shouting out hilarious insults to the performers on stage as the audience roared in laughter.

In Argentina and Uruguay, the circus merged with the theater into a hybrid called the Circo Criollo (Creole Circus). This kind of inexpensive mass entertainment gave voice to a type of popular nationalism that defined itself through a deep distrust, if not an outright rejection, of the state and the rule of law. The story of the rise of the Circo Criollo and its most legendary performer vividly illustrates how this kind of entertainment reflected historical and social change. Since Independence, Argentina had seen the arrival of several circus companies run by foreign impresario-performers who staged shows that variously included clowns, gymnasts, live music, skits, magic, sword swallowing, and knife throwing.[45] In some cases, these circuses hosted pageant-like equestrian processionals and musical performances that highlighted local culture, to the delight of an audience of rural and urban working people who saw themselves and their world reflected to some degree in the arena.[46] It was not until the 1880s, however, that this embryonic combination of circus, theater, and pageant fully matured to become the Circo Criollo. Much of the credit for this transition belongs to the brilliant invention of the performer José "Pepe" Podestá and his family, who created the stage version of the most popular, iconic character of late nineteenth-century Argentinian culture: the outlaw gaucho Juan Moreira.

Pepe Podestá was born to Italian parents in Montevideo, but also spent some of his formative years in Buenos Aires.[47] As a boy and an adolescent, Pepe and his brothers spent their days recreating the gymnastics they had seen at circus shows. In 1873, when Pepe was fifteen, he and his fellow performers successfully staged their first circus under the banner of *Juventud Unida* (United Youth). Two years later, they began traveling the River Plate as contract players with established circuses that wandered

Figure 3.3. José Podestá as Pepino el 88, singing
the "Garbage Song" (1890), from the magazine
Caras y Caretas, 1905. Courtesy of Special
Collections, The University of Virginia Library.

from town to town. His brother Jerónimo and his sister Graciana were
acrobats like himself, and his brother Antonio was a musician and animal trainer. As was common among circus people, other members of the
family joined the business, raising their children to become performers
as well. In this, the first phase of his career, Pepe was a talented and powerful acrobat working on the trapeze and the horizontal bars. Although
gymnasts commonly worked the horizontal bars in the mid to late 1870s,
Podestá was the only athlete who used the enormously difficult combination of three horizontal bars in his act.[48]

Figure 3.4. José Podestá as Pepino the 88, and his burro, Pancho (1890), from the magazine *Caras y Caretas*, 1905. Courtesy of Special Collections, The University of Virginia Library.

In 1881, while on tour in Uruguay, Pepe's career took a momentous turn when he created a clown called Pepino el 88 (Pepino the 88). Since Pepe and his brothers were fond of joking with each other in Italian, the name Pepino (meaning "cucumber") emerged as a playful, Italianate version of Pepe's own name. The use of "88" came about when Pepe was cutting out a pattern of black circles to patch onto the baggy clown costume that his mother had sewn for him; when he cut the black fabric he had folded in fours, he produced two sets of circular black patches connected to each other, forming the number 88.[49] Pepe pasted this on his costume and became Pepino the 88, delighting audiences with his witty songs and jokes, most of which were inspired by the social and political problems of the day. One of his most famous songs was the "Garbage Song," which mocked the reign of false appearances in society: "The garbage that is swept up / does not stop being garbage / and even if it rises to the air / it is just garbage in the air." In another song, he skewered the corruption of financiers, capitalists, and landowners: "I buy, I sell / homes and land, / I pay and lend like a miser, / and after all / I don't hoodwink anyone, / just those that I can fool." He also made fun of cowardly men who talk big about revolution but who lack the guts to carry out their plans: "Suddenly one of them / gave the alarm / and that 'everyone make a run for it' / broke up that meeting. / And do you know what that noise had been? / Do you know who sent them running? / The braying of my burro / which was a revolution."[50] Pepino the 88 embodied the circus clown as a local satirist and as a Creole voice, and his comedy was based on voicing current events and caricaturing rural and urban people of all ranks. In contrast, the brilliant British clown Frank Brown (popularly known as Flon Blon), the other great clown of late nineteenth-century Argentina, represented a more European interpretation of the clown persona.

If Pepe Podestá had had two careers by the 1880s, the first as a great gymnast and the second as a popular clown, his third act was to become one of the most popular male actors of his day. The vehicle for this reinvention occurred in 1884 when he was tapped to star in the pantomime adaptation of the violent tale of the bandit gaucho Juan Moreira, first made famous by Eduardo Gutiérrez's 1879 bestselling novel. This hugely successful pantomime was followed two years later by another adaptation, in two acts and with dialogue, by Podestá himself. He stripped the novel to its most elementary themes and designed a spare plot that begins with Moreira being abused by the mayor and by an Italian barkeep named Sardetti, who owes him ten thousand pesos but refuses to pay him back. The mayor is a heartless man who leeringly plots to seduce the honest gaucho's wife. Although Moreira exacts his revenge by knifing Sardetti and the mayor, he cannot return to his wife because she has shacked up with another man after being told that her husband has been killed. Moreira drowns his sorrow at a *pulpería* and tells the barkeep that his destiny is to wander the world alone, at war with the police and society. "My life is to always fight the posses and to kill as many police as I can," he defiantly declares, "because they have done all the evil in my life and because of them I find myself persecuted like a beast everywhere I go."[51] The final scene of the play finds Moreira and his friend Julián at a brothel when the police swarm the locale. There is no dialogue in the script—just the stage direction for the police to enter and to face Moreira. In Gutiér-rez's novel, the bandit had died after being stabbed in the back as he tried to climb a wall; Podestá and his troupe improvised an all-out battle with the police in which Moreira dies a heroic death while fighting mano a mano. Indeed, despite all the other dialogue and instructions contained in the script, most of the play was improvised in the arena, with Podestá and his players incorporating new characters and injecting musical inter-ludes into the mix to add color. *Juan Moreira* was not so much a play as a spectacle composed of an assemblage of action scenes, with musical and humorous interludes, performed by actors who primarily delivered their lines facing the audience.

The Podestá stage versions of the story of Moreira took the River Plate by storm, spreading to performances in conventional theaters and even an operatic adaptation, Arturo Berutti's *Pampa* (1897). The popu-larity of Moreira dismayed many intellectuals, who complained of the phenomenon of *moreirismo*, in which rural and working-class men mod-eled the intransigent rebelliousness and criminality of Moreira in their own attitudes and behaviors.[52] One commentator wrote, "Without or-der there can be no progress and without submission and respect to the law and to the magistrate there can be no order . . . The cult of rage is incompatible with submission to authority because it is the basis of *moreirismo*."[53]

While Podestá's adaptation sensationalized crime and idealized its bandit hero, it also served as a theatrical prism for highlighting other aspects of contemporary society, such as the tremendous influx of Italian immigrants into Argentina. In one performance of the play, Jerónimo Podestá delighted the audience by playfully imitating the speech patterns of an Italian circus employee named Antonio Cocolicchio, but lovingly known by his coworkers as Cocoliche. In a separate performance, one of the company's actors, Celestino Petray, appeared on stage in a clownish gaucho costume and mounted on a spindly horse. Jerónimo Podestá wel-comed the mock gaucho by identifying him as Cocoliche. Petray made the audience roar when he responded in a nonsensical blend of mock Italian and Spanish: "Ma quiame Franchique Cocoliche, e songo cregoyo gasta lo güese de la taba!" (My name is Francisco Cocoliche, and I am

Figure 3.5. Cocoliche character, Buenos Aires, circa
1920. Photograph from the private collection of
Oestes A. Vaggi. Courtesy of Ana C. Cara.

Creole to the bone!)[54] The character of Cocoliche gave birth to a new
cultural type, the Italianate gaucho clown, whose ridiculous outfits and
linguistic patois became a perennial favorite in Carnival celebrations.
Embraced by all—even by Italian immigrants—the iconic Cocoliche
shows the enduring impact of the myth of Juan Moreira in the River
Plate and the contribution of the Podestá family to its iconography.

The People's Puppets

Besides theaters, circuses, and the Circo Criollo, the puppet theater in nineteenth-century Spanish America deserves some mention in these pages. Puppet theater is one of the most elastic forms of global performance culture because it traverses all social strata, occupying both a central and marginal position in a society's entertainments. The puppet theater can be as modest as the productions of an itinerant black puppeteer in Havana, a man called José el de las Suertes who played shows on street corners, saloons, and in people's homes.[55] It could also be housed in establishments like Chilean *chinganas* and the theater of Don Chole, and function as comedic entertainments that pushed the limits of what was proper. At the same time, puppets could be a staple of established, elite theater, as in the case of international troupes that brought their puppet programs to different countries, or when a local company was singled out by commentators for being both edifying and entertaining. This was the case with nineteenth-century Peru's greatest puppeteer, Manuel Valdivieso, the son of a leather shop owner who learned his trade on the streets of Lima and began performing at midcentury.[56] His cast of characters included over three hundred puppets and his performances were accompanied by a band of musicians that included a violinist, a guitar player, and a harpist. One member of his crew was Damian, a cross--dressing character who told jokes and performed physical comedy. Abelardo Gamarra, a Peruvian journalist, thought Valdivieso a living treasure because he was a moralist and teacher who knew how to capture the imagination of the common man. Valdivieso's puppets, Gamarra wrote, were the confidants of the man and woman of the street, who saw in them the interpretation of their passions, beliefs, hatreds, and loves.[57] The puppets belonged to the people.

The history of the puppet heroes of nineteenth-century Spanish America has yet to be written. Besides Gamarra's puppets, our gallery of heroes would have to include Don Cristobito, a stock character of the nineteenth-century Chilean puppet theater who is based on Christopher Columbus, but whose persona was deeply associated with Chilean national identity and pride. During the War of the Pacific (1879–1883), the great puppeteer and itinerant humorist Cayetano "El Tile" Vallejo staged a puppet show in the northern town of Copiapo, in which the iconic Don Cristobito defended Chile's national honor against the villainous Admiral Pareja of the Spanish navy. Vallejo whipped the audi-

Figure 3.6. The puppets of Zacatecas, from *Catalogue of a Collection of Objects Illustrating the Folklore of Mexico* (1899) by Frederick Starr. Nettie Lee Benson Latin American Collection, University of Texas Libraries, The University of Texas at Austin.

ence—which was full of children—into a frenzy when he had Pareja grab
Don Cristobito by his private parts and not let go. Don Cristobito cried
out: "Don't touch me there! It's dangerous! Let me go! . . . Don't do that!
Cancel the bets! The damned Spaniard is beating me! Don't squeeze me
so hard, *mister*, listen, *mister*, listen, that is a delicate thing! Ouch! Ouch!
Don't grab me there! What are you anyway, a sissy? . . . Hey, please! The
Spaniard has hold of me by a very bad place! Ouch! Help!"[58] At the same
time, in Peru, the puppets also went to war against the Spanish. In 1868,
a company of puppeteers staged an elaborately staged musical pageant in
Lima celebrating Peruvian resistance to the bombardment of the port of
Callao by the Spanish navy.[59]

Our gallery of iconic puppet heroes would also have to include the
Mexican characters of the Little Black Poet (whom we already met in
Chapter 2), and Vale Coyote, a half-Indian and half-black character whose
commentary on politics and culture was full of wordplay and irony. Vale
Coyote celebrated the people and needled the upper classes by mimicking patriotic speech and brilliantly distorting its cadences, grammar, and
pronunciation.[60] Similarly, in Bogotá, at the popular street corner known
as the *portal de Espina*, the puppeteers had a field day exaggerating and
mocking politicians and their parliamentary speeches and debates, in addition to celebrating national identity through *costumbrista* puppet pageants.[61] Any public figure was a candidate for the glory or humiliation of
being set in motion as a puppet, but what was ultimately most powerful
about this kind of theater was the way in which it validated the culture—
the speech, the beliefs, the experiences, the sensibility—of the street and
the countryside against the mainstream elite values of decorum, refinement, and politeness.

Blood Sports

Another category of spectacle and theatricality that challenged the prevailing views of the cultural establishment was blood sports. A blood
sport is any exhibition, performance, or sport that is predicated on violence between humans, between humans and animals, or between animals. The basest blood sports of all were cockfights and dogfights, which
brought men together for the purpose of placing bets on dueling animals
that fought to the death. Of all the forms of theatricality explored in this
chapter, this was the most primal and primitive because it dramatized aggression and death through the use of animals as proxies. For the crowds

of people who cheered when a cock fell in a heap of bloodied feathers in the arena, or when a bull snorted its last with a sword sunk to the hilt between its shoulder blades, the spectacle was a cathartic celebration of martial skill and bravery and an affirmation of life over death.

In Cuba, as in the rest of the Americas, cockfighting was a deeply ingrained pastime. For much of the nineteenth century, Havana's pre-eminent venue for cockfighting was the Valla de Gallos on the outskirts of the city, a roughly hewn, two-story circular frame building that seated up to a thousand spectators. Street vendors and beggars swarmed its entrance as crowds of people bought tickets and streamed into the building. Once inside, they were enveloped in cigar and cigarette smoke and the loud cheers of hundreds roaring at the cocks fighting in the arena. When a bird was wounded, its handler scooped it up, took a swig from a bottle of rum, and sprayed a mouthful of liquor on its head to reinvigorate it so that it could continue fighting to the death. The handlers tossed the birds at each other and the fight continued, with a rushing of feathers and violent, rapid lunging, until one bird lay incapacitated, in its death throes, on the bloodied dirt.[62] Spanish authorities taxed and regulated this sport, though strict enforcement was rarely possible, especially in rural areas. In 1844, for example, authorities ordered that cockfights take place only on holidays, that blacks be banned from the diversion, and that children be accompanied by adults. The sport was protected, though, because it was so lucrative; city authorities received three *reales* for every fight in which the cocks wore small knife-like blades attached to their heels, and two for battles in which the birds did not wear them. According to one estimate, the revenue from these taxes at midcentury was $14,163 a year.[63]

Some enlightened, liberal intellectuals deplored cockfighting as a symbol of cultural backwardness.[64] Others embraced it as an expression of local color. In the illustrated collection of occupations and types titled *Los cubanos pintados por sí mismos* (The Cubans painted by their own hand; 1852) we find an ambivalent and ironic representation of the *gallero*, the man who makes his living through cockfighting. The author, whose pseudonym is Licentiate Vidriera, praises cockfighting for its ties to classical traditions (specifically to Athens and the feats of Themistocles) and for the ways in which it symbolizes valor and virility. Most importantly, however, cockfighting is a symbol of *Cubanía* (Cubanness), because he claims that Cubans are, by disposition, talent, and the "sublimity" of their skills, the finest cockfighters in the world: "In the same way that poetic Andalucía is, without question, the classical land of bullfighters,

Italy of the *ciceroni*, and Mexico of the beggars, the island of Cuba is the land of cockfighters."[65] Vidriera's praise of the *gallero* is sarcastic because he concedes that during the off-season, the handler becomes a vagrant who frequents saloons and billiard halls. Clearly, it would be much better if this colorful character extricated himself from the world of gambling and spent his time in a nobler branch of industry, such as farming.

Bullfighting also provoked debate and controversy, but its social pedigree was generally greater than cockfighting because of its elaborate pageantry and its association with Hispanic identity and state ceremony. Despite centuries of regulation and admonishment by the Catholic Church, bullfighting remained an important diversion that authorities staged to commemorate public occasions. As in the case of cockfighting, bullfighting was objectionable to enlightened reformers because it indulged in violence and a lack of amity that was contrary to civilized society. Spectators became a mob that celebrated and pleasured in violence, breaking with formulas of Republican sociability and good manners considered central to civilized nations and peoples. The violence of the bullfight hardened the human spirit to violence, rather than nourishing the compassion necessary for constructive forms of association. In the words of the Cuban José Enrique Varona, "The people who become accustomed to seeing blood, spill it easily. . . . Such a spectacle would have pernicious effects among any people; among the Spaniards and their descendants, infinitely more."[66]

It is difficult to overstate how popular bullfighting was in Lima. Foreign travelers marveled at the throngs of thousands, most of them people of color, who walked to the bullring of Acho in the suburb of Lázaro on Monday afternoons and feast days to see the spectacular and bloody contest between man and beast. Along the Avenue of Acho, mulatta women with jasmine flowers in their hair served fermented corn drinks called *chicha* while men and women danced to the rhythms of musicians playing drums and Andean flutes called *tarasiyos*.[67] The whole city seemed to empty itself and to hold its breath. On the avenue, everyone crowded together as they converged on the bullring: the aristocratic *doñas* in their fancy two-wheeled carriages; the mysterious *tapadas*, each with only one eye showing through her enigmatic headdress; gentlemen and military officers on horseback; and tailors, cobblers, and carpenters on foot, alongside Afro-descendant and Indian laborers. The Chilean José Victorino Lastarria, who traveled to Lima in the middle of the century, wrote that blacks and mulattoes would sell their own cots to afford a ticket. "There are some whose visage and rags prove their indigence," he wrote, "and yet, those men present themselves in the stalls as happy and as proud as those who dress the best, and they whistle, and they clap every chance they get, like any taurophile."[68] From inside the stalls of the ring, spectators enjoyed shaved ices spiked with *chicha*, pineapple juices, roasted nuts, candies, sugar plums, boiled corn in plantain leaves, and drinks of water that were served out of the ladle of the water carrier. All the vendors had distinctive cries to advertise their products. A black cigarette seller flamboyantly advertised his cigarettes by methodically mimicking the act of smoking and then loudly smacking his lips and shouting, "How delicious!"[69]

The ring at Acho, built in 1766, is the third-oldest bullring in the world, after the arenas in Seville (1761) and Zaragoza (1764). In colonial Peru, bullfights were variously held in central plazas and other gathering places, ringed by carts and by wooden seating that could be disassembled after the spectacle.[70] The first bullfight in Peru was held shortly after the Conquest, in 1538, to celebrate Pizarro's victory over his rivals at the Battle of Salinas.[71] When Pope Pius V banned bullfighting in 1567, the Cabildo of Lima vigorously lobbied for its reinstatement, arguing that the sport was safe and necessary for the recruitment, training, and maintenance of horsemen capable of defending the kingdom against its enemies. Fortunately for the avid taurophiles of Lima, Pope Gregorius XIII reinstated the sport eight years later, although he decreed that bullfights not be held on religious holidays and that clerics be banned from attending, among other cautions. By the eighteenth century, bullfighting was a deeply entrenched Lima tradition, especially among the humbler classes.

Peruvian bullfighting was a hybrid of Spanish tradition and local innovations. In the first half of the century, Lima's bullfights normally began with the *despejo*, when soldiers in ceremonial uniforms cleared the ring with synchronized marching, formations, and symbolic battling set to music.[72] Another inaugural feature was the placement in the center of the ring of colorful piñata-like figures made out of paper and papier-mâché in the shape of fanciful human or animal characters, which crackled and noisily burst when bulls charged them. One traveler described one such contraption as a "fireship of rockets and squibs."[73] Other times, the paper figures were weighted and balanced on the bottom so that they moved from side to side and sprang back when bulls charged them. With regards to the actual bullfighting, two of the most distinctive characteristics of the Peruvian style were the *capeo a caballo* and the *toro ensillado*. The *capeo a caballo* was the art of taunting bulls with bright cloaks from atop a horse, especially after their initial release into the ring, for the purpose of taking the edge off of their speed and vitality. In the array of *suertes* (trials) to which bulls are put during bullfights, the *capeo a caballo* is celebrated as the national *suerte* of Peru. The *toro ensillado* was bullriding, which could take the form of a test of endurance, skill, or courage, or a clownish entertainment.

The greatest practitioners of the *capeo a caballo* and the *toro ensillado* were men and women of color who became celebrities among commoners and who garnered the sponsorship and protection of affluent fans. In the late eighteenth century, Mariano "El Indio" Cevallos, a Peruvian slave, entertained audiences in Spain by doing the *capeo a caballo*, riding bulls while lancing others, and throwing candies and other favors to spectators.[74] In engravings by Francisco Goya, we see Cevallos atop bucking bulls and, in one image, holding a dagger. The greatest *capeador a caballo* was the freed slave Esteban Arredondo, who rode out into the cheers of Acho smoking a cigar and wearing a wide-brimmed straw hat and a poncho or a white suit.[75] Another legendary figure was Juana Breña, a mulatta virago who rode horses at Acho in wide yellow skirts and in a straw hat with a blue ribbon. Ricardo Palma, Peru's preeminent collector of popular lore, wrote that after a brush with death in the ring in 1825, the mannish woman gave up bullfighting and became a well-known fixture at Lima's Plaza Bolívar, where she worked as a butcher.[76]

Another distinctive feature of the bullfight entertainment in Lima was comedy and clowning. One practice was to use a crew of drunken Indians called *mojarreros* armed with long lances to lie in wait on their stomachs for bulls to charge them. In the charge, the *mojarreros*, who posed no real danger to the beasts, were dispersed and chased by the bulls to the delight of the cheering crowds.[77] Other forms of comedy included the placement of clowns on bulls, or other gags, such as the performances of a very popular *zambo* (half-Indian, half-black) clown called Ño Nuez Moscada. The nickname is something of an enigma: *Ño* is short for "Señor," *nuez* is "walnut" and *moscada* is the participle form of either *muescar* (to brand cattle by cutting a groove in its ear) or *mascar* (to chew or grind). Ño Nuez Moscada, who was well known around Lima as a street seller who specialized in religious and children's booklets, was hired to dress up as a clown and ride out into the ring on top of a pathetic-looking donkey to face a bullock with blunted horns. The Nuez Moscada entertainment represented bullfighting in ridiculous,

Figure 3.7. Angel Valdez, "El Maestro," circa 1860, from *Algo del Perú* (1905) by Ultimo Harabica [Abelardo Gamarra]. Nettie Lee Benson Latin American Collection, University of Texas Libraries, The University of Texas at Austin.

caricature form, with its beloved protagonist and his noble steed being knocked about by the young bull.[78]

The most famous bullfighter in nineteenth-century Peru was another Afro-descendant, Angel Custodio Valdez y Franco (1838–1911), who hailed originally from Nazca.[79] When he was ten years old, Valdez moved to Lima, where he got a job at a cattle ranch and became a passionate fan of bullfighting. After coming under the wing of the Mexican bullfighter José María Vázquez, Valdez began to perform as a matador at Acho in 1857. Valdez performed on foot in an unadorned, straightforward, courageous, and muscular style. Although he was familiar with the *volapie* charge, in which a matador lunges forward for the kill while playing the bull to the right with his cloak, he preferred to kill by receiving the bull's charge directly, which was much more dangerous. He was also skilled at vaulting over bulls with his lance and other colorful moves, such as driving *banderilla* darts into the backs of bulls with his mouth. Legend has it that when this young bullfighter was selected to lead a quadrille of bullfighters during the season of 1860–1861, three racist Spanish toreadors refused to participate. Unperturbed, Valdez fielded and killed all twelve bulls by himself, to the great jubilation of the crowds. His most famous accomplishment was a contest with a notoriously fierce bull called Arabí Pachá in 1885. Arabí Pachá had furiously dispersed several other bullfighters upon charging out into the ring before Valdez calmly walked up behind him and called out his name. Arabí Pachá turned and charged, and Valdez drove his sword into the animal to the hilt, killing him. For such feats, Valdez was arguably the most beloved and respected Afro-descendant in late nineteenth-century Peru.

The symbolic meanings of bullfighting for the construction of identity are various. The popularity of Valdez, among other local talent, underscored the power of popular and ethnic nationalism, which celebrated Peruvian bullfighters as symbols of local identity. Valdez was both a symbol of ethnic pride for the large numbers of Afro-descendants who lived in Lima, as well as a national symbol of *Peruanidad* in comparison to Spanish bullfighters. This latent tension between Peru and Spain also manifested itself to some degree in criticisms that Peruvian bullfighting was savage and barbaric. In a satirical poem, Felipe Pardo y Aliaga noted that in bullfights, "There will be humorous scenes, / Blood, deaths and other things / That will make us die laughing."[80] Another taurophile complained in 1842 in the pages of the newspaper *El Comercio* that Peruvian bullfighting was brutish and bloody in comparison to the elegance and refinement of bullfighting in Spain. "Our bulls are not bad; what is needed are good toreadors," he wrote, "and to banish some abuses that, far from being pleasurable, sometimes make the spectacle nauseous."[81] The critic might have been referring to practices that faded in the second half of the century, such as the gruesome spiking of bulls straight through the head and into the body with long spears levered and aimed from atop stakes planted on the ground, or the use of half-moon blades on staffs to cripple bulls by slicing their leg tendons. The return of Spanish bull-fighters to Peru in 1848, after two decades of absence since the Wars of Independence, helped standardize bullfighting and imported elements of Spanish form and style into the Lima spectacle.

The cultural politics of bullfighting had various meanings in Spanish America. In late nineteenth-century Cuba, liberal thinkers who were restless under Spanish rule associated bullfighting with colonialism and celebrated baseball as a more civilized and democratic alternative to the killing of bulls. For the Mexican public, bullfighting became infused with national pride as local matadors like the legendary mustachioed Ponciano Díaz competed with clean-shaven Spanish matadors like the accomplished Luis Mazzantini. Although Díaz and Mazzantini went out of their way to publicly demonstrate their gallant friendship and mutual respect, trying to build a cultural bridge between both countries, Díaz's Mexican followers resisted the symbolic reconciliation. At one *corrida*, Mexican spectators rained stones on Mazzantini and chanted, "Death to Spaniards!"[82] In the words of a Ponciano follower, "Whoever is not behind Ponciano is not a true Mexican but a *gachupín* who disrespects his country."[83] Like other diversions and forms of theatricality, bullfighting was a blend of tradition and modernity—of Spanish influence and Spanish American innovation.

Of *Angelitos* and Communities

All the examples of theatricality that we have touched on in this chapter involve performances, rituals, and spectacles that helped to cement communal identity and to affirm old traditions or to legitimize new ones. In the countryside, theatricality served the same function, although it did not stage mass celebrations or secular entertainments like Republican fiestas or *costumbrista* plays. Away from cities, the ceremonials of theatricality were primarily spiritual, involving the feasts of the Catholic liturgy and syncretic traditions that wed ancient belief systems to the practices of the church. In the life of a peasant or a villager, theatricality involved religious icons, nativity scenes, and Easter processionals. Such rituals bound the experience of a family to a broader community of believers. An illustrative case in point is the tradition of the *velorio del angelito* (wake of the little angel), which was universal throughout the Spanish-speaking Americas among rural peoples.[84] After the death of an infant or a child, the family dressed the deceased in special clothes, sometimes affixing crowns or wings to the body, or even seating it on a throne in a simulation of a religious icon.[85] When the body rested in a coffin, family members decorated it with flowers and streamers and proceeded to hold dances around it, sometimes passing the small coffin or the body around for dancers to hold as they danced and sang mournful songs. Pastries and other special foods and alcohol were served to the celebrants, all of whom believed that the dead child had the ability to intercede in heaven on behalf of family members and godparents. These funerary fiestas began to fade by the twentieth century, under the combined weight of modernization and vigorous church and civilian prohibitions against its practice. For our purposes, the *velorio del angelito* underlines the deeply symbolic, ritual nature of theatricality, shared to different degrees by all the spectacles and diversions included in this chapter. The ceremonies of middle-class conduct, the celebration of national heroes, the primal thrill of man facing bull, and the puppets that laughed at the enemies of the people were all players in a ritual of community that affirmed a sense of identity, expressed joy, or made sense of lived experience.

CHAPTER 4

Image

On July 28, 1872, Venezuela's largest art exhibit to date opened its doors to the public at the Café del Ávila, a coffee shop located next to the Palacio de Gobierno on the western side of the Plaza Mayor in Caracas, across from the city's cathedral. (The plaza would not be rechristened Plaza Bolívar for another two years.)[1] The exhibit, which contained over two hundred objects of art, was the brainchild of an Englishman named James Mudie Spence, a tourist, art collector, and entrepreneur who had ingratiated himself with the highest echelons of Venezuelan power, including President Antonio Guzmán Blanco.

On the first day of the exhibit, guests of honor crowded the Ávila until 3 p.m., after which curious passersby were allowed to enter. People gathered in groups to look at the paintings, and to talk about what they were seeing. They looked at the watercolors by Felicia Castillo de Amundaray and Ana Gathman, ladies of high society whose works, like those of many of the male artists in the exhibit, were copies of well-known paintings or lithographs. They admired Venezuelan landscapes and scenes of everyday life, such as Ramón Bolet's watercolor of a charcoal delivery man alongside a donkey. There were military-themed paintings, as well as sculptures and the handcolored photographs of the city's best photographers, Próspero Rey and José Antonio Salas. Thousands visited during the four-day exhibit. An awed journalist from the newspaper *La Opinión Nacional* called it a splendid sanctuary of national art that demanded reverence.

At the banquet that the owner of the Ávila hosted for the artists and the crème de la crème of society, dignitaries stood to toast the virtues and friendship of Spence, and to celebrate the powers of art to improve society. Antonio Leocadio Guzmán, the father of Venezuela's president, stood and called the exhibit a dream from which he did not want to wake. It communicated to him the powerful bond of friendship between England and Venezuela, one that promised to help his young republic in its quest for progress. Others spoke about how art played a key role in consolidating national pride and cultivating the spirit and intellect of a people. General Eduardo Calcaño stood up and declared that artists should commemorate Venezuela's glorious, heroic past, and produce art capable of stirring patriotic feelings in their descendants. The speakers agreed that more exhibits should take place, and that the government should support the teaching of the fine arts and sponsor the work of Venezuelan artists.

The Ávila exhibit and the praise commentators showered on it is representative of how cultural elites across Spanish America understood the themes, topics, and values that the fine arts should embody. Yet, alongside this definition of art, there was a different kind of pictorial and sculptural image. A visitor to the Ávila exhibit could find it by simply walking out of the exhibit and sauntering across the crowded Plaza Mayor, past the fruit and vegetable vendors, to look at the varied painted and constructed objects on blankets, stands, and movable carts near the cathedral's heavy wooden doors. The art for sale there included brightly colored paintings of the Virgin Mary, various saints, and Jesus, as well as elaborately dressed wax dolls. One disapproving Protestant traveler wrote: "I was particularly struck with one . . . in which the Virgin, dressed in all the frippery imaginable, was kneeling beside a gigantic crucifix, while a six-year-old angel fluttered above the cross, dressed in silver-embroidered trunk-hose and tartan leggings of the royal Stuart pattern."[2] For the modest housewife or the Afro-descendant shoemaker who bought an inexpensive picture of the Virgin Mary here, their purchase was an icon of religious devotion and domesticity—an instrument for assisting in prayer and reverence. The patrons of the Ávila exhibit, like other nineteenth-century Spanish American critics, considered such artifacts too primitive to be aesthetically pleasing. In 1849, the Chilean writer Miguel Luis Amunátegui complained about the inexpensive religious art of Quito, Ecuador, that flooded the Chilean market. He criticized the flatness of the human form in these paintings, the lack of realistic perspective, the use of bright colors. "They are not human figures," he wrote. "What they delineate are monsters."[3]

The story of these two displays of art, one at the Café Ávila and the other across the plaza, reminds us that the creation and dissemination of pictures reflected contrasting attitudes, expectations, and cultural practices tied to class difference. Religious, devotional art was domestic and spiritual, and defined by an individual's relationship to God, whereas fine painting was framed by the concept of national progress, Europeanized notions of good taste, and forms of consumption and display that were generally linked to privilege. Often, critics speak of high art and low art, but the reality on the ground was much more complex. Like other cultural artifacts, pictures existed on a spectrum that catered to different kinds of people for different purposes. For example, the Peruvian illustrator Pancho Fierro, whom we examine in more detail in this chapter, was the son of a slave, but foreign travelers and members of the elite of Lima collected his illustrations during his lifetime. His art reflected his knowledge of the street, and a sense of humor we may call streetwise, but it was consumed and appreciated by people of influence. In the pages that follow, we explore these telling ambiguities alongside more generalized patterns in art education, aesthetics, technology, and consumption. As with other types of culture examined in this book, pictorial culture was a site of unexpected encounters between old and new, as well as a vehicle for defining and representing different types of identity and cultural memory.

Academic Art

Spanish American governments, art critics, and affluent art patrons supported only art in the European style. This did not mean that Spanish American painters did not paint American subjects, but simply that their works adopted the themes and patterns of composition and execution that defined European painting. In a practical sense, the only way to cultivate such artists in Spanish America was to train them as their European contemporaries were trained, and to facilitate their travel to Europe to perfect their art. More than most cultural forms preferred by states and cultural elites, painting required a considerable investment of capital, and the founding and maintenance of institutions and associations designed to support artists and help them achieve national and international recognition. In eighteenth- and nineteenth-century Europe, the institutions that promoted prestigious artistic endeavors were academies of art, institutions that began to spread to Spanish America in the late eighteenth century. Although nineteenth-century Spanish American academies were often crippled by a lack of funding and political instability, they shaped outstanding artists whose works were as fine as those of their greatest European contemporaries. Even in Spanish American countries without academies, the aesthetic promoted by European academic art was dominant in the teaching of art and the style, techniques and themes that painters adopted.

At its simplest, an art academy was an art school with strong ties to a government that supported the studies of its pupils and instructors by commissioning paintings, sculptures, or architectural designs from it. An academy was a country's most visible and respected arbiter of taste and quality, and a sponsor of juried art exhibitions called "salons." Prior to the rise of the academic model, European artists were organized in guilds, which were associations that facilitated the training of apprentices, regulated market prices, and formed a strong, protective community bond among its members. When academies began to emerge in the seventeenth century, they differed from guilds because of their affiliation with governments and a more comprehensive approach to study: apprentice artists were not simply trained in skills, techniques, and labor, but also in aesthetics, literature, and history.[4] Notions of prestige and refinement, as well as an increasing faith in rationalism and science were aspects of academic training that differentiated it from the guild system.[5]

The earliest academies were formed in sixteenth-century Italy, and important artists such as Leonardo da Vinci, Bertoldo di Giovanni, and Michelangelo were associated with them. The French Royal Academy of Painting and Sculpture, founded in 1648, became widely influential in Europe and helped to inspire the founding of the Academy of Fine Arts in Vienna (1692), the Spanish Royal Academy of San Fernando (1744), and the British Royal Academy (1769). In the nineteenth century, the French Academy and other European academies sought to strengthen morality and civic pride by promoting religious and historical painting. In the prevailing hierarchy of genres, the most prestigious subjects were biblical, mythological, and historical scenes. Below these, in descending order of value, were portraiture, scenes of everyday life, landscapes, animals, and still lives. The study of art at an academy emphasized drawing and the imitation of the works of European masters, as well as aesthetics and mathematics, which was particularly important for architecture students. Academies sponsored frequent art exhibits and recognized the excellence of their finest pupils with prizes, the most prestigious of which were scholarships to travel to a European capital to study the work of the masters directly. The dominant style was neoclassical, which privileged Greek and Roman architecture and literature, and staged sharply delineated figures in a static fashion. In the latter half of the century, romanticism became influential, as well as *just milieu*, a blend of neoclassical and romantic themes and techniques designed to appeal to art patrons.[6] Another feature of academic painting was its smooth, finished texture, reflecting the rejection of brushstroke marks on the canvas, a technique the French called *fini* (finish). In sum, European academic art was tied to political privilege and cultural influence, and was characterized by reverence for the art of antiquity and a polished and crisp pictorial style.

In colonial Spanish America, two royal academies were instituted: the Academy of San Carlos in Mexico City (1781) and the Academy of San Alejandro in Havana (1818). In other parts of eighteenth-century Spanish America, there were tentative steps toward the founding of academies or academy-like schools. The Chilean Academy of San Luis, founded in 1797 by Manuel de Salas with the backing of the governor of Chile, sought to use math and art instruction to improve industry. In Peru, Viceroy Abascal recruited an artist from Quito named Francisco Javier Cortés to lead classes of drawing at the School of Medicine of San Fernando in 1808. One year later, in Caracas, a mestizo artist named Juan José Franco, who had trained at the Royal Academy of San Fernando in Spain, petitioned the city to open an academy but was refused because he was not white.[7] After Independence, the academic project in the arts continued to gain traction. Though briefly interrupted by the War of Independence, and hobbled by financial shortfalls in the first half of the century, the Mexican Academy of San Carlos endured and trained Mexico's most important nineteenth-century painters. Beginning in 1835, Venezuela saw a succession of state-sponsored academies of art, such as the Academy of Drawing (1835), the Academy of Fine Arts (1849), the Provincial Institute of Fine Arts (1852), and the Institute of Fine Arts (1870), among others. Similarly, the drive to institute art academies in Argentina began in 1815 through various institutions that culminated in 1877 with the creation of the Society for the Promotion of Fine Arts, an organization created by a dedicated group of Argentinian artists to promote art and its teaching.[8] Chilean president Manuel Bulnes founded his country's academy of painting in 1849, which for nearly forty years was directed by European headmasters outsourced from Italy and Germany. In Colombia, the Vásquez Academy (1873) embodied the academic project until the founding of the School of Fine Arts (1886), which staged that country's first large-scale, comprehensive exhibit of Colombian art.[9] In Lima, the talented painters Ignacio Merino and Francisco Lazo directed the government-sponsored Academy of Drawing (1841).[10]

Academies varied from country to country because of finances and political conditions. What remained constant was the academic aesthetic of neoclassicism, the smooth canvas finish, the practice of staging juried exhibits, the conferral of scholarships for study abroad in France or Italy, and certain teaching techniques. Students in an academy focused primarily on drawing, which was considered to be an indispensable foundation for painting and architecture. Teaching and learning was based on copying; students copied plaster casts, sculptural busts, and full body sculptures, as well as reproductions of paintings by Renaissance painters.[11] In addition to copying such works, which academies procured from Europe with the financial support of the state, students studied textures such as folded and draped fabrics so that they could draw (and eventually paint) the appearance of clothes on the human body. If a student excelled at a salon exhibit, he might receive a prize to study in Rome or Paris, and compete for a place in European salons. After all, one of the reasons that academic art was sponsored by Spanish American governments was because statesmen and cultural commentators saw it as a way of correcting the view that Spanish America was underdeveloped and unequal in comparison to Europe. The conferral of an international distinction on an artist provided a platform for expressions of cultural nationalism that could be used to rally citizens and public opinion. In 1850, Mexican newspapers celebrated when Italian art patrons and critics acclaimed a large canvas of Christopher Columbus by Juan Cordero, who was working in Florence on a scholarship from the Academy of San Carlos. "Let this serve as an example to destroy that worry that we're incapable of doing anything," wrote a commentator in the newspaper *El Demócrata*. "If all branches had received the impetus that has been given to painting, it is easy to see the happy results that we would have achieved. . . . The Mexican name would be honored by the soldier, the farmer, the artist, etc."[12]

In general, any youngster could enroll in an academy as long as they could provide proof of talent and good character. The Mexican Pedro Patiño Ixtolinque, who directed the Academy of San Carlos in Mexico City from 1825 to 1835, was an Indian who received a twelve-year scholarship from the school in 1788. After working as an assistant to the Spanish director of sculpture, Manuel Tolsá, Patiño became a teacher, and in 1817 applied for the prestigious title of *académico de mérito*, which he received after some controversy and deliberation because of his ethnicity. Shortly after this victory, while his Spanish colleagues were supporting the Spanish monarchy in the Mexican War of Independence, Patiño joined the insurgent forces of General Vicente Guerrero and fought against Spain.[13]

Art academies were also a way for working artisans to acquire skills that they could use to make a living, which was why night classes were particularly popular. The records of the Academy of San Carlos indicate that many of the school's applicants were children between the ages of twelve and fourteen who worked in trades like carpentry, blacksmithing, and shoemaking.[14] At the Chilean Academy, artisans enrolled to learn the basics of drawing, design, and mathematics, but the state sought to create a separate track for such students, channeling them into a night school of drawing expressly designed to support artisans and their children. Domingo Sarmiento praised this school, located in the working-class neighborhood of Chimba, because it promised to protect and dignify the artisan class: "Linear drawing, as popular education," he wrote, "goes straight to the primary object of education, which is to empower the individual to better provide for his necessities, to acquire the means to progress."[15] Besides self-reliance, such alternatives to the academy were also driven by a desire to promote economic development and competition.[16]

Politically and culturally, Spanish American art academies occupied a contradictory space in which European influence and nationalist pride came together. No one questioned that the European model of the academy was the best way to promote national progress in the fine arts, but the slavish imitation of European models, and the preeminence given to European teachers over local ones, caused friction and resentment. Francisco Zarco, one of Mexico's earliest art critics, complained that the Academy of San Carlos, which was run by European instructors, treated Mexican artists like Juan Cordero and Primitivo Miranda unjustly and with disrespect. Antonio Smith, one of Chile's greatest landscape painters, had studied as an adolescent under the Neapolitan Alejandro Cicarelli shortly after the founding of the Chilean Academy, but struck out on his own instead, rejecting his teacher's rigid neoclassicism in favor of a more romantic approach. In 1858, Smith published a caricature of Cicarelli in a magazine called *El Correo Literario*, representing him as a silly-looking man with a pointed nose and large mustaches and sideburns. The inscription reads, "He arrived to these beautiful regions as a painter; he was momentous; he showed boxes full of diplomas, distinctions, and medals, but he did not show any talent."[17] Another tension was subject matter.

Since academic teaching was predicated on copying, and on European models, many academic painters focused on neoclassical, Greco-Latin, or biblical themes, rather than on local, American subjects. Cuba's José Martí was living in Mexico in 1876 when he wrote an article complaining about the imitative nature of the art created by the faculty and students of the Academy of San Carlos. Mexico fascinated foreign commentators and travelers, but why didn't Mexican artists share this interest? To be useful, Martí wrote, the Academy of San Carlos should forget biblical and mythological themes and promote the painting of Mexican types, which would sell easily and be everywhere embraced.[18]

By the end of the century, nationalist, historical painting had taken root in Spanish American academies and become a dominant trend. A select group of talented painters that included Arturo Michelena (Venezuela), Juan Manuel Blanes (Uruguay), Franciso Laso (Peru), and Leandro Izaguirre (Mexico) resolved the paradox of foreign/local by using academic techniques and an academic sensibility to produce vibrant and inspiring works of nationalist art. Since many of their paintings were generally commissioned by governments, they were indeed official art to some degree, but this does not detract from their compositional and symbolic richness. They were not propaganda, but rather sophisticated and beautiful reflections on history. For example, let's consider Arturo Michelena's *Miranda en La Carraca* (1896), which depicts Francisco de Miranda, one of Venezuela's greatest heroes of Independence, in a prison cell at La Carraca Prison in Spain in July 1816. This treatment of Miranda shows him reclining on a straw cot in his prison cell. His sharp-featured face, propped on his right hand, radiates intelligence and learning, especially because of the penetrating gaze of the eyes staring directly out of the painting. Miranda's partially reclining posture, with his left leg on the cot and his right leg on the stone floor, suggests the possibility of motion—of a man ready to stand up in an instant. Although his individual fate, and that of Venezuelan independence, is in that moment in question, as represented by an unforgiving black shadow on the prison wall behind his head, there is also an aura of projected light on the same wall, emanating from the left side of his body, implying both the glory of his contribution to Independence and its eventual triumph. One telling detail is the stool in front of the cot, with a frayed piece of its rope seat come loose, seeming to suggest that the tight weave of history, of an old monarchical social order, has begun to irreversibly unravel through the sacrifice of men like Miranda. If we look carefully, we can see how the painting balances precise draftsmanship (line) with hints of imaginative impressionism (color, tone, and shadow).

Another masterpiece of Spanish American academic art is *El juramento de los treinta y tres orientales* (1877) by Juan Manuel Blanes, a large canvas that depicts a foundational moment in the Uruguayan resistance to Brazil, which in 1824 had annexed the region (then known as the Banda Oriental). The panoramic painting shows the patriot insurgent Juan Antonio Lavalleja and his band of thirty-two *Orientales* planting a flag and vowing to liberate their land. Academic art's signature crispness of line is everywhere evident in the canvas's colorful crowd of thirty-three men, who are cheering, and gesturing with their weapons, hats, and hands. We see gauchos and country people, and mustachioed Creoles in more traditional military uniform. There's a lot to look at, and dwell on, and the painting glows with both color and nationalist pride. Beyond the splendid visuality of the scene—the positioning of bodies, the setting, the

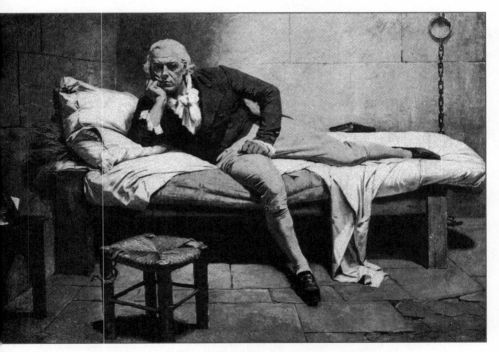

Figure 4.1. *Miranda en La Carraca* (Miranda in La Carraca Prison; 1896), by Julio Michelena, from *Bulletin of the Pan American Union*, 1920.

flag—the painter uses the richness of bodily gesture and facial expressions to evoke in the mind of the viewer the sounds of many voices swearing an oath and cheering. When Blanes went public with the painting in his Montevideo studio, it caused a sensation, with thousands of people coming by to proudly marvel at it.

By and For the People

As indicated at the beginning of this chapter, the popular arts manufactured images that were in many ways antithetical to academic art. The popular image did not attend to the aesthetic values, techniques, and materials that were central to academic art, leading nineteenth- and twentieth-century art critics to call it primitive or naïve, as if its artists were children. Another important difference was that popular art did not circulate publicly as academic art did. The art of the elites wanted to be shown at national and international exhibits and public buildings, while popular art mostly hung at home, or as an offering at a church altar. Yet, the two kinds of image-making intersected through a shared interest in religion. The difference was that the Christian subject was one topic among others for academic artists whereas for popular artists the topic was dominant. For this reason, we may refer to the art available to people of modest means as primarily devotional, meaning that it was designed to be a part of a family's spiritual relationship with God. Nothing was more intimate and personal than this relationship: God, the saints, and the Virgin Mary were not distant companions, but intimates who were bound up with the experience of joy and grief. The devotional image was a vital accessory in this sphere of religiosity. Naturally, middle- and upper-class people also deeply valued devotional imagery, but through education and access to magazines, books, and newspapers, they also cultivated an interest in a wide variety of secular imagery.

Who were the artists who made popular devotional art? Before Independence, artists were organized in guilds that regulated prices, trained apprentices, and supported their members in times of hardship. In the nineteenth century, the preeminence of the academic model of instruction in cities led to the creation of state-sponsored vocational schools for artisans called *escuelas de artes y oficios*, in which youngsters learned reading and writing, as well as illustration, ornamentation, or any other trade that they wanted. Although the guild system no longer existed, most artisans continued to learn through the apprenticeship system, often by

Figure 4.2. Detail from *El juramento de los treinta y tres orientales*
(The oath of the thirty-three Orientales; 1877), by Juan Manuel Blanes.
Courtesy of Museo Juan Manuel Blanes de la Intendencia de Montevideo.

practicing their family's trade alongside their parents and grandparents, or by convincing an established artisan to take them on as a pupil. The artisans sold their devotional paintings and figurines from their modest workshops, or carted the products to plazas, loading them onto rudimentary tables or blankets to display them. They were not people of rank or prestige, as indicated by the fact that their salaries were comparable to those of blacksmiths, carpenters, shoemakers, tin workers, and bakers.[19]

Paul Marcoy, a French traveler who visited Peru in the 1840s, published a valuable account about the devotional art and artists of the legendary city of Cuzco. He noted that the ancient capital of the Inca Empire boasted of only two or three artists who did religious commissions for the affluent and for the less affluent. The subjects of these commissions included shepherds, the Stations of the Cross, busts or full body canvases of the Saints, and many depictions of the Virgin Mary, often copied from engravings. To create such pictures, these enterprising painters had to be very creative: for their paints they mixed local soil, powders from the apothecary, oil from foodstuffs, and the soot of candle smoke. Marcoy visited one of these humble artists in his studio, which was a gloomy room strewn with vegetable scraps, with chickens and guinea pigs hungrily rushing about the floor. Marcoy christened this Indian painter with the name Raphael of the Cancha; "Raphael" was a sarcastic nod to the Italian master (Marcoy's point of view was patronizing in matters of art and taste), and "Cancha" referred to the proximity of the artist's home to a cockfighting *cancha* (ring). Marcoy wrote that artists like Raphael of the Cancha were essentially poor people, "because their naked toes are seen protruding through the holes of their shoes, or their shirt hanging out from their tattered inexpressibles when the wind blows aside the rag of fustian which serves for a cloak."[20]

Artisans like Rafael de la Cancha created images of saints and virgins that were the most ubiquitous imagery in people's homes and businesses throughout Spanish America. In Mexico, the photography studio of Cruces y Campa staged a series of photographs of trades and occupations in the 1860s that illustrates how devotional art was associated with commoners and with women in particular. Cruces y Campa's photograph of a plainly dressed woman ironing shows her in the corner of a bare room decorated with a print of Saint Anthony of Padua holding the baby Jesus.[21] The image of a smiling woman with Indian features who is on her knees grinding corn shows two religious prints on the wall behind her, including one of the Holy Child of Atocha, which represents Jesus as a seated child with long, flowing hair, a plumed hat, a staff, and a basket.[22] Pancho Fierro, a Peruvian illustrator whom we examine in more detail below, painted many street scenes of Lima during his lifetime, and in several watercolors of shops and saloons we find images of the Virgin Mary prominently placed in their interiors.

Devotional pictures often did more than simply represent a religious icon directly. Artisans could infuse their images with the worldview of

Figure 4.3. Woman ironing, by the photography studio of
Antioco Cruces y Luis Campa, Mexico City, circa 1870.
Photograph courtesy of the Collection of Wolfgang Wiggers.

their humble consumers, reflecting distinctive and localized beliefs and symbols. In the Andes, artisans were particularly fond of using imagery that featured Saint James the Moor Killer (Santiago el Matamoros), Saint Isidore, and Saint John the Baptist, icons that indigenous people associated with the pre-Columbian deities who were linked to war, farming, and the natural world. The unnamed artists of these rare, unsigned images depicted the iconic saints in ways that made them appear more Indian than white, and arranged them in ways that modeled an Amerindian cosmology in which the Virgin Mary occupied the upper realm, Saint James and Saint John the middle realm, and Saint Isidore the lower realm, which was associated with the soil and its tilling. Painted with the same pigments used in other crafts, these pictures were often placed on a mixture of textile and hardened clay, as if to suggest that the image had been cut from a mural. The pictures were also devoid of shading and conventional European perspective and proportionality.[23]

One of the most distinctive and individuated forms of popular devotional art was the Mexican *retablo*, a religious painting on tin that depicted a saint or the Virgin Mary. The sheets of metal ranged in size primarily from 7" x 10" to 10" x 14."[24] One kind of *retablo* was the *milagro* (miracle), a picture offered to a sacred icon in gratitude for a promise honored in a moment of life versus death or a tremendous personal crisis. In nineteenth-century central and northern Mexico, the painting of *retablos* on inexpensive sheets of tin became a common practice among local artists, who prepared them to order for their humble customers. Specifically, the *milagros* combined the pictorial depiction of tragedy with a handwritten script that explained the crisis and the miracle in question. In one, Mrs. Ignacio Hernández offers thanks to Christ for healing Mr. José María Gómez, who had been severely burned when he fell into a pot of hot lard in 1861. The *retablo* illustrates both the accident and the image of Christ. In another, Rafael Luján presents an illustrated *milagro* to thank Christ for saving him from falling over a precipice while he was riding a runaway mule.[25]

Such *retablos* had equivalents in other parts of Spanish America in delicate silver charms shaped like parts of the human body, which were offered at church altars in gratitude for favors received, or to request them. Whatever form an *ex voto* took, it was always defined as a token of sincere gratitude and devotional reciprocity. It was not a work of "art" to be analyzed, collected, and exhibited for secular purposes. Rather, it was an intimate and spiritual object that carried within it the faint echo of the prayers that countless men and women offered to the heavens, for favors requested and received.

By a Woman's Hand

In nineteenth-century Western culture, middle- and upper-class women were identified with the so-called domestic or private sphere, meaning that their intellectual, emotional, and social lives were defined by the home and by family life. Attributes such as sensitivity, fragility, and virtue constituted a narrow feminine realm and defined what it meant to be a mother, a wife, a daughter, or a sister. In Spanish America, as in Europe, this domestic definition of women did not preclude their education in the fine arts, nor their occasional public recognition as poets, novelists, musicians, or painters. Indeed, the heightened sense of feeling associated with women could authorize them as artists with something valuable to say about feeling and beauty. As a mother of future citizens, and the companion of man, a well-educated woman was key to the betterment of society, and to the material and spiritual well-being of the modern family. "The dangers and benefits of a woman's level of education to man are so great," wrote the nineteenth-century Venezuelan historian Rafael María Baralt, "that in all truly educated and civilized societies the molding of the heart of woman, and of her understanding, has been the object of exquisite care."[26]

In the arts, what held most Spanish American women back was the lack of independence that domesticity imposed on them. Young women who shone in adolescence as publicly recognized artists more often than not faded away after getting married and having children. Even unmarried women struggled to maintain their vocation because of the rigors of helping their mothers and sisters keep a household. As illustrators and painters, women were also limited in academic settings by prohibitions against their taking courses of study about human anatomy.[27] For this reason, talented women educated at an academy might be more adept at drawing hands, feet, faces, and draped clothes than the human form, or might be encouraged to pursue primarily landscapes, still lives, and devotional, religious painting, which presented the human form in more static and formulaic poses. Early art critics noted these limitations and criticized them, observing that if a woman could have equal access to the aesthetic instruction offered to a man, she could be as great if not greater than any male peer. In a review of women's paintings exhibited at the Chilean Salon of 1883, an anonymous commentator wrote, "The education of woman is restricted to a circle of ideas so narrow that it cannot embrace those grand realms that a work of art must materialize in order to dignify itself as art."[28] The Mexican writer Leopolda Gasso y Vidal expressed similar ideas in a Mexican women's magazine in 1885, in a blunt feminist critique of women's art education. She objected that women were condemned to painting landscapes and fruit baskets when they were capable of much more, especially in an age that recognized that women were as bright as men, and as important to society. Women artists should be free to cast aside "puerile pursuits that situate us on the same level as children and which deviate us from the mission we are called to bring to fruition." There is no conflict between domestic labor and the life of the mind and artistic creation, Gasso y Vidal wrote, because new technologies have made the maintenance of the home easier.[29]

Despite such challenges and obstacles, the annals of Spanish American academic painting reveal skilled women artists who achieved honors and recognition in an art establishment controlled exclusively by men. The majority of these women belonged to the upper classes. The most cursory reading of the biographies of the women who attended the Mexican Academy of San Carlos reveals that the majority belonged to the old colonial aristocracy, the affluent merchant class, or to families associated with the highest echelons of political power. The two most celebrated women painters of nineteenth-century Chile, Magdalena and Aurora Mira, hailed from a wealthy, conservative landowning family with strong ties to the art establishment and political class. Rebeca Oquendo Díaz, nineteenth-century Peru's most successful woman painter, was educated in Europe and received a college degree from the Sorbonne in Paris, where she also competed at several salons among the best academic painters from around the world. The axiom that privilege begets opportunity applies to these and other talented women. In an art world plagued by unreliable state funding, opening up academies to the education of the daughters of the aristocracy was a way to cultivate the good will of wealthy families and help to generate patronage, commissions, and other forms of political and monetary support. For example, the Academy of San Carlos ingratiated itself with the aristocratic Italian-Mexican family of Maria Guadalupe Moncada y Berrio by naming the twenty-two-year-old woman honorary director of the school, as well as giving her the honorific *académica de honor*, a prestigious faculty title, on the strength of a single painting. Little is known about this fascinating artist, who studied with Francisco Goya and socialized with Lord Byron.

What did women paint? Often the work they exhibited at local exhibits consisted of copies, which was an acknowledged way for men and women to showcase their skill. As we have already seen, academic training was firmly entrenched in copying the paintings of the masters as well as copying lithographic reproductions of famous paintings. One of the finest women painters of mid-nineteenth-century Mexico, Josefa Sanromán, copied paintings by her mentor, Pelegrín Clavé, the Spanish director of the Academy of San Carlos, as well as works by her older sister, Juliana, who also studied under Clavé. The sisters painted still lives and then proceeded to copy each other's works. One painting by Josefa is a copy of Clavé's striking portrait of adolescent Juliana, her head covered by a dark shawl, as she takes off a cream-colored glove to begin painting at her easel. The culture of the copy also overlapped with a preference for religious themes and figures, which were also often copied from printed reproductions of European originals. One Mexican painter who deviated from this common practice was Julia Escalante, who resolutely affirmed her originality and self- confidence by conceiving and executing secular topics of her own, such as a *costumbrista* rendition of the *lechero* (a milk delivery boy) or a delicate portrait of Graziella, the tragic heroine of an 1852 book by the French writer Alphonse de Lamartine. The Peruvian Rebeca Oquendo Díaz was similarly ambitious, as evidenced by the paintings that she submitted to the Paris Salon of 1872: a treatment of the characters of Faust and Margaret by Goethe, and a stylized portrait of a Neapolitan boy holding a wooden flute in his hand, a painting for which she won a prestigious silver medal.[30]

The paradox of emergent, modern women's art is that although women artists set out to express themselves in a world that generally subordinated their intelligence and creativity to that of men, they were able to produce works of art that could be as complex, expansive, and rich as that of their male peers, if not surpassing them altogether. A closer look at one painting, *Ante el caballete* (Before the easel), will help illustrate this point. Magdalena Mira's portrait of her father, Gregorio Mira, standing with his arms crossed in front of a painting on an easel, won the gold medal at the Chilean salon of 1884. The bald-headed Mr. Mira, with assertive white sideburns, is centered on the canvas and framed by canvases sitting on the studio floor to his right and by a chair to his left. In front of him stands the easel and the painting that he is contemplating with a mixture of severity and studiousness; he asserts his command over the painting by intrusively pushing his left foot past the horizontal wooden crossbar that joins the front legs of the easel. The gray wall of the studio surrounding his shoulders seems to radiate motion and texture, as if it were a pool of water with highlights and ripples glancing off his body. The brushstrokes are warm and thick and the likeness of Mr. Mira is realistic and accurate. With the foreknowledge that the artist is the subject's daughter, it is hard not to see in the painting an affectionate and intimate rendition of a woman artist commemorating her yearning for her father's approval, and by extension, the approval of her father's proxies: the men who juried art exhibits or served as art critics. There is, however, another way to interpret this canvas, one that is predicated neither on biographical and contextual interpretation nor on the idea of woman as a subordinate to patriarchy. *Ante el caballete* beautifully connotes something that is quite elusive and intangible: thought, evaluation, and assessment. Magdalena Mira has situated the viewers of her painting, who are also standing "before the easel," in the same role as its main character. She has taken as her theme not a thing or a person, but the very experience of looking at art, regardless of its theme. What at first glance might seem like an intimate and personal painting, conditioned by woman's subordination to man, proves to be universal, provocative, and philosophically challenging.

In short, the art produced by academically trained women was not hidden or private, but publicly exhibited in national salons and national and international industrial fairs where it was commented on in print by men who deemed themselves experts. Paintings by women were a common sight at Spanish American salons, and many successful works by women traveled overseas to be shown at world's fairs attended by thousands of people.[31] Regrettably, the cultural challenges that impeded women from making a living from their art careers, as well as the Western tradition of identifying art with male genius and inspiration with feminine beauty, made most women artists fade from twentieth-century histories of nineteenth-century Spanish American art. But they were there, and some were as accomplished as their male contemporaries.

The Streetwise Illustrations
of Pancho Fierro

As we saw in Chapter 2, one of the most important cultural movements in nineteenth-century Spanish America was *costumbrismo*, or the representation of local types and scenes. *Costumbrismo* deeply influenced literature and journalism, as well as the theater, and it was equally important to the history of painting and illustration. The pictorial representation of an exotic slice of Spanish American life was pioneered in the travel accounts or paintings of Europeans like Alexander von Humboldt, Johann Moritz Rugendas, Claudio Gay, and Jean-Baptiste Debret, among others.[32] The eyes of Enlightenment Europe had turned to the New World, producing beautiful pictorial works and inquiries into its archaeological past, fauna, and ways of life. After the Wars of Independence, Spanish American writers and illustrators increasingly sought to evoke their world through writings and pictures that highlighted its cultural distinctiveness and its vivid folklore and local customs.

There are different kinds of pictorial *costumbrismo*. One early variant was print *costumbrista* illustration, as exemplified by books like *Los cubanos pintados por sí mismos* and *Los mexicanos pintados por sí mismos*, which contained illustrated sketches of local tradespeople like water carriers, musicians, barkeeps, coachmen, and servants. Painters in the academic tradition also gravitated toward *costumbrismo*. One of the finest Mexican *costumbristas* was José Agustín Arrieta, who painted compelling scenes of daily life, like the *pulquería* scene discussed in Chapter 2, and the beautiful portrait *El chinaco y la china* (n.d.), a man and a woman in picturesque dress from Arrieta's hometown of Puebla. Another outstanding *costumbrista* painter in the academic style was the Uruguayan Juan Manuel Blanes, who was famous for his nationalist paintings of military heroes and battles. Blanes painted the most emblematic, beautiful, and idealized paintings of the gauchos ever to be produced, forming a series known as the *Gauchitos*. These radiant paintings of gauchos standing alone or in pairs against the horizon of the plains project a mythical and timeless quality.[33] *Costumbrismo* was so all-encompassing in this period that it even affected the production of folk art by artisans, whose pottery, murals, and sculptural figurines began to represent local types and scenes.[34]

There was another kind of *costumbrismo*—one that straddled streetwise or rural popular art and middle-class or elite taste. One of the most iconic creators of this kind of art was the Peruvian, Afro-descendant illustrator Pancho Fierro (1807–1879). The illegitimate son of a white priest named Nicolás Mariano Rodríguez del Fierro and a slave named María del Carmen, Fierro was born in a working-class Lima neighborhood called Huérfanos (orphans).[35] Although details of Fierro's life are scarce, we may get an idea of his world by noting that his brother was a shoemaker and his close friend José Alleguez ran a small tobacco stand in the bustling arcade called Escribanos on the western side of the Plaza Mayor of Lima, across from the archbishop's palace and the city's cathedral, and alongside lottery ticket vendors, paperboys, moneychangers, and notaries.[36] At one point, Fierro's home and studio was behind the cathedral, on Santa Apolonia Street, among a row of modest businesses and street sellers specializing in religious prints, crucifixes, Christmas crèches, and colorful wood and plaster saints. When he worked there he was listed as a "sculptor," suggesting that he made a living manufacturing these devotional objects.[37] At another time, he rented a small room a few blocks from the Plaza de Armas where he painted colorful placards advertising bullfights. At the end of his life, he and his family were living in the bustling Indian neighborhood called Cercada, whose enterprising vendors supplied much of the city with fruits, vegetables, and fowl.[38]

Besides devotional objects and bullfight advertisements, Fierro painted murals in the interior patios of the homes of the affluent, as well as murals commissioned by businesses. His most famous work of this kind, destroyed in a fire in 1888, was a large mural for a *pulpería* that depicted the old medieval motif of the world turned upside down. Such imagery was central to the old traditions of Carnival and a symbolic way to ironically represent the cruelty of the world. Ismael Portal, who claimed to have known Fierro and to have seen the mural, described it as containing a closed carriage drawn by men, with two white horses' heads sticking out of its windows; a fisherman caught in a fishing line held by a small fish; and a bull stabbing a man with the sharp, barbed flags used to torment bulls in bullfights. Portal's description ends there with an ellipsis, suggesting that there were more figures.[39] Since Ricardo Palma described a similarly themed mural in another part of the city, it is probable that Fierro's *pulpería* mural contained similar if not identical elements, for example: schoolchildren beating their teacher, a cow slaughtering a butcher, a burro whipping a man, and a prisoner hanging a judge. Other common motifs associated with *pulpería* murals included upside-down, crucified Saint Peters, sirens, and Saint Lawrences roasted on a fire.[40] Fierro's world-upside-down mural was so well known that people took to calling the *pulpería* on its corner "The World Upside Down," and a well-to-do gentleman hired Fierro to do another version of it inside his home.[41]

Fierro is today remembered for his prolific production of vibrant handpainted watercolors of local characters and types, who are depicted in gentle caricature and in a simple yet compelling style. He painted the traditions of Carnival, such as the processionals of *Gigantes* and *Papahuevos*, which were grotesque, marionette-like floats. He depicted household altars, elite sitting room gatherings, religious penitents, street food vendors, barbershops, bodegas, and *pulperías*. Fierro also depicted urban celebrities, many of whom were Afro-descendants, such as the bullfighter Esteban Arredondo, a friar known as Friar Tomato, the dignified war veteran Sargeant Zapata, and Master Hueso, a well-known and respected dance instructor. Taken together, Fierro's vast body of work recreates life in nineteenth-century Lima, highlighting the distinctive places and practices of everyday city life, as well as the foibles of noteworthy locals. The color of his illustrations make them jump off the page, and they show admirable detail. Many of Fierro's compositions also show skill in implied motion and action; a picture of the eccentric gentleman known as Corporal Cruzate, who was notorious for exploding in rage every time he heard clapping, shows him in a top hat, trotting toward some youngsters in straw hats in the background who are taunting him by merrily clapping their hands.[42]

It is tempting to assume that Fierro was just an unschooled illustrator and streetwise journalist of urban life who produced art on the margins of elite culture. Yet, the ways that the market affected his work tells a more complicated story.[43] Fierro's body of work was conditioned by a long European tradition of illustrated collections of costumes and street sellers, as well as late eighteenth-century and early nineteenth-century illustrated travel books, all of which motivated tourists to commission similar illustrations from local artists to keep as mementos of their travels to exotic lands. For example, in the 1830s, Fierro sold forty-nine watercolors to Léonce Angrand, the French consul in Lima, who wrote that the artist was self-taught and that he made a good living selling his paintings to foreign travelers. Indeed, we know that works by Fierro were bought by another collector, a Chilean diplomat named José Miguel de la Barra, and by Martha Wheelwright, the wife of an affluent North American industrialist and shipping entrepreneur who did busi-

Figure 4.4. *Women in Procession for the Festival of San Juan de Dios*, by Pancho Fierro (circa 1853). Digital image courtesy of the Getty's Open Content Program.

ness in Lima in the 1840s. Mrs. Wheelwright sent Fierro's originals to the Chinese city of Canton, which at that time had thriving workshops that specialized in reproducing color illustrations for resale in Europe, the United States, and even Peru. Travelers in Peru, eager to buy souvenirs and mementos, probably bought such Chinese copies believing that they were the work of local artists like Fierro, who found himself in the unenviable position of competing with pirated versions of his work from across the Pacific. Another purchaser of Fierro's work was the Peruvian educator Agustín de la Rosa Toro, who commissioned paintings on specific subjects from Fierro, possibly directing him to represent the subject matter in a particular way.[44]

Fierro's bullfight placards, murals, and work as a religious artist have not been preserved or attributed to him, preventing a more complete assessment of who he was as an artist. Be that as it may, Fierro's remarkable story and art, however fragmentary and indeterminate, remind us that secular, nonacademic art in nineteenth-century Peru was produced in an artisanal economy that served both the local commercial class and foreign travelers. It was unabashedly local in its focus on urban types, practices, and costumes, but it was also a type of folk art designed to satisfy a foreign yearning for local exoticism. Rather than expressing an exclusively separate and popular form of Peruvian art, Fierro's watercolors are a hybrid of local pride and made-to-order art shaped by souvenir culture and the expectations of faraway travelers.

Daguerreotype

In August 1839, the Frenchman Louis-Jacques-Mandé Daguerre went public with a chemical process that allowed the fixing of sharp photographic images on copper sheets plated with silver. The invention was not his alone, however. He collaborated with another inventor named Joseph Nicéphore Niépce, who had fixed a photographic image on a plate of pewter in 1827. After Niépce's death, Daguerre continued alone until he succeeded in developing a functional photographic process that took the world by storm in 1839. The daguerreian image was startlingly sharp and beautiful but its long exposure times required human sitters to remain motionless anywhere from five to ten minutes. The process was also arduous for the photographer, who had to sensitize and treat the photographic plate with several chemical baths in wooden cases designed to keep out the light. When Daguerre announced his process and began to publicize how to render and preserve images on silver-plated copper, two Englishmen, William Henry Fox Talbot and John Herschel, made advancements in the art of fixing images on paper, a process that Talbot initially described as "photogenic drawing" and Herschel called "photography." Paper photographs, initially called "talbotypes," lagged far behind daguerreotypes in popularity for nearly two decades before making them obsolete. By then, however, the daguerreotype had profoundly changed the Western world by inaugurating astonishing new ways of seeing and understanding visuality, the self, and landscape.

Photographers began making daguerreotypes in the Americas the same year that Daguerre announced his invention. In the United States, daguerreotypes were taken in New York City six weeks after the announcement of the invention, and in Mexico City two months after that, in December 1839.[45] In one of the most exotic chapters of the nineteenth-century transatlantic exchange of technology, the daguerreotype landed in South America in early 1840 via the French ship *L'Orientale*, which was both a floating school (for French and Belgian students interested in maritime careers) and a commercial expedition.[46] Captain Lucas's ship carried daguerreian equipment, which his young and well-spoken chaplain, the abbot Louis Comte, knew how to use. After departing France on September 30, 1839, *L'Orientale* arrived in Brazil in January 1840. In Río, Comte took at least three daguerreotypes, one of the Imperial Palace and two of city scenes: a public market and a fountain. *L'Orientale* continued on its journey and docked in Montevideo and Valparaiso, Chile, where its crew astonished the locals by showing them daguerreotypes and performing live demonstrations of the new image-making process.

In the 1840s, daguerreotypes were exotic and desirable commodities in Spanish America.[47] The ability to purchase such images of oneself and of loved ones entailed new interpretations of portraiture, a transition of older forms of representation to new ones, and a cultish appreciation of newness and technology. Early on, people compared daguerreotype portraiture to more established forms of image-making, such as miniature paintings and silhouettes. The astonishing fidelity of daguerreotypes was a bit too harsh for some, who preferred to use them as an underlying image to be painted over or retouched by an artist.[48] Spanish American advertisements for the daguerreian process also underline that photographers appealed to potential customers by promoting their scientific expertise and their access to accoutrements and innovative processes imported from Europe or the United States. To own a daguerreotype was to stake a claim on an object created by a professional with tools and materials imbued with the aura of newness, scientific innovation, and foreignness.[49] Daguerreotypes also had less ideological associations, such as the fear of death and the desire to preserve memory. One 1857 advertisement from Medellín, Colombia, reads, "Those who wish to carry with them the image of the loved one, of the friend, of the mother, of the son, should hurry soon to the portraitist. . . . Buy your portraits while there is still time to do so with precision; because the day that sickness and death disfigure the object of the sought-after portrait will be too late, it will then be impossible to secure it accurately."[50]

The daguerreotype was an expensive investment, especially if procured from sought-after artists, who were European or from the United States.[51] The difficulties and the equipment needed to make daguerreotypes circumscribed the process to cities and towns, although photographers did travel the countryside to take images of landowners, public officials, and other local notables.[52] In mid-nineteenth-century Medellín, an inexpensive daguerreotype cost between five and ten pesos, which was equal to the average monthly wage of a laborer.[53] For a person of means who was not rich, and who made an average of 35–50 pesos a month, a daguerreotype cost nearly a week's worth of pay. In the same period, in Mexico City, daguerreotypes of different sizes were sold for anywhere between two and sixteen pesos. To put this in context, the monthly salary of a footman or a chambermaid in a house of means was between five and seven pesos a month.[54] In Lima in 1860, for the price of a daguerreotype measuring two inches by two inches, a person could buy approximately four pounds of beef, the most premium of foodstuffs.[55] It would not be until the ascent of tintypes (inexpensive photographs on tin) and cheap paper photography in the 1860s that access to photography became more widespread.

The Serialized Image

The era of the daguerreotype spanned the 1840s through the beginning of the 1860s, but it shared the stage with other popular photographical processes. The ambrotype (image on glass; *ambrotipo* in Spanish) and the tintype (*ferrotipo* in Spanish) were similar to the daguerreotype insofar as they were one-of-a-kind images, rather than pictures produced serially from an original negative. Both were examples of a wet process that used a sticky substance called "collodion" to sensitize the plate that received the image. The sharpness of ambrotypes was superior to that of the cheaper tintypes, which tended to be have much less contrast and a gray hue. Further experiments with the collodion process enabled the ascendance of paper photography, which became dominant in the second half of the nineteenth century. After sensitizing a glass plate with collodion and other substances, the photographer created a negative image that was pressed to a sheet of paper coated with ammonium chloride and albumen (egg whites). The most popular albumen prints of the nineteenth century were the enormously popular *cartes de visite*, measuring 1 ½" by 3 ½," and cabinet cards, overgrown versions of the *carte de visite*, which measured 4" by 5 ½." What was distinctive about the *carte de visite* photographs, known in Spanish as *tarjetas de visita* or *retratos tarjetas*, was the use of a camera with multiple lenses that created eight negative images on the same plate, which then could be pressed onto albumen paper to produce a master containing multiple photographs. The developer cut this master print into eight separate pictures that he pasted on pieces of card stock. Throughout the 1860s and 1870s, the *carte de visite* was arguably the most accessible, ubiquitous form of photography known to European, North American, and Spanish American consumers.

The *carte de visite* was designed to be mass produced and as such it contributed to the idea of the image as a serialized collectible. One example of this phenomenon was the global use of the *carte de visite* to represent a person as someone refined and respectable. In general, the vast majority of people represented on *cartes de visite* did not smile or pose in interesting or memorable ways. The photograph represented their attempt to conform to a standardized social type by dressing conservatively and striking a preestablished pose that constrained their body and made it look elegant and decorous. Props used for bust or full-body portraits included small tables for resting an arm, Doric columns, curtains, and large books. The paper construction of the photograph allowed people to sign or write a brief message on the back. This personalization was important because it was customary for people of the upper and emergent middle classes to present each other with these images as tokens of friendship. These photographs ultimately landed in the recipient's photo album, which constituted a kind of pictorial representation of his or her social world. The album of a well-to-do impresario and person of influence might include numerous photographs of the men who came into contact with him for business and leisure activities, whereas the album of a family of more modest means might contain more family photographs and represent a smaller community of people.[56] For the impresario, the album could attest to a sphere of influence extending out into the public realm of politics and commerce, while the other album was circumscribed by a more domestic sphere.

The *carte de visite* also lent itself to uses other than mapping human relationships and preserving a family's memory. The format was also used

E. GARREAUD Y Cᴬ   Calle del Ucayali. 26, LIMA

Figure 4.5. *Carte de visite* of Señorita Abruyes and servant girl,
from the photography studio of Garreaud y Compañía, circa 1870.
Courtesy of the Library of Nineteenth-Century Photography.

Figure 4.6. *Carte de visite* of a gentleman and two *tapadas* of Lima, from the photography studio of Garreaud y Compañía, circa 1870. Courtesy of the Library of Nineteenth-Century Photography.

to market images of important political and cultural figures, such as presidents, royalty, famous performers, and even writers. It was customary for photo albums to contain a pictorial representation of the world of international celebrity, alongside the photographs of family, friends, and acquaintances. An average nineteenth-century Mexican photo album from the 1870s would contain *cartes de visite* of international figures like Napoleon III of France and Abraham Lincoln, as well as Mexicans like President Benito Juárez and his family, and Guillermo Prieto and Ignacio Manuel Altamirano, two writers who appear in the pages of this book.[57] In Lima, a collector would likewise have been able to acquire images of international celebrities, as well as cards depicting famous Inca rulers. Thomas Hutchinson, who traveled to Peru in 1873, reported seeing such *cartes de visite* on display on an advertising placard and realized that the suspiciously familiar images were portraits of English kings from Oliver Goldsmith's well-known *History of England* (1764) that had been retouched by hand to include feathers and other details that symbolized Amerindian features.[58]

Another collectible image that was available to Spanish American consumers during the era of the *carte de visite* was *costumbrista* photography that depicted people engaged in different trades and occupations, such as the water carrier, the wood peddler, a woman grinding corn on her knees, a food vendor on her haunches, and an Indian woman breastfeeding a child.[59] In Lima, one of the most popular collectibles was images of the legendary *tapadas*—women wearing *sayas* and *mantos*. In the eighteenth and early nineteenth centuries, Peruvian women of distinction wore tight, form-fitting dresses called *sayas* that revealed their silk-stockinged feet. A *tapada* would affix the *manto* (black silk shawl) to her waists and then pull it over her head with one hand so that only one eye was visible through a crease. The fashion of *tapadas* (meaning "covered ones") was a colonial tradition designed to promote modesty in public, but its critics complained that it became a pretext for women to disguise themselves and pursue inappropriate amorous intrigues in public. For nineteenth-century Peruvians, the *tapada* was an exotic figure that conveyed mystery and sensuality, as well as nostalgia for vanished traditions. Photography gave this phantom of Lima's colorful past a new lease on life, circulating her enigmatic visage onto mantelpieces and into photo albums.

Memento Mori

One of the most common types of nineteenth-century photography in Spanish America, as in the rest of the Western world, was mortuary photography. Photographs of the dead served a variety of purposes, such as assuaging grief, strengthening faith in God, and indulging lurid curiosity about deceased celebrities, but they were all object lessons about the fragility of human life and power. Such photographs were objects of *memento mori* (Latin for "remember thy death") that made people aware of their mortality, as well as of the threatening world of sickness, politics, and conflict that surrounded them.

One type of memento mori had as its object deceased children. This was not a new practice among people of means, who in the colonial period commissioned paintings of their dead children to memorialize them, but it was indeed new for the poor, who used the affordability of paper photography to participate in this pictorial tradition for the first time. For the middle and upper classes, photographs of dead children preserved their memory in photo albums or framed pictures, often presenting them as if they were living or sleeping peacefully. The extraordinary paper photograph of Estanislao Harvey Beausejour (1850s) of Lima uses the four- or five-year-old body as a posable mannequin; the seated figure is dressed in checkered trousers, dress shoes, and a fancy jacket fringed at the neck.[60] The left arm of the corpse rests on a side table, underneath a white handkerchief and next to a small straw hat with a black band around it. The eyes are open and the face's blank expression is not unlike that of a living subject. Were it not for the known provenance and history of this photograph, we might assume that little Estanislao was alive.

The memento mori of families of more modest means also used photography to reinforce and bear witness to their belief that their departed child had become a kind of guardian angel in heaven, looking over the spiritual destiny of the family. Their photographs, in contrast to those of more middle- or upper-class subjects, drew on rich religious symbolism and became devotional icons. As described in Chapter 3 of this book, the *angelitos* tradition in Spanish America treated the death of an infant as a cause of ritualized celebration, based on the belief that the child would intercede for the family in heaven. In the mortuary photography of Mexico, village and rural people hired photographers to capture images of their *angelitos* resting on a table covered with a white tablecloth, decorated with a wreath of flowers on their heads. The use of palm leaf in such

Figure 4.7. Mexican postmortem photograph, circa 1910.
Courtesy of the Library of Nineteenth-Century Photography.

photographs was particularly symbolic because it referred to the story of the Assumption of the Virgin Mary, who had received a palm leaf from an angel before being reunited with Jesus and the apostles in Heaven.[61] Since the Virgin had not been conceived in sin, her assumption provided the representational and conceptual framework for imagining the journey of the *angelito*, who was also unstained by sin.

Whether tinged with grief or religious faith, *memento mori* that depicted children were private images for personal use. To different degrees, such photographs invoked memory as a form of consolation, or the hope that the death of the body would lead to resurrection. There was another kind of photographic memento mori that was public, and which intertwined voyeurism and profit. Photographs of murderers, their accomplices, and the firing squads charged with executing them circulated among consumers eager to vicariously experience the horror of crime and the satisfaction of justice served. Such was the case with the Peruvian mass murderer Manuel Peña Chacallaza, an Indian who murdered fourteen members of a family in 1871 and who escaped from jail twice. Many inhabitants of Lima carried *carte de visite* photographs of Chacallaza, a man of delicate and austere features with a thin, frowning mustache, for the ostensible purpose of identifying him on the street. Similarly, in 1874, the inhabitants of Medellín bought cheap photographs of the scene of the crime where eighteen-year-old Daniel Escovar and his accomplices had slaughtered a family with axes and knives.[62] Another popular subject were death-row inmates posed with their soon-to-be firing squads.[63] Such images provided a catharsis of some kind by evoking the triumph of justice in the face of terrible crimes, but they also invited viewers to explore whether evil was visible on a person's face, or if any remorse or fear loomed in the eyes of the condemned. If photography could capture an absolute likeness of a person or an otherwise ineffable glance of the eyes, scrutinizing such photographs promised a revelation about the human condition. Indeed, the quest to know the criminal mind and spirit had its scientific counterpart in the anthropologists and police who used photography to understand and record criminal deviancy. For example, in Puebla, Mexico, state law decreed that each penitentiary should have an office of criminal anthropology to perform autopsies, preserve the craniums and brains of the dead, and take photographs of each living prisoner.[64] All these items became a part of the prison's museum collection, which served as a scientific laboratory for the study of crime.

One of the most beautiful memento mori in the history of Spanish American photography comes from Uruguay and depicts the body of Colonel León Palleja after his death in battle against the forces of Paraguay during the War of the Triple Alliance, which pitched Uruguay, Argentina, and Brazil against Paraguay from 1864 to 1870. Javier López, a war correspondent working for the Montevideo photo studio of an Irishman named Thomas Bate, staged the photograph to represent Palleja as a noble fallen hero, surrounded by his loyal men. In the photograph, the body rests on a pallet propped up on wooden blocks, but López arranged four soldiers in uniform around the body in such a way to suggest that their long rifles were handles for carrying the platform holding the body. In the background, soldiers stand by the pallet, their heads bowed before the bearded Palleja, whose left hand rests elegantly on his torso. The photograph is more reminiscent of a neoclassical painting than a candid and spontaneous image; there's a timeless, mournful quality about it, as if handsome Palleja were sleeping peacefully under the watchful gaze of his men. Bate's photographs circulated widely in the River Plate and Brazil, both as news coverage and as nationalist propaganda. In one advertisement, Bate boasted that he had printed fifty thousand prints of his first series of photographs from the front.[65] Palleja's celebrity as a death object extended to many other Spanish Americans, such as the Argentine presidents Domingo Sarmiento and Justo José Urquiza, the Peruvian president Nicolás de San Román, and Emperor Maximilian of Mexico, whose body and clothes were luridly photographed after his execution in 1867.[66]

Posada's Calaveras

The illustrations of the Mexican José Guadalupe Posada (1852–1913) are the most internationally recognized and commercially reproduced images from nineteenth-century Spanish America. This is ironic because in his lifetime Posada was not a prestigious artist but a salaried commercial illustrator at Mexico City's most important print shop, which was run by Antonio Vanegas Arroyo. As we saw in Chapter 2, Vanegas Arroyo supplied Mexico City and the rest of the country with a vast amount of printed matter that was sold for a few cents a piece in a variety of shops and street stalls, as well as by barefoot boys called *papeleros* (paperboys). His shop's output included sensationalized accounts of true crime, song and joke books, embroidery patterns for women, and satirical verses and illustrations, to mention just a few. The back cover of one of the booklets printed at his shop shows a revealing picture of its interior, with two customers at the counter and other significant figures. One customer is a well-dressed gentleman in black and the other a commoner in a broad-brimmed sombrero. Next to them, three barefoot boys of varying sizes hold stacks of print to sell on the street and deliver to shops.[67]

The specifics of Posada's biography are thin. He hailed from Aguascalientes and was the son of a baker. Posada took courses at the Academy of Arts and Trades in Aguascalientes, an important vocational school that taught artisans reading, writing, and math, as well as trades, such as printing, blacksmithing, and carpentry.[68] By age eighteen he had joined a local print shop as an illustrator and caricaturist. In 1888, after running his own print shop in the city of Leon, and a stint as a teacher of lithography in a high school, the middle-aged Posada settled into a prominent position with Vanegas Arroyo in Mexico City. There he produced thousands of illustrations and designs, thanks in part to emergent photomechanical processes of image reproduction.[69] This process involved the transferring of a handmade illustration through the exposure of a photographic negative onto a specially treated metal plate. The plate then received a chemical bath that etched the metal and preserved the image in relief on its surface. After retouching by hand, the etched plate was mounted on a printing block with type and placed in a hand-operated printing press for inking and contact with paper.

The majority of Posada's output as a commercial illustrator was produced at a very rapid pace, probably with the assistance of one or two clerks who mounted type, helped touch up metal plates, and laboriously ran the press. Although Posada was a versatile artist with experience in fine illustration, he employed a looser pictorial style for Vanegas Arroyo to appeal to the general populace and to produce volume and variety.[70] When not transferring and adapting photographic portraits onto printing plates, Posada drew the human form in either exaggerated, caricature form or with clean, simple lines, in a style reminiscent of the illustrations we might find in Victorian children's literature (graceful lines and rounded bodies).[71] His most iconic images are *calaveras*—jocular skeletons and skulls that are associated with the folk imagery of the Mexican Day of the Dead. Although Posada's *calaveras* (literally meaning "skulls") are the most universally recognized examples of this kind of iconography, he did not invent it but rather adopted a preexisting pictorial tradition.

Mexico's celebration of the Day of the Dead on November 1 and 2, inspired by the Catholic feasts of All Saints Day and All Souls Day, and by ancient pre-Columbian traditions, is one of the country's most popular and internationally recognized fiestas. During this celebration, Mexicans erect colorful altars to the dead in their homes, on which they offer the departed *pan de muerto* (sweet bread), candied fruits, and savory foods like tamales or mole. These candlelit altars, decorated with orange and yellow *cempasúchil* flowers and the magenta blooms of the *mano de león*, traditionally display the image of the departed as well as some of his or her personal possessions.[72] People also visit the dead at cemeteries, where they decorate gravesite markers with flowers and candles, and eat and drink in the company of the dead. The universal belief of the celebrants of the Day of the Dead was and is that the dead return to earth to partake of the prayers and offerings of their relatives. According to tradition, failure to honor the dead not only is an affront to them, but also tempts fate.[73]

The Day of the Dead is also distinctive because it depends on the manufacture and sale of a wide variety of decorations and sweets that are used in the celebration, notably handpainted sugar *calaveras*. Although the precise historical origin of the *calavera* motif is unknown, scholars agree that it emerged through a blending of pre-Columbian and medieval European beliefs about death, such as the iconography of the "Dance of Death." One of the most distinctive features of the Mexican *calaveras* of the Day of the Dead is their playful and jocular nature; the *calaveras* channel an attitude toward death that is festive and fun rather than somber. The logic of this is that the *calavera* does not need to abide by social convention and its pretensions, nor does it bow to anyone, however powerful or rich. Like death, the *calavera* is a great leveler—an entity whose grinning visage and mocking poses reveal the truth. This is underlined by the two primary meanings of *calavera* in Spanish, which encapsulate the duality of death and laughter. Besides the literal meaning of skull, *calavera* has been commonly used since the late eighteenth century to signify "rake" and "fool."[74] The verb *calavarear* is "to behave imprudently," and the past participle *calaverada* denotes "an inappropriate action or joke." The nineteenth-century Hispanic embodiment of this kind of *calavera* was the fictional protagonist of *Don Juan Tenorio* (1844), by the Spanish playwright José Zorrilla. This play, which featured gothic cemetery scenes, ghosts, and sensual immorality, was typically staged in nineteenth-century Spain on All Saints Day and in Mexico during the Day of the Dead. The custom of attending the play was so popular that one writer joked that Mexicans might forget to honor a dead relative on the Day of the Dead, but they never forgot to pay their respects to Tenorio.[75]

All these cultural associations were at work when Posada began printing illustrations of *calaveras* for Vanegas Arroyo. In particular, he illustrated *calaveritas*, satirical poems about people, living or dead, that consumers bought to celebrate the Day of the Dead. Such broadsides and caricatures began to appear in the 1840s, sometimes drawing from the scenes and setting of Zorrilla's *Don Juan Tenorio*. By the end of the century, Posada and other illustrators who worked for Vanegas Arroyo were producing a wealth of cheap broadsides covered with caricatures of skeletons and skulls and populated with biting satires about life in modern Mexico City.

One example of Posada's outstanding work in the *calavera* genre is the double-sided broadside with the heading "Gran calavera eléctrica / que se les va a regalar / calavera muy fachosa de pura electricidad" ("The grand electrical calavera / being given to you / the ridiculous calavera made out of pure electricity [my translation]). On the front side of the sheet, Posada shows a full-bodied *calavera* gesturing at a pile of skulls at the cemetery of Dolores, with lines of electricity shooting out of its eye sockets as a seated *calavera* stares back with the same lines emanating from its eyes. In the background, on the right, is a trolley with *calavera* passengers. Beneath this half-page illustration, we read a playful poem about the convergence of different classes of people at the cemetery to celebrate the Day of the Dead. The poem takes electricity and its mul-

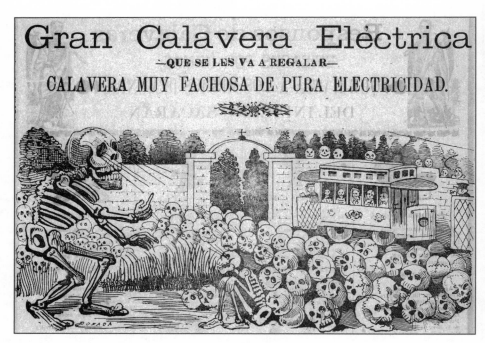

Figure 4.8. *Gran calavera eléctrica* (The grand electrical calavera; 1907), by José Guadalupe Posada. Courtesy of the Library of Congress, LC-DIG-ppmsc-04585.

tiple meanings (technological progress, fearful magic, drunkenness) as a guiding thread to represent the fiesta of death at the cemetery in an outlandish way: the dead rise from their graves to dance with the living, the devilishly fast trolley cars come and go, monstrous policemen beat and arrest celebrants, and people eat dogs cooked in mole sauce and rat tripe too. In these and other pictorial *calaveras* by Posada, no one escapes the fate of becoming a skeleton and everyone is a player in the gruesome comedy of life and death. Posada was an equal opportunity offender: no one escaped from his critical eye, whether it be the men in power, or the desperate and tragic people of the street. His jangling skeletons and gaping jawbones, so charged with life and humor, were chattering about how Mexicans lived, interacted, and laughed. His visual iconography, so familiar today throughout the world as a symbol of Mexicanness, is iconoclastic, raw, and compelling.

The Moving Image

The nineteenth century saw extraordinary technological advancements in printing and image reproduction: cumbersome woodcuts gave way to the more nuanced and finer lines of lithography, expensive daguerreotypes gave way to cheap paper photography, and hand-drawing and hand-etching was replaced by chemical and mechanical processes. New technologies also infused the experience of looking at images with wonderment, as shown by devices designed to create optical illusions, or to heighten the vividness of pictures. One of the simplest was the stereocard, a rectangular piece of card stock that contained two identical images on it, side by side. To enjoy the stereocard, the viewer placed it in a special viewing device and looked at it through binocular-like lenses that combined the two images into a unified and vivid three-dimensional one. Other nineteenth-century optical devices and effects included panoramas, theatrical enclosures in which large-scale murals or canvases were manipulated through light and motion to create the illusion of movement or simply a beautiful, luminous effect. The most spectacular development of them all came in late 1896, when motion pictures began to be filmed and screened in Mexico City and Buenos Aires, and then, in 1897, in Havana, Bogotá, Caracas, and other Spanish American capitals. The arrival of motion picture technology foreshadowed a tremendous, hemispheric shift in how culture circulated nationally and transnationally; mass culture, which reached its apotheosis in the middle of the twentieth century through radio and television, had begun to emerge. Visual culture was about to spill out of its discrete nineteenth-century compartments and reach more people than ever before. In short, the industrialized image, dressed in celluloid film, was prepared to take the stage and inspire wonderment on a grand scale.

CHAPTER 5

Musicality

NINETEENTH-CENTURY WRITERS considered music, like all the other forms of culture explored in this book, to be an instrument for promoting progress and national reconciliation. The Argentinian judge of all things civilized and barbaric, Domingo Sarmiento, wrote that music softened the hearts of men and guided them away from the temptations of sloth and vice. In his seminal book *Facundo: Civilization and Barbarism*, he underlined that Argentinian culture was permeated with musicality; in cities, educated young men played the piano or the flute, while in the countryside, rustics on guitars accompanied by drums sang primitive and colorful songs about war and everyday life. This generalized predilection for music, Sarmiento wrote, would one day help to create a beautiful and distinctively national musical culture. On a more profound level, he also intuited that the music of Argentina was a product of complex cultural exchanges: he saw striking similarities between the songs of the mestizo plainsmen and the songs of the Indians, as well as between the guitar styles of Buenos Aires and of Spain. He perceived that different cultural traditions had blended in the past and were evolving into something new and national in the present.[1]

Sarmiento's reflections highlight three key points that help us frame the cultural history of nineteenth-century music: (1) The elite view was that music was a civilizing force; (2) Musical identities are determined by social class and regionalism; and (3) Music was a site of transculturation. We could say the same about literature, or art history, but there was something more elusive about nineteenth-century music because its sounds and melodies were performed in real time without being preserved for posterity through audio or film. Although we can trace what critics, educators and contemporaries said about music, it is much more challenging to recreate the ineffable and intimate experience of musicality. For example, Sarmiento was deeply moved by an 1844 performance of the opera *Lucia di Lammermoor* (1839) by Gaetano Donizetti in Santiago, Chile, and struggled to find the words to evoke what he had heard and why it was so special. Music had a vaporous quality, he wrote in his review, magically real yet insubstantial and fleeting, like the airy stuff of human feelings and dreams.[2]

The pages that follow underline some of Sarmiento's insights and echo his quandary about how to put music into words. This chapter outlines key cultural templates that were intrinsic to nineteenth-century musical culture, such as clubs, national anthems, popular songs, and dancing styles. In a way, we are trying to follow the musical notes on a printed musical score to discern the melody of an unrecorded performance. Gone is the ambient sound of that past moment, the quality and tone of the instruments, and the errors or improvisations that made a performance distinct. Much may be lost, but not all; as we work through our score, we begin to discover revealing continuities and shared melodies beneath the varied soundscapes of nineteenth-century Spanish America.

Musical Sociability

In other chapters we have seen how important social clubs were to nineteenth-century Spanish American life. Elite clubs like Santiago's Club del Progreso blended the functions of party hall, bar, restaurant, and lounge. Reading clubs and literary salons like the gatherings held at Juana Manuela Gorriti's home in Lima brought the educated together to read and talk about literature and the arts. Urban people of humbler origins belonged to mutualist trade organizations designed to educate and to protect them and their families, as well as to provide them with leisure activities that fostered community. In short, clubs and associations were the institutional cornerstones of the modern idea of sociability—the practice of peaceful, orderly, and purposeful social interaction. Spanish Americans also experienced music in community, seeing it variously as a symbol of social refinement, joyful celebration, and a form of witness about the trials and tribulations of life. In the colonial period, musical experience was primarily defined by state and church ceremonies that commemorated important occasions related to the Spanish monarchy or the celebration of religious feast days. Although both of these inter-twined domains—the political and the religious—remained important in the postcolonial era, they were overtaken by a musical culture defined by leisure and secular associationism.

The dominant form of elite urban musical sociability in Spanish America, as in Europe and the United States, was the *sociedad filarmónica* (philharmonic society). *Filarmónicas* brought together professional and amateur musicians to perform for their members, who paid membership and subscription fees to support the organization. "A philharmonic society is a temple consecrated to the most eloquent of arts," declared one Cuban enthusiast in 1840. "It strengthens the bonds of friendship, en-courages the dispirited, and fosters frankness."[3] Chilean journalists cele-brated the inauguration of a *filarmónica* in Santiago in 1826 by observing that it would help heal the wounds that the War of Independence had inflicted on the body politic and break up the monotony of elite leisure habits, then limited to taking nighttime strolls around the central plaza or playing cards at home.[4] In theory, at least, music promised a kind of social utopia. The promoters of Mexico City's most successful and influ-ential *filarmónica* wrote in 1866 that the organization would not distin-guish between nationalities or political parties. Rather, they argued, it was a club defined by the concepts of decency, politeness, good manners, talent, and the diligent study of music.[5] The affluence and exclusivity im-plied by words like "decency" and "manners" was reinforced by signing and membership fees that kept out the poor. For example, the monthly subscription fee of five pesos for the Filarmónica of Bogotá in 1846 was only one peso short of the monthly salary of the club's hired coachman.[6] Some clubs admitted members only through a nomination process in which existing members put individuals forward to be vetted by an ad-visory board. National dignitaries and their families received honorary memberships, and professional musicians were exempted from paying fees as long as they provided their services to the organization.[7] In short, to be prestigious, elite *filarmónicas* were to be composed of prestigious people.

The seeds of the *sociedades filarmónicas* were sown in the homes of the elite, where friends and family gathered to enjoy musical perfor-mances. The desire to add more musicians and dancers, and to imitate European musical societies, promoted the transition from homebound musical *tertulias* (social gatherings) to the more structured and semi-public *filarmónicas*. These new clubs were not abruptly moved outside of the domestic sphere but continued to be staged at the homes of a select few of their patrons and members. As a rule, *filarmónicas* had anywhere between one hundred and three hundred subscribing members, so the homes that hosted performances had to be large, such as the patrician home of the Fernández Recio family on 39 Santo Domingo Street in Santiago, Chile, or of the Rosell family on Doña Josefa del Puente Street in Lima, Perú.[8] In Havana, Cuba, which had a highly developed circuit of elite *filarmónica* organizations that were markedly more aristocratic than those on the mainland, musical events and dances were held at the palatial homes of the crème de la crème, such as those of Mercedes Santa Cruz y Montalvo, known as the Countess of Merlin, and Teresa de Garro y Risel y Herrera, the Countess of Fernandina. In 1839, Fanny Calderón de la Barca, the Scottish wife of a Spanish diplomat, described hundreds of people dancing at the house of the Countess of Fernandina. She wrote, "Diamonds on all the women, jewels and orders on all of the men, magnificent lustres and mirrors, and a capital band of music in the gallery."[9] In contrast, Bogotá's *filarmónica* in 1867 secured access to the facilities of the Central University for its performances, while one of the protectors of Mexico's *filarmónica*, Dr. Ignacio Durán, the director of Mexico City's School of Medicine, allowed the club to use the beautiful grounds of the imposing Palace of Inquisition.[10]

Filarmónica orchestras were small, the largest consisting of between twenty and forty professional and/or amateur musicians.[11] The instrumentation available to most of the clubs might include fortepiano, piano, guitar, viola, violoncello, flute, clarinet, and harp.[12] That said, it was not uncommon for *filarmónicas* to host performances that consisted of only two or three instruments and a voice. In the *filarmónica* of Santiago (1826), most performances consisted of trios, many of which combined string instruments with piano. Similarly, most of the concerts of the *filarmónica* of Mexico City (1866) consisted of the singing of opera arias, which did not require extensive instrumental accompaniment.[13] Concerts took place in the evening and were structured in two parts, each containing five or six separate musical performances.[14] Most of the music performed was the most popular music of the day, meaning simplified arrangements drawn from Italian opera, as well as waltzes, polkas, quadrilles, and contradances. It was catchy and familiar music, rather than academic or esoteric music. The composers Joseph Haydn, Giaochino Rossini, and Giuseppe Bellini were perennial favorites, while composers like Wolfgang Amadeus Mozart, Ludwig van Beethoven, and Robert

Schumann were admired but underperformed.[15] One nineteenth-century Chilean music critic complained that fathers insisted on teaching their daughters to play dance music and opera samplers on the piano rather than more salutary compositions like Beethoven's "Moonlight Sonata" or "Sonata Pathétique." An article published in a Buenos Aires magazine emphasized the same point, arguing against opera arrangements and dance music, and in favor of Beethoven and Mozart, because they helped to prevent frivolity among women and cultivate good taste.[16]

People of lesser means, whether they were city-dwellers or from the countryside, also formed musical associations that were called *filarmónicas*. In cities, mutualist *filarmónicas* thrived alongside other trade organizations designed to promote community or financial security among the artisan class, which included tailors, bakers, carpenters, clerks, shoemakers, and other tradespeople. In the capital of Chile, the Filarmónica de Obreros (Workers' Philharmonic) was the preeminent musical club for artisans and urban workers, hosting dances and musical and theatrical performances for its members. Its mission was to provide wholesome, cultural entertainment for the working class, as underlined by stringent entrance requirements that banned criminals, disruptive conduct, and risqué dances like the *cueca* and the *aurora*.[17] For liberals and conservative commentators alike, it was a shining model of how an "apolitical" mutual aid organization could cultivate morality and good conduct among the working class and contribute to the greater good. One friend of the Chilean labor movement, Antonio Bórquez Solar, recalled attending a dance at a worker's club of this kind, and provided this admiring sketch of an orderly, family-friendly affair:

> For three hours I was enchanted by the order, discretion, and culture
> of the dancers. The girls, simply but elegantly dressed, and without
> excessive adornments, spoke little and smiled at their suitors.
> The mothers, silent in their seats, followed the movements of the
> dance with attentive eyes. There was in them complacency and a
> mute acceptance of life. Perhaps they were just then resting from
> all their chores in the home. The most elaborate dances proceeded
> under the direction of a headmaster who wore a wide red silk sash,
> and spectacles behind which shone an imperious and vivacious
> gaze. The young men, in their gestures and movements, had a
> certain affectation. But nothing, nothing could alter the tranquil
> atmosphere, the muted joy.[18]

Whatever the contradictions and inequalities of nineteenth-century Republican life, tradespeople and elite commentators accepted the idea that working people could cultivate an innate sense of true, social nobility in spite of their lack of titles and affluence. Mexico's José Tomás de Cuéllar, a tireless *costumbrista* journalist and novelist, went as far as to say that Mexican society would redeem itself and become productive, peaceful, and procreative only when one hundred dandies on posh Plateros Street were replaced by one thousand honest workers with calloused hands.[19] Organizations like mutualist *filarmónicas* provided a stage for working people to validate themselves as a noble class of people, to say nothing of providing opportunities for women and men to socialize in ways that were considered proper.[20]

Another type of musical club that publicly used the label *filarmónica* was the village band. For example, Indian musicians in the Peruvian village of Santo Domingo de Chincha Alta founded the Filarmónica del Orden (Philharmonic of Order), which essentially functioned as a guild and a society for the betterment of Indians. The *filarmónica* instructed its members to seek musical gigs for the band and chorus anywhere they could find them, and to devoutly honor their patroness the Virgin of Guadalupe. The *filarmónica* allowed membership only to pure-blooded Indians and considered rival bands as inferiors and antagonists who represented disorder and underdevelopment in the musical realm. "Any member who agrees to play with the other rebel bands," the *filarmónica*'s combative bylaws intoned, "will be penalized with a fine of twenty silver soles, the sum of which will be distributed to the entire Society, based on the rank of each member."[21] In Mexico, village bands were also generally implicated in power plays with other bands that served as proxies for rival villages or a rival political faction within the same village. In any case, the humble village *filarmónicas* proved themselves to be a vital staple of the rhythms of traditional life by offering concerts during religious holidays and civic celebrations.[22] On the weekends, the sounds of brass bands were common in public plazas, where people of all classes congregated to people-watch and to be seen. Whether or not they served as an extension of religious or secular power, such village bands had little in common with elite *filarmónicas* and other musical associations, which did not define themselves as guilds but rather as clubs of leisure.

Though most nineteenth-century Spanish American musical associations carried the same catchall label of *filarmónica*, in practice they were either elite organizations, urban-mutualist associations, or specialized musical unions or guilds. All three categories were shot through with issues of class or ethnic identity, and the policing of that identity, but there was something else that they shared—something more timeless: the pleasure of melody, rhythm, and companionship.

The Popularity of Musical Theater

The most beloved music among nineteenth-century Spanish American elites was Italian opera and Spanish zarzuelas. People attended the opera to enjoy musical theater, but in cities like Buenos Aires (home of the Teatro Colón), Montevideo (Teatro Solís), and Santiago (Teatro Municipal), the opera house itself functioned as an architectural symbol of modernity and luxury. Havana's Teatro Tacón (1830), which could seat over three thousand, sparked the admiration of cosmopolitan North American and European travelers, who considered it one of the finest opera houses in the world.[23] The Teatro Guzmán Blanco (1881), situated in the heart of Caracas, was built in an elliptical shape and had neoclassical columns, a portico, and stained glass windows. Its seating capacity was over two thousand and its sumptuous interior featured three galleries, an ornate crystal chandelier that hung from the ceiling, and foyers decorated with paintings of notable Venezuelans. During the breaks in performances, which sometimes extended past midnight, the ladies and gentlemen of Caracas wandered the halls of the opera house, eating ice cream and pastries and drinking wine and other spirits.[24]

The opera that predominated throughout the nineteenth century was Italian. This was in part because of the large number of Italian opera companies (some as small as a traveling family, others as large as an elaborate circus) that began to crisscross Spanish America from the end of the Wars of Independence onward. Some traveled a US/Cuba circuit, some a Mexican/Central American itinerary, and other companies a South American circuit that included Venezuela, Brazil, Uruguay, Argentina, and Chile.[25] The most popular composers that these companies performed were Vincenzo Bellini, Gaetano Donizetti, and especially Gioachino Rossini and Giuseppe Verdi.[26] Rossini, who authored the worldwide hit *The Barber of Seville* (1816), as well as dozens of operatic comedies and melodramatic historical dramas, loomed large in the minds and hearts of sophisticated Spanish Americans. One Mexican critic wrote in 1868 that Rossini's extraordinary achievement sprang from the cheerfulness of his melodies. Similarly, others referred to the brightness of his music by calling him an angel or a celestial cherub, the musical embodiment of inspiration.[27] Such comments were probably responding in part to Rossini's adoption of the style of singing known as bel canto, which emphasized the vocal virtuosity of individual singers through smooth phrasing, complex melodic lines, and delicate and gradual crescendos in the volume of a singer's voice.[28] Rossini also applied this logic to his crowd-pleasing overtures by incorporating a gradual increase in sound, culminating in a dramatic finish.

Giuseppe Verdi was Rossini's only real rival for the hearts and ears of Spanish American audiences. In Chapter 3, we noted that his opera *La traviata* (1853) was one of the most well-known and frequently staged works in the nineteenth century. The melodies of *La traviata*'s "Sempre libera" aria and its *brindisi* (drinking song) are to this day nearly universally known in the West by even the most casual listeners of classical music. After Verdi's death, one Buenos Aires magazine eulogized him by saying that even people who had not attended the numerous productions of his operas were familiar with bits and pieces of memorable arias from *La traviata*, *Ernani* (1844), *Rigoletto* (1851), *Il trovatore* (The troubadour; 1853), *Aída* (1871), and others.[29] As we saw above, this was due to the fact that at family gatherings and *filarmónicas* the most commonly performed pieces of music were extracts from operas in simplified piano arrangements, and amateur vocal performances. In other words, opera hits not only were heard in complete, formally staged opera productions, but were also frequently experienced in private homes.

In the second half of the century, a lighthearted kind of operetta from Spain called the *zarzuela* took all of Spanish America by storm. Unlike operas, which had no spoken words, zarzuelas mixed dialogue with song, dance, and pageantry. Their tone and subject matter also favored lighter themes, with comedy and happy endings being more common than in Italian operas. Early in its history, in the seventeenth century, zarzuelas dealt with mythological themes and highlighted pastoral themes. After going out of style in the eighteenth century, zarzuelas made a dramatic comeback as a conspicuous expression of Spanish musical nationalism. The new nineteenth-century zarzuelas distinguished themselves from the baroque ones by having a wider variety of settings, including contemporary ones; by highlighting the lower classes; and by accenting Spanish identity and idioms.[30] The nineteenth-century zarzuela genre was so popular that by one estimate tens of thousands of zarzuelas were produced in Spain between 1850 and 1950.[31]

One of the most beloved Spanish zarzuelas in Spain and Spanish America was *La verbena de la Paloma* (The celebration of Paloma; 1894) by Ricardo de la Vega and Tomás Bretón, the plot of which is a convoluted love story set against the colorful local characters who frequent Madrid's La Latina neighborhood during a festival in honor of the Virgin of la Paloma. In Buenos Aires alone, this one-act musical was performed four times a night in several theaters concurrently. In Mexico, it was performed a hundred times between 1894 and 1895, and it was parodied by a Mexican sequel titled *La verbena de la Guadalupe* (The celebration of Guadalupe; 1896) by Armando Morales Puente.[32] Spanish Americans also wrote zarzuelas, especially in Mexico, where over 350 were composed at the end of the nineteenth century and the beginning of the twentieth.[33] The most famous and successful of them all was *Chin-Chun-Chán* (1904) by Rafael Medina and José Elizondo, with music by Luis G. Jordá, which was staged in Mexico, Argentina, and Spain. This brilliantly crafted theatrical trifle was a comedy about a man who flees his wife by checking into a Mexico City hotel disguised as a Chinaman, where the staff and everyone around him confuse him for a distinguished Chinese guest they are expecting named Chin-Chun-Chán. The zarzuela brimmed with elaborate musical entertainments and dancing, social commentary, and wordplay centered around the fake Chin-Chun-Chán's attempts to sound like a Chinaman. It was a smash hit.

In short, zarzuela was a transatlantic and transnational merging of Spanish and American theatrical and musical tastes. Zarzuela was easy to relate to because it was performed in Spanish and because its songs were catchy and memorable. It was less pretentious and tragic than opera, and its penchant for comedy and local speech made it familiar and relatable.

New World Choreographies

In his memoirs, the Mexican poet Guillermo Prieto recalled different types of dance parties that took place in mid-nineteenth-century Mexico. The gatherings of country people featured women wearing aprons and men in short trousers, and included popular dances such as *el dormido* (the sleeping man), *el perico* (the parrot), and *el malcriado* (the rude man). At the fancy balls of the elite, you could see women with layered underskirts and fancy headdresses, and men in gloves and tails, dancing European imports like contradances, quadrilles, waltzes, and polkas. The middle classes enjoyed those dances as well but held their parties in charming homes decorated with flowerpots, birdcages, and religious icons of the Virgin of Guadalupe or Saint John Nepomucene. The women there wore light gingham or muslin dresses, while the young men wore skinny trousers that narrowed at the ankles. A more charged and risqué environment was found at the *bailes de escote* (dances of the low-cut dresses), attended primarily by a restless swarm of soldiers, law students, shopkeepers, salesclerks, fallen women, and other urban types who could not be categorized as middle-class. It was here, as the smoke of countless cigarettes and cigars hung in the air, that men forged friendships and partnerships, and men and women arranged marriages and one-night stands.[34]

Prieto's evocation of these entertainments illustrates how difficult it is to generalize about dancing culture; dancing was defined by shifting social networks and spaces, and by choreographies that largely faded with the advent of the twentieth century. Unlike literature and art, the story of dance was not written down or brushed onto a canvas, but rather developed through an elusive and ephemeral process of adaptation and innovation. Like other community-building cultural forms, dancing was a vital and socially significant activity; it was a pleasurable and ordinary activity that people of all walks of life and social ranks associated with musical experience and community. The ideal of sociability realized itself through dancing, and so did the choreographies of courtship and seduction. For intellectuals invested in theories of social engineering, dancing was also a cultural metric for measuring civilization and barbarism. In his widely disseminated conduct manual, Manuel Antonio Carreño broke dancing down into an elaborate social ballet composed of an intimidating set of prohibitions and instructions about the appropriate posing and sequencing of bodies and gestures.[35] José María Mora, a Spanish writer who became a respected and influential member of the nineteenth-century Chilean intelligentsia, was so concerned about the dangers of unregulated dancing that he proposed the formation of a state-sponsored corps of dancers that would perform at public events and teach commoners how to dance in ways that were respectable and decent.[36]

The story of modern Spanish American dancing is the story of a complex exchange between European, African, and New World rhythms, choreographies, instrumentation, and traditions. The primary foundation of this process of cultural adaptation and transformation originates in two types of European dance that were widespread in nineteenth-century Spanish America: choral dancing (e.g., the contradance, the quadrille, and the cotillion) and closed-couple dancing (such as the waltz and the polka). A third type of dancing, open-couple dancing, was exemplified by the seventeenth-century European dance called the "minuet," in which couples moved ceremoniously around the dance floor doing elaborately choreographed curtseys, bows, and poses. The minuet was the highest expression of elite refinement and upper-crust culture during the first half of the century, although some communities of Afro-Cubans adopted it for its elaborate theatricality. One observer from 1819 went as far as to write that Afro-Cubans honored the regal ancestry of the minuet better than the elites: "I cannot express the astonishment I felt on seeing these blacks, of graceful figure, going up to their partners, holding their dress-hats in their hands, and then covering themselves with a dignity that begins to be rare even in Ancient Europe."[37] This Caribbean cross-pollination aside, the impact and influence of the minuet was less important and enduring than that of choral dancing and closed-couple dancing, to which we now turn.

Choral dancing was for groups of people rather than for couples. Originating in mid-seventeenth-century Europe, English country dancing (or, as the French called it, the *contradanse*) became a dominant dance paradigm for nearly two centuries. Contradancing, still practiced

Figure 5.1. Choral dancing, from *Colección de bailes de sala* (1862) by Domingo Ibarra. Nettie Lee Benson Latin American Collection, University of Texas Libraries, The University of Texas at Austin.

today in Europe and the United States among enthusiasts of folk music, arranged dancers in parallel lines or circles and set them in structured, sequential movements or choreographies called "figures." Sometimes, there was a caller (in Spanish, a *bastonero*), whose job it was to call out the figures to be danced by the dancers. In the longways format of the contradance, a row of men and a row of women lined up on the dance floor opposite each other. The man and woman at the head of the lines (the first couple) would do a set of figures that the other dancers would have to copy, with the set moving down the line. Then, when all had performed their figures, the first couple would do another set, repeating the process. The figures of the contradance included the promenade (in Spanish, *paseo*), a graceful, stylized walk down the middle of the longways corridor; the chain (*cadena*), in which men and women pass each other and exchange places, sometimes moving all the way down the line by reproducing the figure with new partners; the star (*molino*), in which a subset of dancers move in a circle while crossing their hands together in the center; the allemande (*alemanda*), which consists of two partners linking arms and tracing a circle while leaning away from each other; and the sieve (*cedazo*), which might feature couples dancing a kind of waltz in 2/4 time or "passing through" arches formed by the outstretched arms of other dancers.[38]

The quadrille (*cuadrilla*) and cotillion (*cotilión*) dances were other types of eighteenth-century choral dancing descended from contradancing.[39] In the quadrille, four couples arranged themselves in a square and proceeded to dance a series of figures in which partners changed positions, curtsied, circled around each other, and diagrammed diagonals inwards and outwards on the dance floor.[40] Originally, the cotillion (from the French for "petticoat") was danced in a circular or closed-square formation, but by the nineteenth century it had become something quite distinct: a rowdy and extravagantly theatrical party dance in which various couples mimicked comical scenes or allegorical stories through theatrical choreographies. Props such as ribbons, piñatas, mirrors, chairs, and ropes, as well as a variety of party favors, made the cotillion a festive favorite for closing a party in the wee hours of the morning.[41] At one fancy ball held in Mexico City in 1900, the cotillion opened with a gentleman dressed in eighteenth-century costume, along with two sumptuously dressed pages. This was followed by pages who pulled a flower-laden cart full of coiffed ladies waiting to be asked to dance. At one point, dancers and partygoers took delicately constructed balls of confetti and threw

"El diabolo," figura de Cotillón.

Figure 5.2. Cotillion dance, from the magazine *El Mundo Ilustrado* (1908). Nettie Lee Benson Latin American Collection, University of Texas Libraries, The University of Texas at Austin.

them onto the floors and at the bodies of other attendees, covering the premises with fine, snow-white confetti.[42] Another famous cotillion dance was one in which women swung a long skipping rope that men had to hop over without getting caught or tripping.

Two of the most popular closed-couple dances in nineteenth-century Spanish America, as in the rest of the Western world, were the waltz and the polka, both of which landed in the New World in the first half of the century. In the waltz, which was usually danced in ¾ time, the man held his partner's arm outward while she rested her arm on his other shoulder. The couple bobbed and spun across the floor, spinning around with their bodies joined together. Mexico City's most famous mid-century dance master, Domingo Ibarra, wrote that the waltz should be danced only by experienced and careful dancers because there was so much risk of stepping on toes and long skirts. As if that were not enough, he instructed that each dancer should maintain great composure throughout in order to communicate refinement and class.[43] Because of its closed-couple formation and its speed, the waltz implied a more intimate and physical encounter between a man and a woman than what was found in contradancing or quadrilles. In a culture that prized the containment and taming of the body and its passions, this is why the waltz was risqué: it put a woman up close against the body of a man for a dance that led to the sensual symptoms of physical exertion (heavy breathing and sweating).[44]

The polka was cut from the same cloth. In its nineteenth-century iteration, the dancers held their bodies either in a position similar to that used in the waltz, or in a side-by-side position in which the dancers wrapped their arms low around each other's backs. The polka used promenades and reverse turns like waltzing, but its footwork, consisting of step, close, step, and hop, was different.[45] The overall effect and rhythm was more dynamic and vigorous. Throughout Europe and the United States, a polka craze called "polkomania" took off in the 1840s, generating extravagant trends in fashion. At least in one instance, the polka rose up in arms. In 1847, it swept Mexico City, spawning an association with a short-lived conservative revolt against the liberal president of Mexico, Valentín Gómez Farías, who had moved to expropriate the property of the Catholic Church during the US-Mexico War. The so-called Polkos Revolt acquired its name not only because its supporters were people of affluence and conservative inclinations who loved the polka, but also because the supporters of Farías claimed that the uprising provided tacit support to the US war effort against Mexico, led by President James K. Polk.[46]

Figure 5.3. Couple dancing, from *Colección de bailes de sala* (1862) by Domingo Ibarra. Nettie Lee Benson Latin American Collection, University of Texas Libraries, The University of Texas at Austin.

The story of New World choreographies is more than the tale of how Spanish Americans adopted European dances to imitate the cultures of the Old World. It's also the story of how European and African dances were Americanized by the inventiveness and traditions of local musicians and dancers. Take, for example, the *pericón* dance of Argentina and Uruguay, which also spread westward to Chile. Although today it's firmly associated in the imagination of the people of the River Plate with country life and colorfully dressed gauchos, the *pericón* emerged as a local reinvention of contradancing, with interdependent couples using the longways or the quadrille formation to execute individual figures, such as the bridge (*puente*), borrowed from Spanish contradancing, or the basket (*canasta*), which is similar to a French contradance figure. Alongside these

Old World appropriations, the *pericón* also absorbed figures and choreographies from local performers, such as the legendary clown and acrobat José Podestá, whose circus played a key role in promoting and spreading the dance throughout Argentina and Uruguay.[47] (We already met Podestá and his circus in Chapter 3.) Musically, the *pericón* often featured the call-and-response tradition of gaucho singers who, accompanied by a guitar, competed to best each other with witticisms and boasts. Imagine a country scene on a field with country men and women arrayed in longways. The music begins: we hear the thick and deep voice of the gaucho singer Chiclina, strumming his rustic guitar with heavy downstrokes, intoning: "Pericón and pericón, / whip that bird! / Let the gauchos have fun!"[48] This is the epitome of an American cultural moment, not because the sounds and the motions were invented in isolation by Chiclina and his rural cohort, but because they coalesced through the alchemy of a variety of cultural forms and influences.

The contradance was also instrumental in the development of new kinds of dancing in the Caribbean. Improvisational Afro-Caribbean musical performers put their stamp on contradance melodies by adopting rhythms such as the habanera, *tresillo*, and the *cinquillo*, and by syncopating the music (stressing the weak or down beats in a given rhythm). Under such circumstances, what was a body to do? The music begged for more than just the feet to move: it demanded that bodies sway, and for the hips to do things that might seem indecorous to stuffy nineteenth-century moralists. In the contradance, the final figure of the *cedazo*, which drove dancers into each other's arms for a waltz-like swing around the dance floor, began to overpower the rest of the choreography.[49] The longways lines, the quadrille squares, and most of their elaborate figures took a backseat to a new kind of dancing, one that joined bodies together intimately. In Puerto Rico, this variation on the contradance led to a choreography known as *merengue* or the *contradanza merengueada* (neither of which should be confused with the contemporary Dominican dance of the same name). "The invention of that dance must be the joint product of a poet, a musician, a crazy man, and the devil," wrote one disapproving observer about this mid-nineteenth-century dance. The upper halves of the bodies of the dancers made them seem like saints, he continued, but the lower halves seemed like "the joining of glory and hell, of truth and lie."[50] In Cuba, a parallel transition occurred, creating similarly risqué closed-couple dances—first the *danza*, and later on the *danzón*. For moralists, these new dances represented the unacceptable eruption of barbaric African sensuality into mainstream Cuban society. As another indignant critic wrote, "Who does not know that the bass notes of our *danzas* constitute the echo of African drums?"[51] The rise of such dances and their spread throughout the Caribbean (and to Mexico, where *danzón* became popular as well) signaled an irrevocable combination of European choreographies with African rhythms.

The tango, which began to rise to prominence at the end of the nineteenth century before taking Argentina and Europe by storm in the new century, was also the product of transculturation. The urban poor of Buenos Aires, especially Afro-Argentines, combined the polka, the habanera, and other musical and choreographical influences to develop the *milonga*, a closed-couple dance that pressed bodies into a tight embrace while the hips of the dancers moved provocatively. The *milonga* laid the foundation for the dance that is today known as "tango," a word commonly used in the nineteenth century to refer to Afro-descendant dancing and rhythms.[52] At the beginning of the twentieth century, the *milonga* and the emergent tango expanded its sphere of influence beyond the urban poor and people of color, becoming the iconic dance of Argentines. A similar phenomenon occurred in neighboring Chile with the *zamacueca*, an Afro-Peruvian open-couple dance in which the dancers swayed forward and backward from each other while flicking handkerchiefs over each other's heads. Although the Chilean *zamacueca* was at first controversial, it became wildly popular across all classes of people by the 1830s. What had begun as a dance tradition of the commoners became a national treasure and symbol of Chileanness. "I'd much prefer a *zamacueca*," one famous government minister said, "to the office of President of Chile."[53]

All the fashionable and transgressive choreographies described here coexisted with a large array of traditional dances that had been passed down from generation to generation in modest rural communities from northern Mexico down to Tierra del Fuego. During Christmas in the Mexican village of San Miguel de las Peras, near Oaxaca, Indian boys and girls in guarache sandals performed the Dance of the Sombrero: circling a hat on the ground, they approached and backed away from it to the music of a trio of Indians playing small mandolins. In the Bolivian village of Tiahuanaco, near Lake Titicaca, Indians commemorated the potato harvest and the sun with rhythmic male dancers wearing plumed headdresses that shielded their heads like large umbrellas, and with female dancers whose elaborate paper hats featured mirrors and stalks of quinoa, representing the sun and its beneficent, life-giving powers.[54] And slaves and freedmen, their bodies gleaming with sweat, danced to a circle of pounding drums in the Venezuelan seaside village of Choroní, as their descendants do today.

Martial Melodies

Music has been a part of military life and war for centuries, and nineteenth-century Spanish America was no exception. The armies of Independence, like their colonial predecessors, featured battalions composed of musicians whose music lifted morale and directed the actions of men during a battle. Common trumpet calls included "the march," "saddle up," "retreat or return to quarters," and the infamous *deguello* (literally "to slit the throat"), which was used to unleash combat without quarter or mercy. (One of the most legendary uses of the *deguello* was by Santa Anna's forces at the Battle of the Alamo in 1836.)[55] In 1814, when General José de San Martín forged his legendary Army of the Andes to undertake the liberation of South America, he formed two musical divisions: the Eighth Battalion and the Eleventh Battalion. The musical warriors in both divisions carried drums, fifes, trumpets, and cymbals and were led by standard-bearers and an officer with a long staff.[56] The Eleventh Battalion was a striking sight to see: it was composed of former slaves dressed in baggy Turkish trousers and short vests.[57] Both the Eighth and Eleventh were not sideline groups but combat-ready units with a specific role to play on the battlefield. At the decisive Battle of Chacabuco, San Martín's Army of the Andes joined with the forces of the Chilean Bernardo O'Higgins and defeated over two thousand royalists with the help of these battalions. At one perilous moment during the fight, General O'Higgins placed himself at the head of the Eighth Battalion and personally led the musicians forward into the thick of the action, as they played a rousing march that inspired all the patriots within earshot to fight and to push harder.[58]

When not motivating soldiers on the battlefield, the musical battalions of the armies of Independence performed at balls and celebrations for officers and the rank and file. As they traveled from one faraway town to another, they adopted local tunes and dances, taking them to the next town and beyond. The bands also helped to disseminate European melodies and choreographies to out-of-the-way places that were less likely to be familiar with operas and songs popular in cities and abroad. In this way, military bands spread musical and dance traditions across wide geographical areas. For example, a Chilean military band sent to liberate Peru as a part of an expeditionary force in 1822 became caught up in the Peruvian craze for the *zamacueca* dance and brought it back to Chile where, by 1840, it had spread across all social classes and become the country's national dance. From there, the *zamacueca* continued to spread, across the Andes into northern Argentina, where it developed yet another version of itself.[59] In the Caribbean, military bands performed a similar role, moving local tunes and rhythms from island to island during periods of conflict and deployment. When Spain sent military regiments from Puerto Rico and Cuba to quell a rebellion in the Dominican Republic in 1861, Puerto Rican musical styles (specifically its brand of *merengue*) took root in Santo Domingo and among soldiers from Cuba, who then took it back with them to their island.[60] Besides these functions, military bands also took on a public, commemorative role, providing pomp and circumstance, marching music, and entertainment at nationalist celebrations and religious holidays. They performed at the beginning of bullfights, as well as in public plazas on the weekends.

National anthems were the epitome of military music in nineteenth-century Republican life. These earnest musical marches were designed to trigger feelings of loyalty in all who heard them at public and ceremonial functions. By most dispassionate, contemporary aesthetic standards, their formulaic lyrics were unoriginal and devoid of beauty, but once the anthems were adopted and institutionalized, people began to appreciate them as songs that bound them symbolically to their fellow citizens, and which could inspire feelings of patriotism. Generally, these anthems were military tales of sacrifice and triumph that provided a lesson for future generations to follow. Let's sketch their generic themes here, beginning with divinity. Anthems present the sacrifices the nation demands of its citizens, as well as the inevitability of its triumph, as conditions and outcomes linked to the will of God. No citizen should worry about how terrible things might seem because the heavens are aligned with the cause of the nation, ensuring its survival and future. For example, the second verse of the Mexican anthem rallies citizens by declaring that God has already written the country's everlasting fate on the heavens. Victory is predestined in the celestial realm. In the anthems of Ecuador and Venezuela, God either approves of the sacrifices demanded by Independence or actively encourages people to fight for freedom. Another repeatable theme is unity. Victories on the battlefields of the past and the battlefields of the future are possible only when citizens come together to form one solid, composite mass with the single-minded goal of protecting their motherland and its children. The Venezuelan anthem, which is Pan-American in its focus, intones, "Joined by bonds formed in the heavens, all of America is one nation." The Mexican anthem, in contrast, personifies disunity and then has it die like an enemy on the battlefield. Finally, another shared theme is historical memory, which presents the glories of the past as the foundation on which future triumphs and accomplishments rest. The songs clamor for citizens to remember the sacrifice of the heroic generations of the past, because it illustrates the price of freedom and glory. In sum, national anthems were formula songs, rigid like statues and columns, stained with the blood of heroes and martyrs, and unwaveringly firm in the conviction that tomorrow would bring glory to a chosen people.[61]

The Songs of the People

In Chapter 2 we explored popular song as a conduit for the expression of a literature of the people in contrast to the print consumed by more educated and refined readers. We underlined that print genres such as gauchesque poetry in Argentina and Uruguay were modeled on satirizing, celebrating, or imitating the voice of unlettered gaucho singers, and as such provided a bridge between oral and print cultures. Now we return to the same topic, but with an emphasis on the origins and evolution of popular song traditions. Perhaps nowhere else in the arena of nineteenth-century Spanish American culture, with the possible exception of religious practice, do we see a stronger trace of Spanish tradition than in the *cantores* (singers) who took Spanish forms and Americanized them. The nineteenth century was the last flowering of these New World song traditions that began in the sixteenth century and continued to evolve until the twentieth. Modern life and culture chipped away at these traditions and wore them down by introducing new ones. Although *romances, coplas, décimas*, and *corridos* continue to be sung in the twenty-first century, they are much less widespread and influential than they were a century earlier. What was once a living and breathing thing, familiar to all, became a museum piece or an isolated ethnic activity.

One of the oldest and most enduring forms of popular song in Spanish America was the *romance*, a kind of ballad. *Romance* refers to a genre of poetry that was well established in Spain as early as the fifteenth century and that was associated with orality and song. (The meaning of the word *romance* is related here not to love, but rather to a distinction between Latin and the local "Romance" languages derived from it, in this case Spanish.) In Spanish literary history, *romances* are periodized as belonging either to a lesser-known and largely unpreserved medieval tradition of oral literature (*romancero viejo*) or to a more print-oriented tradition that began in the sixteenth century (*romancero nuevo*), when these songs became a popular type of cheap print culture. Collected in *cancioneros* (songbooks), the *romances* of the *romancero nuevo* could be songs that had circulated for several generations without any known author, or new compositions by well-known authors that followed the conventions of the genre. Although the *romancero nuevo* repurposed oral tradition and song as static reading material, people of all social classes preserved these printed *romances* through music, singing the print and passing it on to others, who in turn altered it and transmitted their own versions inside and outside of their families. And since the boom of the *romancero nuevo* coincided with the Conquest and the colonization of the New World, Spanish *romances* quickly spread throughout the Americas between the sixteenth and eighteenth centuries, as far north as New Mexico and Louisiana, and all the way south to Argentina. Because they were primarily transmitted through song, *romances* were the earliest and most popular form of storytelling entertainment in early Modern Spain and the New World.

The *romance* is a narrative poem without stanzas composed of an indeterminate number of octosyllabic verses that uses assonant rhyme, meaning that sound-alike vowels in the last word of each line form the basis of the rhyme rather than the consonants. Generally, every two verses of a *romance* compose a unified phrase, and only even-numbered verses are rhymed. Despite these rules, the *romancero tradicional* evidences many variations in line length and rhyme structure: after all, *romances* were passed on from generation to generation and were subject to continual revision and reinvention. There are *romances* on every imaginable subject, from epic tales about the wars between Christians and Moors in Spain, to love stories, captivity narratives, lurid crime stories, religious tales, and commentary on current events. In Spanish America, many of the old Spanish romances endured into the twentieth century with multiple variants in different countries.[62]

One of the earliest known *romances*, first transcribed in 1421, "The Lady and the Shepherd" (*La dama y el pastor*), was sung for generations in California, New Mexico, Mexico, Cuba, Chile, and Argentina, and probably everywhere else on the continent.[63] The romance is structured around a dialogue between a beautiful young lady of means and a shepherd. The woman is pretty forward because she tries to entice the shepherd to spend the night with her by flattering him, and by offering him gold, mules, and property, all of which the shepherd declines because he wishes to return to stay with his herd of cattle in the mountains. In the end, however, the shepherd realizes his lost opportunity but it is too late. One of the pioneering collectors of New World romances, Aurelio Espinosa, transcribed "The Lady and the Shepherd" in 1915 as sung by a fifty-five-year-old woman named Dionisia Monclovia from New Mexico. Here is the part of the romance that Dionisia sang to convey the shepherd's regret and the lady's cruel reply:

> [Shepherd]: Lass, owner of my soul,
> lass, I come again;
> lass, when you spoke to me,
> Your words I did not understand.
> Forgive me, great lady,
> If I offended you in some way.
>
> [Lady]: When I wanted to, you didn't want to,
> and now that you want to I don't want to,
> so weep for your loneliness,
> since I wept for mine first.[64]

Individual singers like Dionisia were not the only channels for the dissemination of such *romances*. One of the most well-known *romances* in the New World was called "Delgadina," although it was also known as "Algarina," "Antolina," "Ambarina," "Agadenta," and "Guadina," among others.[65] This sixteenth-century ballad tells the story of a girl who, after refusing to have sex with her father, the king, is locked up in a room, from which she mournfully begs her family to bring her a drink of water. The name Delgadina is a variant of *delgada* (thin), reinforcing the *romance*'s theme of starvation and punishment. This disquieting ballad was one of several that endured for generations in child's play, especially among girls. In the eighteenth and nineteenth centuries, girls formed circles, held hands, and sang versions of romances like "Delgadina" in unison as they skipped clockwise and counterclockwise, making different figures and sometimes acting out scenes from different *romances*.[66] In addition to singing "Delgadina," these *juegos de corros* or *de ruedas* (chorus or circle games) helped to preserve many other old songs and romances, among them "Don Gato" (Don Cat), "Arroz con leche" (Rice with milk), "Mambrú se fue a la guerra" (Mambrú went to war), and "Hilo de Oro" (The gold thread). Variation defined all these compositions, the lyrics of which were the product of the inventiveness of countless singers—adults and children—who thought to change the words and make the songs their own.

Besides preserving and disseminating individual romances like the ones mentioned above, the *romanceros* provided New World *cantores* with a model and inspiration to follow in composing songs born out of local experiences and current events. One of the close relatives of the *romance* was a kind of song known as a *corrido* that was found in nineteenth-century Chile, Venezuela, Argentina, Guatemala, and Mexico.[67] However, it was in Mexico where this kind of song took deep root, becoming an influential form of popular music that has thrived until the present day. The word *corrido, corrío,* or *carrerilla* means "fast" and originally referred to a style of singing in which a *cantor* sang a romance fast and uninterrupted.[68] Mexican *corridos* are commonly composed of quatrains (four-line strophes), sixains (six), septets (seven), or octets (eight), and each line is generally octosyllabic or longer, with an *abcb* rhyme scheme. That said, Mexican *corridos* are varied enough that insisting on metrical formulas alone to define them is not enough. Their thematic focus and style is key. One of the defining characteristics of the *corrido* is that it tells a specific story about real life and people, such as bandits, bullfighters, lovers, and criminals. Another important feature of the *corrido* is the repeated use of certain expressions and formulas, such as the dating of an event at the beginning of the ballad, an inaugural greeting and announcement of the topic of the song, a farewell at the end, the use of colloquial language, and the inclusion of stock phrases, such as "Vuela vuela palomita" (Fly, fly away, little dove), as well as invocations to the Virgin of Guadalupe.[69]

One of the most popular types of nineteenth-century *corridos* is the tale about a bandit, such as songs about Jesus Arriaga (alias Chucho el Roto), Heraclio Bernal, and Gregorio Cortez, one of the most celebrated folk heroes of the US-Mexico border. In these *corridos*, the bandit embodies machismo and rebellion against an unjust status quo represented by the military, the police, the rich, and the state. They are often primitive, tragic figures whose admirable virility is destroyed by Judas-like associates. All these qualities are in evidence in the "Corrido of Heraclio Bernal." First, we discover that the protagonist is a hero of the people:

"Bernal was so brave, / on his horse Jovero. / Bernal did not steal from the poor. / Rather, he gave them money." Whatever his virtues, however, Bernal is not soft: "In the mountains of Durango, / he killed ten Spaniards. / He ordered that their skins be tanned / to make himself boots." In the end, he is betrayed by one of his men, and the *corridista* bids the dark hero farewell: "Fly, fly away, little dove,/ to the top of the walnut tree. / The roads are empty. / They've already killed Bernal / . . . Fly, fly away, little dove,/ to his resting place as well / and weep a little / for the man who was brave." The *corrido* closes, in classic fashion, with the following lines: "Here goes my farewell / as the peacock lifts off to fly: / This is the end of the song / about the tragedy of Bernal."[70] *Corridos* like this one about Heraclio Bernal belong to a vast, transnational body of popular songs spanning centuries. The *corrido* began as a successful outgrowth of the Spanish *romance* but it evolved to become something original, and distinctly Mexican and American.

Another song tradition from Spain that took root throughout the New World were *coplas* (quatrains). These four-line poems were very popular among singers in medieval Spain and subsequently across the Atlantic because their brevity allowed for concise, humorous, and proverb-like compositions that were easy to remember and modify. Moreover, the simplicity of the *copla* made it an excellent frame for improvisational singing. The meter of the *copla* form was varied, but it usually featured octoyllabic lines with an *abcb* or *abba* rhyme (these were *copla de romance* and the *redondilla*, respectively). Another popular structure was a combination of heptasyllabic (five) and pentasyllabic (seven) lines with an *abcb* rhyme (the *seguidilla*). Coplas were used in *contrapuntos*, in which two singers took turns singing *coplas* to best each other, as well as to voice the lyrics to dances like the *zamacueca*.[71] If the flavor of the romance was defined by its narrative, storytelling function, the *copla* was defined by its irreverence and proverbial sententiousness, which prized a memorable turn of phrase above everything else. Male *copleros* liked to brag about their machismo, joke about the women they pursued, or complain bitterly about their *suegras* (mothers-in-law). It didn't matter if you were a mestizo, an Afro-descendant, a wealthy Creole landowner, a peasant, or a drunk strumming a guitar on the stool of a *pulpería*: if you were musically inclined, you knew how to sing *coplas*, combining traditional standards with those of your own invention. Everywhere in nineteenth-century Spanish America, from the countryside to city streetcorners and markets, we find the wit of the *copla*.

People started collecting and publishing collections of Spanish American *coplas* at the end of the nineteenth century and the beginning of the twentieth, and when we review them in comparison to some of the most popular ones from Spain, it becomes clear that the New World *copla* tradition preserved Spanish originals, modified others, and created new *coplas* out of the experiences, worldviews, and environment of different Spanish American peoples.[72] Here's a sampling of various *coplas* that were in circulation in the nineteenth century:

Jacinta gave me a piece of ribbon,
Leona gave me a piece of rope.
For Jacinta I would give my life,
for Leona my heart.
    [Argentina, Venezuela, Colombia, Puerto Rico]

—Mariquita, give me a kiss.
Your mother orders it.
—My mother is her own boss.
I'm the boss of my own business.
    [Spain, Chile, Argentina, Mexico]

One of the girlfriends I had
had all the f's:
she was flaccid, frivolous, fuzzy,
ferocious, fragile, and frigid.
    [Spain, Colombia, Venezuela, Mexico]

I ride down from the plains
on my honey-colored horse.
Like a herd of cattle
I am trampling singers underfoot.
    [Venezuela]

I am like a hot green pepper—
spicy but much sought after.
They call me the negress,
the haughty negress.
    [Panama][73]

Sometimes early folklorists and commentators of the New World *coplas* assumed that a particular *copla* was American when it was actually Spanish in origin. The power of a good *copla* was such that it could take root on both sides of the Atlantic and thrive. Most importantly, the *copla* tradition was full of local invention and vitality; it preserved *coplas* that no one remembered as being Spanish, recasting them as local songs while also generating countless new ones that were never transcribed or otherwise preserved for posterity.

The third Spanish American song tradition that was widely popular in the nineteenth century was called the *décima*. Although the *décima* was famously canonized in Spanish literature through Vicente Espinel's *Diversas rimas* (Various rhymes; 1591), it was never as popular there as in the New World, where it was adopted by singers of all colors and ranks to tell stories, to moralize, to philosophize, and to boast.[74] The *décima's* structure was much more complex than that of the *copla* and the *romance* but it was ideally suited for improvisational singing, as well as for musical dueling between two or more *decimistas*. The *décima espinel* (named after the abovementioned author of *Diversas rimas*) is considered the classic form: a forty-four-line, octosyllabic poem divided into five stanzas, the first of which was a quatrain and the other four consisting of ten lines each. Its *abbaaccddc* rhyme was consonant. What was special about the *décima* was the relationship between that initial quatrain and the four stanzas that followed. The opening quatrain was called the *planta*, and functioned as a text or theme that the rest of the poem, called the *glosa* (gloss), was supposed to respond to, to explain, or to expand. But that was not all. Each stanza in the *glosa* was supposed to have as its last line one of the lines of the *planta*. In other words, the *décima* was a way of commenting on an inaugural thought or proposition by glossing or exploring each one of its lines through the following four stanzas.

The *contrapunto* tradition, which set two singers in competition to determine who was the wittier improviser of words, took a variety of forms, but the *décima* format was the most structured and challenging of them all because of the relationship between the *planta* and the *glosa*. In nineteenth-century Chile and Peru, two rival *decimistas* and their rowdy followers would gather in a makeshift rural saloon or a city bar to musically spar, with one singer throwing down a *planta* for the other to gloss. Or, they would jointly gloss a *planta* called out by an audience member or a presiding judge. On the US-Mexico border, rival *decimistas* sometimes sent satirical *plantas* in writing to rivals, or posted them in public places, to stoke the fires of competition in advance of a musical duel.[75] Unlike the *romance* and the *copla*, the *décima's planta* and *glosa* structure invited dialogue, challenge, and collaboration.

In the colonial period, religious themes were common in the *décima* tradition, but the nineteenth century saw a boom of satirical, historical, and otherwise secular compositions. Most *décimas*, like oral culture writ large, were never collected, but some existing transcriptions give us an idea of what these songs were like. Below is a complete *décima* that was well known in Salta, Argentina, at the end of the nineteenth century, and which documents the sarcastic reaction of Salteños to the threat of a war with Chile over a border dispute. The word *roto*, meaning "a low-class person," is here used to refer to Chileans, and Korner is a famous Chilean general. To highlight the dialogue between the *planta* and the *glosa*, the *planta* and the sequential repetition of each of its lines in the *glosa* are italicized:

The rotos will soon be upon us
with their rifles loaded
and their cannon packed
with grapeshot made out of beans.

Let's flee like partridges
scared by those cannon,
which aimed at the heels
hit the target on the nose.
They are happy artillerymen
because they are devoted to Korner;
With their little cannon
that don't make much noise,
firing shots without smoke.
The rotos will soon be upon us.

Let the bugles call
and the drums roll.
We begin to see the glimmering
of their polished swords.
Here the spurs of our quaking soldiers
now begin to ring.
They tremble in agonizing fear

despite being in cavalry formation
as they watch them come
with their rifles loaded.

Let us, the Argentines, tremble.
We're such useless gauchos.
Trembling in fear of the guns
in the hands of those pigs,
who aim so precisely
that we will be drowned.
And as we are suffocated that way
the cornet will call,
bayonets will be fixed
and their cannon packed.

That will be very horrible.
I am horrified to think about it,
and simply imagining it
I get out of breath
and I stretch my neck way out
and I lift my prayers upward
like the faithful do.
And devotedly I begin to pray
that the Heavens will not let them kill us
with grapeshot made out of beans.[76]

This example—humorous as long as you're not Chilean—underlines that the *décima* form was well designed for developing a story or a theme. For this reason, *décimas* worked well as populist journalism about local and national events, as well as for entertainment.

Music and Change

All of nineteenth-century Spanish American music was popular in the sense that it appealed to a particular group that confidently claimed it as belonging to its cultural identity. Young elite women grew up learning how to play the greatest hits of the musical theater on the piano, or to sing their favorite opera arias at family and public gatherings. Like their gaucho neighbors to the south, the plainsmen of Venezuela, the *llaneros*, strummed small four-stringed guitars with the accompaniment of maracas, and sang boastful *coplas* and *décimas* while their friends cheered them on. In Havana, the drums sounded at a celebration hosted by an African *cofradía* (mutual aid society). Every musical constituency had its own worldview or function; there was music for pleasure and leisure, for reaching toward God, for war and discipline, and for keeping memory alive across the generations. In this chapter we explored how certain musical trends and forms (*filarmónicas*, military bands, *coplas*, and so on) crossed national borders. And yet, enveloping these repeatable forms was a large, heterogeneous, and ever-changing soundscape resistant to generalization and easy classification. Some writers and travelers thought to try to represent parts of this soundscape with words, but much of its diversity faded without being recorded, or transformed itself into something new as it evolved over time. Music was, and continues to be, a living tradition, molded by identifiable patterns while also erupting into unexpected melodies and rhythms that create new genres and choreographies.

Change

THERE ARE TWO OVERARCHING THEMES in this book. The first is that there are historically legitimate grounds for generalizing about nineteenth-century Spanish American culture. In the preceding chapters, I have underlined cultural practices that were shared by a broad cross-section of people from different nations. These cultural commonalities included *costumbrismo*, the ideology and practice of good manners, Spanish song traditions, elite social clubs, and the popularity of certain kinds of print. These and other phenomena sprang from shared historical experiences, institutions, technologies, and aesthetics, all of which contributed to the creation of a transnational cultural realm. The second theme is the dynamic interaction between different kinds of culture, a phenomenon that scholars have variously called "transculturation," "creolization," or "hybridity." For example, the stories of the Mexican Day of the Dead, New World contradancing, and the interplay between European travel books and *costumbrismo* demonstrate how cultural experience and artistic creation are based on the mixing of a variety of ethnic, national, and regional influences.

In these pages we have also seen how important the idea of "the modern" was to nineteenth-century Spanish American elites, who applied and interpreted it in a variety of ways. As outlined in the Introduction, the guiding principles of these interpretations were the civilization and barbarism dichotomy, the conservative-liberal divide, urbanism, and elite nationalism. The culture of nonelite peoples provided a marked contrast—even a challenge—to these principles. Their culture was defined by the old traditional ways (such as religious practice), and by forms of expression that affirmed their ethnic identities and questioned elite categories of what was socially and cultural valuable. Elite and nonelite cultural outlooks often converged and interacted in everyday life and the arts, but they also diverged because the cultural transmission of ideas, values, and entertainments was limited by barriers of distance, education, and literacy. It was not until the twentieth century that massive numbers of people of different classes were able to experience politics and culture on a grand collective level. This is not to say that the twentieth century was a period of utopian equality and unchallenged communitarian experience—far from it; I am suggesting that culture, in its mode of transmission, began to circulate more widely than before, reaching more people than was ever possible in the nineteenth century. I am invoking "mass culture," a concept that is intertwined with "mass media" (radio, television, film, cheap print) and "mass politics" (often marshaled by populism).

There are so many ways of conceptualizing the difference between nineteenth- and twentieth-century culture that the comparison threatens our ability to provide a coherent framework. There are differences of degree, such as the continued expansion of cities in the twentieth century, the rise in literacy rates, and the growth of the middle class. There are also differences that hinge on the emergence of political or cultural movements that promoted the rights and status of people who had been marginalized, subordinated, or vilified in the nineteenth-century: feminism, indigenismo (the celebration of Indian identity), Negrismo (the celebration of Afro-descendant identity), and gay rights. In the political realm, the rise of Marxism-Leninism thrust Spanish America into the middle of the Cold War, producing iconic figures like Che Guevara and fueling a powerful strain of anticolonialist literature, music, art, and political thought. These and other developments created a conversation and a cultural atmosphere that was fundamentally different from the nineteenth-century cultural world sketched in the preceding chapters. They are some of the game changers that might help us write a twentieth-century sequel to this book. But if we zero in on culture and how it travels, the number of people it reaches, and the geographical scope of its impact, we can see that mass culture is the most important difference between the nineteenth century and what came afterward.

The rise of radio, television, and film, as well as the further expansion of forms of cheap print (like newspapers, comics, and pulp novels), enabled larger numbers of people than ever before to experience culture collectively, as a shared national, or Pan-American phenomenon. Consider, for example, the tremendous success of the Peruvian *telenovela* (soap opera) *Simplemente María* (Simply María; 1969–1971), which held practically the entire nation rapt during its run of over four hundred episodes. The story of María—a humble maid and seamstress who climbs the social ladder while dealing with all kinds of sentimental and family entanglements—celebrated social mobility and hard work and explored the challenges of moving from the countryside to the city to reach middle-class status. Rich people, middle-class people, and poor people all found something to relate to in this story. When María's wedding was filmed in Lima, thousands of people showed up for the filming and treated it like a real event in the life of a real person. In the words of one news article, "Last Saturday, fiction became reality. . . . María wed Esteban in a real Church. . . . Several people fainted, gripped by their emotions."[1] *Simplemente María* was also a runaway hit outside of Peru. The *telenovela* had originally begun as an Argentinian radio soap opera in 1948, and was later produced for television in Argentina twice (1967 and 1980), and later in Brazil (1970), Venezuela (1970), and Mexico (1989). There was a film adaptation and other radio versions, including a widely popular Spanish one. The impact of María's story was so great that in Peru and elsewhere, women flocked out to buy Singer sewing machines of the same kind used by the heroine to conquer success.[2] None of the most popular nineteenth-century stories or cultural fads could reach the staggering numbers of people that televised programs like *Simplemente María* could reach.[3] Class differences, geographical distance, and the separation of the sexes could all be temporarily overturned in the process of consuming a popular, mass culture product like a *telenovela*. At the end of each episode of *Simplemente María*, people of different ranks still found themselves circumscribed by their separate socioeconomic realities, but they all had experienced something together in real time and could share a conversation about it with people different from themselves.

Mass media was not only about entertainment and the consumption of love stories; it also provided vehicles for developing nationalist consciousness and promoting political action or inaction. Radio and television embedded certain kinds of music and stories into a larger story about what it meant to be Argentinian, or Mexican, or Venezuelan, or so on. To a large degree, the tango became a deeply felt symbol of Argentinian national identity because it dominated the country's radio waves in the 1930s and 1940s. Modern Mexican musical nationalism also emerged at the same time, as radio stations took a variety of regional musical genres and began to package them to their listening audience as *música típica* (typical or popular music).[4] Governments and dictators in different countries soon recognized the tremendous power of the mass media and intervened in shaping or censoring what was transmitted out to the public. One good example is Colombia's first television transmission on June 13, 1954, which began with the national anthem and a speech by President Gustavo Rojas Pinilla. Rojas Pinilla had come to power via a coup and was quite eager to take advantage of both radio and television to bolster the legitimacy of his regime among the masses. During the same period, similar phenomena occurred in the Dominican Republic, which infused most of its programming with propaganda celebrating its dictator Rafael Trujillo, and in Argentina, where the populist regime of Juan Domingo Perón blanketed the country with celebrations of Peronism and the country's first lady, Evita.[5]

Mass culture also raises key questions that are not applicable to the nineteenth century. For example, how was Spanish American popular culture standardized or made generic in its transition from lived, localized experience to something manufactured for repeated, mass consumption? How did the export and translation of US comic book icons, such as Superman and Batman, cowboys, and Walt Disney characters, affect the culture industry in Spanish American countries? To what degree can we speak of a transnational mass culture through cultural products like soap operas, televised beauty pageants, and comedy programs? The answers to such questions are reserved for students of twentieth-century Spanish American culture.

These concluding observations and questions might suggest that twenty-first-century Spanish America is separated from the nineteenth century by a wide gulf, but that is not entirely true. The past endures into the present, sometimes in tangible forms, and at other times in more ghostly ways: the popularity of soap operas like *Simplemente María* descends from the transnational *folletines* of the nineteenth century; contemporary transnational urban musical genres like reggaeton spark cultural anxieties similar to those provoked by dances like the *danzón* and the *milonga*; the pomp and circumstance of nineteenth-century Republican festivals continues to be employed into the twenty-first century, as evidenced by the 2013 state funeral of Venezuela's president, Hugo Chávez; Mexican *corridos* continue to thrive in the present as *narcocorridos* (drug ballads); urban poverty and overcrowding still drive conversations about the future of the Spanish American city; and foreign cultural products—European in the nineteenth century, North American in the present—continue to exert tremendous cultural influence.

Nineteenth-century iconography, architecture, and mythology also live on beneath Spanish American's twenty-first-century exterior. The monumental heroes, the grand dreams for a utopian future, and the nationalist mythologies and sense of belonging all began in the nineteenth century. It's a period that provides us with a framework and a vocabulary for understanding key aspects of what came afterward, and remains today. This is why the nineteenth century is not strange when we encounter it; it is familiar and recognizable, like an *abuela* (grandmother) whose stories can help us understand and appreciate the present. Let's listen to her.

SUGGESTED READING

THE FOLLOWING RECOMMENDATIONS for further reading are primarily of English-language books, as well as some other sources that are broad and introductory in nature. They are not intended to be exhaustive, but rather a starting point for further study. For a more expansive list of sources in both Spanish and English, please see the endnotes to each chapter and the Bibliography. Publication details provided here are only for titles not included in the Bibliography.

INTRODUCTION *Cultures*

Nineteenth-century Spanish American cultural history: A good place for a beginner to start is John Charles Chasteen's excellent primer *Born in Blood and Fire: A Concise History of Latin America*, which includes valuable discussions of cultural and literary materials relating to the nineteenth century. Angel Rama's enormously influential *The Lettered City* proposes a framework for reading Latin American culture through the prism of the urban ideal. Two of his chapters deal with the nineteenth century, but readers would do well to read the whole volume to appreciate the impact and context of his arguments. *The Burden of Modernity: The Rhetoric of Cultural Discourse in Spanish America*, by Carlos Alonso (New York: Oxford University Press, 1998), is an excellent framing analysis that helps us understand the nineteenth century. One of the most cited and debated books in interdisciplinary nineteenth-century Latin American studies is *Foundational Fictions: The National Romances of Spanish America*, by Doris Sommer (Berkeley: University of California Press, 1991), which provides a model for understanding the relationship between literature and politics in this period. Lee Skinner's *History Lessons: Refiguring the Historical Novel in Nineteenth-Century Latin America* (Newark, DE: Juan de la Cuesta, 2006) expertly guides us to understand the role of historical memory in building literary nationalism. Carlos Forment's *Democracy in Latin America, 1760–1900, vol. 1: Civic Selfhood and Public Life in Mexico and Peru* is an inspired work of intellectual, cultural, and social history, full of great detail about journalism, religion, and the association of people. William G. Acree Jr.'s original and expansive *Everyday Reading: Print Culture and Collective Identity in the Río de la Plata, 1780–1910* explores the power of print in nineteenth-century Argentina and Uruguay through popular literature, consumer culture, and the history of education. William H. Beezley's *Mexican National Identity: Memory, Innuendo, and Popular Culture* is an outstanding exploration of the culture of commoners, such as its expression in music, lottery games, and puppets. One of the most original and useful books on late nineteenth-century literature and culture is *On the Dark Side of the Archive: Nation and Literature in Spanish America*, by Juan Carlos González Espitia (Lewisburg, PA: Bucknell University Press, 2010). Finally, there are many outstanding anthologies of historical and cultural essays, including *A Cultural History of Latin America: Literature, Music and the Visual Arts*, edited by Leslie Bethell (New York: Cambridge University Press, 1998); *Latin American Popular Culture: An Introduction*, edited by William H. Beezley and Linda Ann Curcio-Nagy (Wilmington, DE: Scholarly Resources, 2000); *Building Nineteenth-Century Latin America: Re-Rooted Culture, Identities, and Nations*, edited by William G. Acree Jr. and Juan Carlos González Espitia; *A Companion to Latin American Literature and Culture*, edited by Sara Castro-Klaren (Malden, MA: Blackwell, 2008); and the fantastic multivolume reference work *Literary Cultures of Latin America: A Comparative History*, edited by Mario Valdés and Djelal Kadir. Pamela Murray's *Women and Gender in Modern Latin America* (New York: Routledge, 2014) contains excellent secondary essays on women and gender in the nineteenth century, as well as key period primary texts. For more on gender, see *Plotting Women: Gender and Representation in Mexico*, by Jean Franco (New York: Columbia University Press, 1989); Ana Peluffo's *Lágrimas andinas: Sentimentalismo, género y virtud republicana en Clorinda Matto de Turner* (Pittsburgh: Instituto Internacional de Literatura Iberoamericana, 2005); and Lee Skinner's essay "Constructions of Domesticity in Nineteenth-Century Spanish America" (*Bulletin of Hispanic Studies* 88, no. 7 [2011]).

Facundo Quiroga and Domingo Sarmiento: The secondary literature in this area is especially rich. A good place to start is with the historical and cultural context on nineteenth-century Argentina detailed in Nicholas Shumway's *The Invention of Argentina*, which contains ample sections about gauchos and Domingo Sarmiento, as well as many other canonical topics. The excellent Kathleen Ross translation of Sarmiento's *Facundo: Civilization and Barbarism* contains a useful introduction by Roberto González Echevarría. Other valuable sources on Sarmiento and his world include the anthology *Sarmiento: Author of a Nation*, edited by Tulio Halperín Donghi, Iván Jaksić, Gwen Kirkpatrick, and Francine Masiello; Ariel de la Fuente's *The Children of Facundo*; and Diana Sorensen's *Facundo and the Construction of Argentine Culture* (Austin: University of Texas Press, 1996), which examines the reception of Sarmiento's book in Argentina. "The Other's Knowledge: Writing and Orality in Sarmiento's *Facundo*," by Julio Ramos, in his *Divergent Modernities: Cultural and Politics in Nineteenth-Century Latin America*, is a rewarding interpretation of the classic work.

Civilization and barbarism in nineteenth-century Spanish America: *The Poverty of Progress: Latin America in the Nineteenth-Century*, by E. Bradford Burns, is a good place to start, as are "The Essay in Spanish America: 1800 to Modernismo" by Nicolas Shumway and "The Essay of Nineteenth-Century Mexico, Central America, and the Caribbean," both in *The Cambridge History of Latin American Literature*, vol. 1, edited by Roberto González Echevarría and Enrique Pupo-Walker. Martin Stabb's book-length intellectual history of Spanish America, *In Quest of Identity: Patterns in the Spanish American Essay of Ideas* (Chapel Hill: University of North Carolina

Press, 1967), provides excellent sketches about late nineteenth-century positivism and race. Juan Pablo Dabove's *Nightmares of the Lettered City: Banditry and Literature in Latin America, 1816–1929* is an interdisciplinary sourcebook of critical thinking about bandits and how liberal thinkers framed the problem of barbarism. Another way of exploring the civilization/barbarism dichotomy is through the concept of modernity, which Spanish Americans used to judge their cultural and historical situation in comparison to Europe and the United States. In *The Burden of Modernity: The Rhetoric of Cultural Discourse in Latin America* (New York: Oxford University Press, 1998), Carlos Alonso historicizes the contradictions of nineteenth- and twentieth-century Latin American writers who, on the one hand, embraced the ideal of modernity while also struggling to authorize their own voices by way of a rejection of it. In the first chapter of his book *The Inverted Conquest: The Myth of Modernity and the Onset of Modernismo*, Alejandro Mejías-López provides a road map to debates about modernity and argues that the subordination of nineteenth-century Spanish American modernity to European modernity is unconvincing. Victor Goldgel Carballo's exciting *Cuando lo nuevo conquistó América: Prensa, moda y literatura en el siglo XIX* (Buenos Aires: Siglo Veintiuno, 2013) frames Spanish American debates about modernity within the broader cult of the new in the Western world. For explorations of gender and modernity, see *Between Civilization and Barbarism: Women, Nation, and Literary Culture in Modern Argentina*, by Francine Masiello (Lincoln: University of Nebraska Press, 1992).

CHAPTER 1 *Cities*

Introducing the nineteenth-century Spanish American city: Jay Kinsbruner's *The Colonial Spanish-American City*, despite its focus on the colonial era, provides a brisk and complete historical context for understanding modern urbanism. Rama's *The Lettered City* (see above) is an ambitious blending of literature, history, and philosophy. James Scobie's "The Growth of Latin American Cities, 1870–1930," in Bethell's *Cambridge History of Latin America*, vol. 4, maps the history of cities in an accessible yet comprehensive way, as do all of the chapters contained in *Planning Latin America's Capital Cities, 1850–1950*, edited by Arturo Almandoz Marte. Ramos's *Divergent Modernities* contains analyses of how nineteenth-century cities were represented as metaphors of modernity by key Spanish American writers, especially José Martí. For more on the status of Paris in nineteenth-century Spanish America, see chapter 1 of Marcy Schwartz's *Writing Paris: Urban Topographies of Desire in Contemporary Latin American Fiction* (Albany: State University of New York Press, 1999).

Eyewitness and literary accounts: Personal testimony and literature are excellent vehicles for understanding nineteenth-century urbanism. In this category, *I Saw a City Invincible: Urban Portraits of Latin America*, edited by Gilbert M. Joseph and Mark D. Szuchman (Wilmington, DE: Scholarly Resources, 1995), provides some excellent primary documents about nineteenth-century cities. John Charles Chasteen's translation of the 1903 Mexican best-selling novel *Santa*, by Federico Gamboa (Chapel Hill: University of North Carolina Press, 2010), features breathtaking descriptions of crowds, establishments (including whorehouses), and sounds at the turn of the twentieth century. *La gran aldea* by Lucio Vicente López and the novels of Eugenio Cambaceres provide vivid sketches of nineteenth-century life in Argentina. *Times Gone By: Memoirs of a Man of Action*, by Vicente Pérez Rosales (New York: Oxford University Press, 2003), contains descriptions of life in Santiago, Chile, including the wonderful chapter "Why the Santiago of 1814 to 1822 Can't Hold a Candle to the Santiago of 1860." Traveler accounts such as Samuel Hazard's *Cuba with Pen and Pencil* and Fanny Calderón de la Barca's *Life in Mexico* are also rich in urban detail.

Criminality, prostitution, and hygiene: One of the strongest strands in contemporary scholarship about nineteenth-century Spanish American cities relates to crime and hygiene. On the subject of prostitution, Donna Guy's *Prostitution in Buenos Aires* and Tiffany A. Sippial's *Prostitution, Modernity, and the Making of the Cuban Republic 1840–1920* (Chapel Hill: University of North Carolina Press, 2013) are both comprehensive, excellent sources. William French's article "Prostitutes and Guardian Angels: Women, Work and the Family in Porfirian Mexico" (*Hispanic American Historical Review* 72, no 4 [1992]) charts the anxieties and aspirations of the nationalists and hygienists who tried to define women's place in society. For guidance on nineteenth-century criminality, I recommend the scholarship of Carlos Aguirre, who has published and edited widely on this subject, including his monograph *The Criminals of Lima and Their Worlds: The Prison Experience, 1850–1935* (Durham, NC: Duke University Press, 2005). For Mexico, see James Alex Garza's *The Imagined Underworld: Sex, Crime, and Vice in Porfirian Mexico* (Lincoln: University of Nebraska Press, 2007), and Pablo Piccato's *City of Suspects: Crime in Mexico City, 1900–1931* (Durham, NC: Duke University Press, 2001). Esteban Echeverría's canonical short story "The Slaughterhouse," contained in the *Oxford Book of Latin American Short Stories* (New York: Oxford University Press, 1997), helps us frame the theme of civilization and barbarism in relation to city life. Lee Skinner's article "Carnality in 'El matadero'" (*Revista de Estudios Hispánicos* 33, no. 2 [1999]) is one of the best guides to this story. For hygiene in Argentina, see the much-cited *Ficciones somáticas: Naturalismo, nacionalismo y políticas médicas del cuerpo (Argentina 1880–1910)*, by Gabrielle Nouzeilles (Rosario, Argentina: B. Viterbo, 2002), and Christopher Abel's *Health, Hygiene and Sanitation in Latin America c. 1870 to c. 1950* (London: Institute of Latin American Studies, 1997).

CHAPTER 2 *Print*

Reading and print culture: Acree's *Everyday Reading* provides a broad overview of the relationship between reading and printing in Uruguay and Argentina. Acree's introduction to the John Charles Chasteen translation of the astonishing best seller *Juan Moreira*, by Eduardo Gutiérrez, contains a friendly and expert exploration of the circulation of this hit during the nineteenth century. For insight into printing and politics in Mexico and Peru, see Carlos Forment's *Democracy in Latin America, 1760–1900, vol. 1: Civic Selfhood and Public Life in Mexico and Peru*. Susana Zanetti's *La dorada garra de la lectura* (Rosario, Argentina: B. Viterbo, 2000) is a collection of essays about nineteenth-century reading practices, including the reception of Jorge Isaacs's *María*, and gender and reading. *Tropes of Enlightenment: Simón Rodríguez and* *the American Essay*, by Ronald Briggs, sketches the relationship between typography, reading, and political subjectivity in the first half of the century. *The Political Power of the Word: Press and Oratory in Nineteenth-Century Latin America*, a collection of essays edited by Iván Jaksić (London: Institute of Latin American Studies, 2002), contains important chapters, including Rebecca Earle's "The Role of Print in the Spanish American Wars of Independence." Juan Poblete has published extensively on print culture in this period, and his "Reading National Subjects," in Castro-Klaren's *A Companion to Latin American Literature and Culture*, is a succinct overview of the political, social, and subjective experience of reading. Moreover, his book *Literatura chilena del siglo XIX: Entre públicos lectores y figuras autoriales* (Santiago: Editorial Cuarto Propio, 2003) stages his framework in a case study about Chile. For an insightful introduction to serialized literature, which was the primary mode for transmitting literature in this period, see "Novels, Newspapers, and Nation: The Beginnings of Serial Fiction in Nineteenth-Century Mexico," by Amy E. Wright, in Acree and González Espitia's *Building Nineteenth-Century Latin America*. Belem Clark de Lara and Elisa Speckman Guerra's *La república de las letras: Asomos a la cultura escrita del México decimonónico* is an outstanding three-volume anthology of critical essays on reading and publishing in Mexico. The first part of Ramos's *Divergent Modernities* contains an overview of the Republic of Letters, as well as illuminating case studies. In a related vein, Beatriz González Stephan's award-winning *La historiografía literaria del liberalismo hispanoamericano del siglo XIX* (Havana: Casa de las Américas, 1987) explains the meaning that intellectuals attributed to literature and how they structured it into nationalist narratives. About late nineteenth-century Spanish America, there are several useful studies. *The Spanish American Crónica Modernista, Temporality, and Material Culture: Modernismo's Unstoppable Presses*, by Andrew Reynolds (Lewisburg, PA: Bucknell University Press, 2012), explores the mechanics of publishing and the circulation of print and its relationship to the content of Modernista literature. Mejías López's *The Inverted Conquest* examines the transatlantic dialogues of late nineteenth-century writers, as does Adela Pineda's study of transatlanticism in late nineteenth-century literary magazines, *Geopolíticas de la cultura finisecular en Buenos Aires, París y México: Las revistas literarias y el Modernismo* (Pittsburgh: Instituto Internacional de Literatura Iberoamericana, 2006).

Journalism and *costumbrismo*: One of the standard works on journalism in this period is Aníbal González's *Journalism and the Development of Spanish American Narrative* (New York: Cambridge University Press, 1993). Flor María Rodríguez Arenas's *Periódicos literarios y géneros narrativos menores: Fábula, anécdota y carta ficticia (1792–1850)* (Doral, FL: Stockcero, 2007) is a fascinating compendium about the diversity of nineteenth-century newspaper publishing. Victor Macías González's "The Lagartijo at the High Life: Notes on Masculine Consumption, Race, Nation and Homosexuality in Porfirian Mexico," in *The Famous 41: Sexuality and Social Control in Mexico, 1901*, edited by Robert McKee Irwin, Edward J. McCaughan, and Michelle Rocio Nasser, explores magazines and gender in the late nineteenth century. In the same volume, readers will find Robert Buffington's "Homophobia and the Construction of Working-Class Masculinities: Mexico City, 1890–1910," which dwells on working-class newspapers and their response to the state and the upper classes. *Revista Iberoamericana*'s 2006 collection of essays about newspapers in nineteenth-century Spanish America, titled *Cambio cultural y lectura de periodicos en el siglo XIX en América Latina*, contains an outstanding variety of essays on a variety of periods and nations, including illuminating historicist contributions by Lee Skinner, Celia del Palacio Montiel, Alvaro Kaempfer, and Kirsten Silva-Gruesz, among others. For the definition of *costumbrismo*, see "The Brief Narrative in Spanish America: 1835–1915," by Enrique Pupo-Walker, in González Echevarría and Enrique Pupo-Walker's *Cambridge History of Latin American Literature*. Stephen M. Hart's treatment of the subject in *A Companion to Latin American Literature* (Rochester, NY: Tamesis, 2007) is a valuable synthesis. Rafael Ocasio's *Afro-Cuban Costumbrismo: From Plantations to the Slums* (Gainesville: University Press of Florida) examines *costumbrismo* in relation to blackness.

CHAPTER 3 *Theatricality*

The history of the Spanish American theater: There are few overviews of the history of the Spanish American theater in the nineteenth century. The two most notable ones are Frank Dauster's "The Spanish American Theater of the Nineteenth-Century," in González Echevarría and Pupo-Walker's *Cambridge History of Latin American Literature*, and Emilio Carilla's "The Romantic Theater in Hispanic America," in Gerald Gillespie's *Romantic Drama*. More specific accounts, typologies, and overviews may be found if readers consult national case studies, such as *Historia del teatro argentino en Buenos Aires*, by Osvaldo Pellettieri (Buenos Aires: Galerna, 2001); *Historia del teatro argentino: Desde los rituales hasta 1930*, by Beatriz Seibel; *El teatro en Venezuela*, by Leonardo Azparren Giménez (Caracas: Comisión de Estudios de Posgrado UCV, 2002); and several historical entries corresponding to different national theater traditions in the *Encyclopedia of Latin American Theater*, edited by Eladio Cortés and Mirta Barrea Marlys (Westport, CT: Greenwood Press, 2003).

Popular diversions: Beezley's *Mexican National Identity* contains indispensable explorations of puppetry and other diversions among nonelites. For insight into bullfighting, see the illustrated volume *Plaza de Acho: Historia y tradición, 1766–1944*, by Héctor López Martínez, and *On Becoming Cuban: Identity, Nationality, and Culture*, by Louis A. Pérez Jr. (Chapel Hill: University of North Carolina Press, 1999), which contains a discussion of the cultural meanings of bullfighting and baseball in Cuba. For an overview of popular diversions in different national contexts, see *A Cultural History of Cuba during the U.S. Occupation, 1898–1902*, by Marial Iglesias Utset, and "The New Order: Diversions and Modernization in Turn-of-the-Century Lima," by Fanni Muñoz Cabrejo, in Beezley and Curcio-Nagy's *Latin American Popular Culture since Independence: An Introduction*. The writings of Raúl Héctor Castagnino are must reads for anyone exploring the Creole Circus in the Southern Cone: *El Circo Criollo: Datos y documentos para su historia, 1757–1924* (Buenos Aires: Lajouane Editores, 1953) and *Centurias del circo, teatro gauchesco y tango* (Buenos Aires: Editorial Perrot, 1959) are two important works. Beatriz Seibel's *Historia del circo* is a more recent account, as is the excellent "The Art of Assimilation and Dissimulation among Italians and Argentines," by Ana C. Cara (*Latin American Research Review* 22, no. 3 [1987]). Acree's introduction to the English translation of *Juan Moreira* (mentioned above) includes Moreira's theatrical afterlife. For Mexican circuses, see *La fabulosa historia del circo en México*, by Julio Revolledo Cárdenas (Mexico City: Consejo Nacional para la Cultura y Artes, 2004), and *Los payasos, poetas del pueblo*, by Armando de María y Campos (Mexico City: Editorial Botas, 1939), which, although dated, is a fine journalistic account of the subject. Although it is focused on the pre-Independence period, Juan Pedro Viqueira Albán's *Propriety and Permissiveness in Bourbon Mexico* is an outstanding discussion of diversions that endured well into the nineteenth century. Finally, José Joaquín Fernández de Lizardi's classic novel *The Mangy Parrot*, available now in a lovely English translation by David Frye, is a brilliant compendium of anecdotes about early nineteenth-century Mexico that features many popular diversions.

Fiestas, carnivals, and commemorations: Stephanie Merrim's award-winning study *The Spectacular City, Mexico and Colonial Hispanic Literary Culture* (Austin: University of Texas Press, 2010), although centered on the colonial period, is key for understanding the relationship between urban space and theatricality. Will Fowler's anthology *Celebrating Insurrection: The Commemoration and Representation of the Nineteenth-Century Mexican Pronunciamiento* contains several essays that explore the staging and meanings of Republican fiestas in Mexico. In particular, I recommend Pedro Santoni's "Salvas, Cañonazos y Repiques: Celebrating the Pronunciamiento during the U.S.-Mexican War." *Heroes and Hero Cults in Latin America*, edited by Samuel Brunk and Ben Fallaw (Austin: University of Texas Press, 2006), contains articles by John Charles Chasteen, Shannon Baker, and Víctor Macías González that pertain to state fiestas or republic commemorations in our period. Matthew D. Esposito's *Funerals, Festivals, and Cultural Politics in Porfirian Mexico* is an excellent case study about funerals as commemorative practice in Mexico. My own monograph *The Cult of Bolívar in Latin American Literature* contains an analysis of Fermín Toro's account of the repatriation of Bolívar's remains in 1842, as well as accounts of monuments and the concept of monumentalist nationalism. David H. Brown provides a thorough immersion into the history and symbolism of Afro-Cuban fiestas and carnivals in *Santería Enthroned: Art, Ritual, and Innovation in an Afro-Cuban Religion*. Also, *Cuban Fiestas*, by Roberto González Echevarría (New Haven, CT: Yale University Press, 2010), is a beautifully written evocation, interpretation, and history of popular festivities on the island. For Carnival celebrations elsewhere in Latin America, two essays by John Charles Chasteen provide vital descriptions and interpretations: "Black Kings, Blackface Carnival, and the Nineteenth-Century Origins of the Tango," in Beezley and Curcio-Nagy's *Latin American Popular Culture*, and "Anything Goes: Carnivalesque Transgressions in Nineteenth-Century Latin America," in Acree and González Espitia's *Building Nineteenth-Century Latin America*. Micol Seigel's "Cocoliche's Romp: Fun with Nationalism at Argentina's Carnival" (*TDR: The Drama Review* 44, no. 2 [2000]), contains rewarding descriptions and an analysis of how the clown created by the Podestá theatrical troupe became a stock Carnival character. For Cocoliche, Cara's "Art of Assimilation and Dissimulation" (mentioned above) is an indispensable source.

Conduct manuals: For readers interested in conduct manuals, Beatriz González Stephan has published several seminal studies on Manuel Antonio Carreño, including "De fobias y compulsiones: La regulación de la barbarie" (*Hispamérica* 74 [1996]), and "Modernización y disciplinamiento: La formación del ciudadano; Del espacio público y privado," in *Esplendores y miserias del siglo XIX*, edited by Beatriz González Stephan, Javier Lasarte, et al. (Caracas: Monte Avila Editores, 1995). Also, María Fernanda Lander, in *"El Manual de urbanidad y buenas maneras* de Manuel Antonio Carreño: Reglas del ciudadano ideal" (*Arizona Journal of Hispanic Cultural Studies* 6 [2002]), links Carreño's key text to nineteenth-century Spanish American novels. Although not focused on Spanish America, Leigh Mercer's *Urbanism and Urbanity: The Spanish Bourgeois Novel and Contemporary Customs* (Lewisburg, PA: Bucknell University Press, 2013) provides useful insights that can serve as a point of comparison to the middle- and upper-class Spanish American experience. The same can be said about Jesus Cruz's *Rise of Middle-Class Culture in Nineteenth-Century Spain* (Baton Rouge: Louisiana State University Press, 2011), which contains ample discussions of the cultural and intellectual roots of conduct manuals.

CHAPTER 4 *Image*

General art history: Nineteenth-century Spanish American art history is relatively understudied in English language scholarship in comparison to European and US art. *Art in Latin America: The Modern Era,* by Dawn Ades, is an excellent introduction and has beautifully illustrated chapters about nineteenth-century Latin American art. The relationship between European traveler artists and *costumbrismo* is explored in detail in this book, as well as the political uses of art during and after Independence. The studies "From Prehispanic to Post-Romantic: Latin America in Portraits, 500 B.C.—A.D. 1910," and "Portraiture and the Age of Independence," by Miguel A. Bretos, are both featured in *Retratos: 2,000 Years of Latin American Portraits,* edited by Elizabeth P. Benson (New Haven, CT: Yale University Press, 2004). Also, see *Historia del arte iberoamericano,* by Ramón Gutiérrez and Rodrigo Gutiérrez Vinuales (Barcelona: Lunwerg, 2000), and Gerald Martin's two chapters covering the nineteenth century in Bethell's *Cultural History of Latin America.*

Visual culture studies: In a more interdisciplinary vein, there is a growing body of scholarship on the nineteenth century that is commonly termed "visual culture studies." In *Images of Power: Iconography, Culture and the State in Latin America,* edited by Jens Andermann and William Rowe (New York: Berghahn, 2005), there are excellent essays by Magali Carrera and Beatriz González on corporeality, gender, and visuality in nineteenth-century Mexico and Venezuela. Andermann's *The Optic of the State: Visuality and Power in Argentina and Brazil* (Pittsburgh: University of Pittsburgh, 2007) establishes the connections between state-sponsored social control and visuality. "The Development of *Costumbrista*: Iconography and Nation-Building Strategies in Literary Periodicals of the Mid-Nineteenth Century," by Erica Segre, in her book *Intersected Identities: Strategies of Visualization in Nineteenth- and Twentieth-Century Mexican Culture,*(New York: Berghahn, 2007) charts the relationship between words and illustration in culture and provides insights applicable to other national contexts. My essay "Tecnologías de la mirada: Ignacio Manuel Altamirano, la novela nacional y el realismo literario" (*Decimonónica* 10 [2013]) examines how three nineteenth-century Mexican writers use metaphors related to photography and other optical technologies to define the social role of writing.

Women and art: *Pintoras mexicanas del siglo XIX*, edited by the Museo Nacional de San Carlos in Mexico City (Mexico City: Instituto Nacional de Bellas Artes/Secretaría de Educación Pública, 1985), contains substantial biographies of individual artists, as well as an excellent introductory essay. *Las artistas plásticas de Lima*, by Sofía Karina Pachas Macedo, is primarily focused on the period following 1891, but it provides an excellent overview of women's art before that year. Ana Francisca Allamand's *Magdalena y Aurora Mira: Pioneras del arte femenino* (Santiago: Origo, 2008) is a beautifully illustrated appreciation and study of the art of these two seminal painters from Chile.

The photographic arts: *Image and Memory: Photography from Latin America, 1866–1994*, edited by Wendy Watriss and Lois Parkinson Zamora (Austin: University of Texas Press, 1998), features essays that touch on nineteenth-century photography in Uruguay, Colombia, and Guatemala, as well as an overview by Boris Kossoy titled "Photography in Nineteenth-Century Latin America: The European Experience and the Exotic Experience." Keith McElroy's *Early Peruvian Photography: A Critical Case Study* is a richly detailed, interdisciplinary examination about how photographs were made, thought about, and sold in Peru. His account includes discussions of pricing, rivalries between different photographer-impresarios, and the layout of photographic studios. Also outstanding are Olivier Debroise's *Mexican Suite: A History of Photography in Mexico* and Sara Facio's *La fotografía en la Argentina: Desde 1840 hasta nuestros días* (Buenos Aires: La Azotea, 1995). Finally, *The Encyclopedia of Nineteenth-Century Photography*, edited by John Hannavy (New York: Routledge, 2008), contains useful, substantive entries about several Latin American nations.

Folk art, Pancho Fierro, and José Guadalupe Posada: The secondary bibliography on Spanish American folk art is strong, and one of the finest sources is *Art and Faith in Mexico: The Nineteenth-Century Retablo Tradition*, edited by Elizabeth Netto Calil Zarur and Charles Muir Lovell (Albuquerque: University of New Mexico Press, 2001). Essays featured in this beautifully illustrated volume explore the origins, worldview, and regional variation in nineteenth-century Mexican *retablos*. For the colonial and nineteenth-century arts of the Andes, see *Pintores populares andinos* by Pablo Macera. To understand Pancho Fierro, readers must examine the indispensable scholarship of Natalia Majluf, especially *Tipos del Perú: La Lima criolla de Pancho Fierro*. Another required text is the gorgeous catalog published by the Pinacoteca Ignacio Manuel Merino, *Acuarelas de Pancho Fierro y sus seguidores*, which contains large color reproductions of Fierro's work with delightful and informative annotations by Ricardo Palma. The work of José Guadalupe Posada has recently inspired a wave of excellent scholarship in English, including Patrick Frank's *Posada's Broadsheets: Mexican Popular Imagery, 1890–1910*, and Thomas Gretton's groundbreaking study of Posada's technique, "Posada's Prints as Photomechanical Artifacts" (*Print Quarterly* 9, no. 4). Another excellent study is Rafael Barajas Duran's *Posada mito y mitote: La caricatura política de José Guadalupe Posada y Manuel Alfonso Manilla* (Mexico City: Fondo de Cultural Económica, 2009). One of the invaluable contributions of this book is how the author highlights Posada's fellow artist in the Vanegas Arroyo studio, Manuel Manilla. Manilla and other Mexican caricaturists have been obscured by Posada's international popularity.

CHAPTER 5 *Music*

Spanish American music history: Daniel Mendoza Arce's *Music in Ibero-America to 1850: A Historical Survey* is a brisk and comprehensive survey that scholars will find useful as a stepping-off point. Gerard Béhague's *Music in Latin America: An Introduction* (Englewood Cliffs, NJ: Prentice Hall, 1979) has a brief, descriptive chapter on notable themes and composers in the nineteenth century. Forment's *Democracy in Latin America*, mentioned above, contains reflections and statistics about the musical experience in nineteenth-century Peru and Mexico. Although focused on European musical history, William Weber's *Music and the Middle Class: The Social Structure of Concert Life in London, Paris and Vienna between 1830 and 1848* is a brilliant introduction to the European context and cultural institutions that elite Spanish American lovers of music sought to emulate. *The Garland Handbook of Latin American Music*, edited by Dale Olsen and Daniel Sheehy, contains excellent entries on the musical traditions of Latin American nations, including sections on music history that pertain to the nineteenth century. Alejo Carpentier's *Music in Cuba*, edited by Timothy Brennan (Minneapolis: University of Minnesota Press, 2001), is a rich account of Cuban music history by one of that country's most celebrated writers. Carlos Raygada's hard-to-find 1964 book, *Guía musical del Perú*, provides an outstanding outline history of Peruvian music. Carlos Luis Álvarez Mendoza's *Presencia de la música en los relatos sobre Venezuela de los viajeros de la primera mitad del siglo* is an exceptionally rich and useful sourcebook of traveler accounts describing the musical worlds of Venezuela. Donald Thompson's *Music in Puerto Rico: A Reader's Anthology* (Lanham, MD: Scarecrow Press, 2002) is much briefer, but also of interest. For nineteenth-century Chilean and Argentinian music history, readers will benefit from the memoirs of José Zapiola, *Recuerdos de treinta años: 1810–1840*. Finally, Janet Lyman Sturman's *Zarzuela: Spanish Operetta, American Stage* is necessary reading for understanding the tremendous popularity of light opera in Latin America.

Spanish American dance history: The best place to start to understand European dances imported into Spanish America is the classic work by Curt Sachs, *World History of the Dance*. Ralph G. Giordano's *Social Dancing in America* is about the United States, but its background and descriptions of European dances are useful and accessible starting points for beginners in the field of Spanish American dance history. John Charles Chasteen's *National Rhythms, African Roots* brilliantly maps out the terrain of nineteenth-century Latin American music history, as does Peter Manuel's dazzling *Creolizing Contradance in the Caribbean*, which is a must read. Christian Spencer Espinosa's "Imaginario nacional y cambio cultural: Circulación, recepción y pervivencia de la zamacueca en Chile durante el siglo XIX" is a case study of how one dance evolved and changed over time. To understand the rise of the tango, see *Tango: The Art History of Love*, by Robert Farris Thompson (New York: Pantheon, 2005), and Ana C. Cara's "Entangled Tangos: Passionate Displays, Intimate Dialogues" (*Journal of American Folklore* 122, no. 486 [2009]).

Popular song traditions: With regards to the *romance* ballad tradition, *Cantemos al Alba: Origins of Songs, Sounds, and Liturgical Drama of Hispanic New Mexico*, by Tomás Lozano, has a strong overview of the genre and many examples from the

US Southwest and Mexico. The edited Spanish-language volume titled *Romancero*, edited by Paloma Díaz-Mas, also defines the main currents and historical origins of romances in the Spanish-speaking world. The legendary Spanish scholar Ramón Menéndez Pidal founded modern *romancero* studies and many of his classic books, including *Los romances de América*, explore the spread of *romances* to the New World in detail. For the history of Mexican and Mexican American *corridos*, the book *"With His Pistol in His Hand": A Border Ballad and Its Hero*, by Américo Paredes, is a fascinating overview of the genre and a beautifully crafted work of nonfiction. Other well-known studies include *The Mexican Corrido*, by Merle E. Simmons, and several works by Vicente Mendoza, including *El romance español y el corrido mexicano: Estudio comparativo*. Moreover, "On the Paredes-Simmons Exchange and the Origin of the Corrido," by Guillermo E. Hernández (*Western Folklore*, Winter/Spring 2005), provides insight into debates about the origin of the *corrido*, and María Herrera-Sobek's *The Mexican Corrido: A Feminist Analysis* (Bloomington: Indiana University Press, 1990) offers a counterpoint to generic or formalist analyses of the genre. *La décima en el Perú*, by Nicomedes Santa Cruz, and the *Diccionario de coplas populares anónimas*, edited by Francisco Acaso, provide valuable insight and examples. "La copla española en América Latina," by Andrey Kofman (*La Colmena* 79 [2013]) compares Spanish *coplas* with Spanish American ones and provides a structuralist analysis of the New World *copla* tradition.

NOTES

INTRODUCTION *Cultures*

1. Mayer (1809–1879) was an affluent and educated world traveler. He published popular books about Mexican history and antiquities, including *Mexico as It Was and as It Is* (1844), and an important abolitionist novel titled *Captain Canot; or, Twenty Years of an African Slaver* (1854). He served the Union in the Civil War, founded the Maryland Historical Society, and was an influential promoter of the cultural life of Baltimore.

2. My account of Mayer's experiences is drawn from *Mexico as It Was*, 54–57. I also consulted Hardy, *Travels in the Interior*, 3–4; García Cubas, *El libro*, 205; and Prieto, *Memorias de mis tiempos*, 104.

3. Zarco, "Operas y toros," 595. The article is signed with the pseudonym "Fortun."

4. Ortiz, *Contrapunteo cubano*, 96–97. For debates on transculturation, see Millington, "Transculturation."

5. See Zárate, *Facundo Quiroga*, 129–30. My account of the assassination is a composite based on multiple accounts in Zárate.

6. De la Fuente, *Children of Facundo*, 125–27 and 130–33.

7. All the songs cited here are from Zárate, *Facundo Quiroga*, 15–40. My translation.

8. See Sarmiento, "El camino," 153–57.

9. Quoted in Botana, "Sarmiento and Political Order," 143. Translation by Botana.

10. Carrizo, "Del cantar popular."

11. Bilbao, *El evangelio americano*, 27. My translation.

12. My account of positivism's themes is informed by Harwich Vallenilla, "Venezuelan Positivism," 339–40. For accounts of Mexican positivism, see Zea, *El Positivismo en México*; and Elizabeth Fowler, "Mexican Revolt against Positivism."

13. Harwich Vallenilla, "Venezuelan Positivism," 339.

14. Quoted in Burns, *Poverty of Progress*, 53. Translation by Burns.

15. Martí, "Our America," 294.

16. Anderson, *Imagined Communities*, 7.

17. Carreño, *Manual de urbanidad*, 24. My translation.

18. Rama, *Lettered City*, 1–2, 17, 31, and 63.

19. Keen, *History of Latin America*, 201.

20. For popular nationalism, see the puppet theater section in Chapter 3 of this book, and also Beezley's *Mexican National Identity*, 4–10.

21. Tulio Halperín Donghi emphasizes this argument in *Contemporary History*, 74–76.

22. My synthesis is drawn from Bulmer-Thomas, "The Struggle for National Identity from Independence to Midcentury," in *Economic History*, 22–30.

23. Chasteen, *Born in Blood*, 180.
24. In this regard, I treat cities as contact zones, to use the influential phrase that Mary Louise Pratt coined: "A 'contact' perspective emphasizes how subjects get constituted in and by their relations to each other" (*Imperial Eyes*, 8).

CHAPTER 1 *Cities*

1. Dávila, *La babel argentina*, 8. My translation.
2. Espinosa, *La reforma*, 47. My translation.
3. Unless otherwise noted, my précis of the colonial city is drawn from Kinsbruner, *Colonial Spanish-American City*, 23–32. On the subject of slaughterhouses, I also consulted the 1525 ordinance of Hernán Cortés, in *Escritos sueltos*, 75–86.
4. Quoted in Rama, *Lettered City*, 4. Italics in the original.
5. Child, *Spanish-American Republics*, 422. In 1906, an Uruguayan congressman called for a more concentrated and taller Montevideo to better impress foreigners and make the delivery of municipal services more effective. See Cámara de la Asamblea General, *Diario de sesiones*, 505.
6. Ruhl, "Lhasa of South America," 600.
7. My approximate statistics are drawn from Fernández Armesto, "Latin America," 374; Mejía Pavony, "Los itinerarios," 24; Clemente Travieso, *Las esquinas de Caracas*, 29; Socolow, *Bureaucrats of Buenos Aires*, 305; Hunefeldt, *Liberalism in the Bedroom*, 18; and Low, *On the Plaza*, 59.
8. Rudé, *Europe*, 54.
9. Almandoz Marte, "Urbanization and Urbanism," 15.
10. De Sales Pérez, *Costumbres venezolanas*, 140.
11. Rearick, *Paris Dreams, Paris Memories*, 13.
12. "Correspondencia." My translation.
13. JME, "Policia." My translation.
14. For an overview of Haussmann and his influence in Latin America, including period comparisons of Latin American urban planners with Haussmann, see Almandoz Marte, "Urbanization and Urbanism," 17–18 and 25–28. Also, see Hardoy, "Theory and Practice," 27–29.
15. Almandoz Marte, "Urbanization and Urbanism," 25–26.
16. Vicuña Mackenna, *Pájinas de mi diario*, 182. My translation.
17. Vicuña Mackenna, *La transformación de Santiago*, 12–17.
18. Ibid., 18–20.
19. Ibid., 49–51.
20. Carpenter, *South America*, 215–16.
21. Pérez Oyarzun and Rosas Vera, "Cities within the City," 117.
22. Congreso la Nación Argentina, *Diario de sesiones (1883)*, 1:827.
23. Martí, "Tres héroes," 59. My translation.
24. Armando Rojas, "Muerte y resurrección," 341–45.
25. Conway, *Cult of Bolívar*, 45–47.
26. Tenenbaum, "Streetwise History," 130–32.
27. For nationalist meanings of the Cuauhtémoc monument, see ibid., 139–41. For nationalist appropriation of the Aztec empire in 1836, see "Manifesto," 29.

28. Vicuña Mackenna, "La transformación de Santiago," 25. My translation.
29. Prince, *Lima antigua*, 37–38.
30. Samper Agudelo, *La miseria en Bogotá*, iv. My translation.
31. For more on conservative attacks on nineteenth-century progress, see the section of Chapter 2 in this book about the novel *María* by Jorge Isaacs.
32. Martínez Ortega, "El cólera en México," 38.
33. De Gandía, *Historia de la república argentina*, 777.
34. The general description of *callejones* provided here is drawn from Gamarra, *Lima*, 21–23. For information on the Callejón de Otaiza, see Vargas, "Ligeras reflexiones," 280–81.
35. Aguila Peralta, *Callejones y mansiones*, 58.
36. Martínez, *Censo general de población*, cxxiv. My translation.
37. Rock, *Argentina*, 153; Scobie, "Paris of South America," 177; and Nari, *Políticas de maternidad*, 55.
38. Scobie, "Paris of South America," 177.
39. See Ignacio Manuel Altamirano, "Crónica de la semana," 98.
40. Muñiz, quoted in Vargas, "Ligeras reflexiones," 259.
41. The story of Eduwigis is drawn from Roumagnac's *Los criminales en México*, 180–83.
42. Lara y Pardo, *La prostitución en México*, 19–20. It is difficult to independently corroborate these figures, which Lara y Pardo claimed he had based on hygienic registries.
43. Muñiz, *Higiene pública*, 2. My translation.
44. Modern techniques of regulating prostitution in Mexico began in 1867; see Guzmán, "El regimen jurídico," 86. Similar trends may be found, as follows: For Cuba, see Céspedes y Santa Cruz, *La prostitución*, 268–77; For Uruguay, see Goyena, "Reglamento de la prostitución," 701–4; For Costa Rica: "Decreto #1," 83–95.
45. My précis about immigration, prostitution, and sex trafficking in Buenos Aires is drawn from Guy's *Sex and Danger* 5–7, 25, and 37–76.
46. Obarrio, "Ordenanza reglamentaria," 293–300.
47. Céspedes y Santa Cruz, *La prostitución*, 89.
48. Lara y Pardo, *La prostitución en México*, 1301–31.
49. Cabello de Carbonera, *Blanca Sol*, 181. My translation.
50. Voysest, "Mercedes Cabello de Carbonera," ix–x.
51. Valenzuela, *Mis recuerdos*, 108. My translation.
52. In *Cuba with Pen and Pencil*, the nineteenth-century chronicler Samuel Hazard writes that "almost every small town possesses what is known as El Liceo, an association of the young men of the place, which is encouraged by the presence of ladies, forming an attractive feature in the social life of the smaller places," 554. The account I present of the Liceo of Havana is from Ramírez, *La Habana artística*, 303–11.
53. Ramírez, *La Habana artística*, 311. My translation.
54. Amorena, *Memorandum enciclopédico*, 41–44.
55. Club del progreso, *Club del Progreso*, 10–11.
56. All quotes and details here are drawn from López, *La gran aldea*, 166–200. Translations mine.

57. Losada, "Sociabilidad," 551. For more on entry fees of the Jockey Club at the start of the twentieth century, see Albes, *Viajando por Sud América*, 39.

58. Losada, "Sociabilidad," 551.

59. Congreso de la Nación Argentina, *Diario de sesiones* (1908), 1:745.

60. Koebel, *Modern Argentina*, 56.

61. See Ayala Mora and Posada Carbo, *Historia general*, 277–78; Sowell, *Early Colombian Labor Movement*, 105–8; and Overmyer-Velázquez, *Visions*, 84–85. For the origin of mutual aid societies, see Harrison, *Bourgeois Citizen*, 125–28.

62. See Amunátegui's *Las primeras representaciones dramáticas*, 146.

63. Salazar Vergara, *Labradores, peones y proletarios*, 126–27.

64. For problems with interpreting the nomenclature of cafés, see Gayol, *Sociabilidad en Buenos Aires*, 46. Similar problems extend to other parts of Spanish America, especially in cafés that doubled as dance halls, like the Café Escauriza of Havana.

65. Cuéllar, *La linterna mágica*, 297–98.

66. The descriptions of both the Café de San Juan and the Café del Agua Sucia are drawn from Pereira, *Cosas de antaño*, 7–14 and 274–76.

67. My descriptions of the Progreso's layout and clientele are drawn from García Cubas, *El libro*, 158; and also from Payno, *El fistol del diablo*, 250–51.

68. For more on the clientele of the Café Escauriza, see Estrada y Zenea's "El concurrente a Escauriza," and "La concurrenta a Escauriza." Also, see Betancourt, *Artículos de costumbres*, 17–27.

69. For descriptions of the Aguila, see Child, *Spanish-American Republics*, 299–300; and Velasco del Real, *Viaje*, 57–58.

70. Gayol, *Sociabilidad en Buenos Aires*, 221–40.

71. My conceptualization of the duality of the city is indebted to Mumford, *City in History*, 558; and Ramos, *Divergent Modernities*, 118.

CHAPTER 2 *Print*

1. Acosta's speech was reprinted various times in the nineteenth century. See Lagomaggiore, *América literaria*, 284–87; José María Rojas, *Biblioteca de escritores venezolanos*, 528–34; and Oyuela, *Trozos escogidos*, 329–32. Acosta's speech was also cited by Mercedes Cabello de Carbonera in the literary salon of Juana Manuela Gorriti in Lima in 1876, and later reprinted; see Gorriti, *Veladas literarias*, 8. My translation.

2. "Sociedades literarias en islandia," *Mercurio Peruano*, May 17, 1833, 2–3.

3. Ignacio Manuel Altamirano, "Revistas literarias de México," 78.

4. For Latin American literacy rates, see Mariscal and Sokoloff, "Schooling," 180–81; Van Young, "Limits," 46–47; Restrepo and Aponte, *Guerra y violencias*, 329; Engerman and Sokoloff, *Economic Development*, 146; and Forment, *Democracy in Latin America*, 194 and 217–18.

5. Acree, *Everyday Reading*, 3–7.

6. Calvo, "Latin America," 138.

7. Ibid., 139; Leonard, *Books of the Brave*, 75–90; and Zuñiga Saldaña, "Licencias para imprimir," 164.

8. Silva, "Prácticas de lectura," 89.
9. Arteaga y Alemparte, "Sociabilidad y progreso," 243. My translation.
10. Briggs, *Tropes of Enlightenment*, 135–36.
11. Some of these newspapers were *Las Sombras de Heráclito y Demócrito* (The shadows of Heraclitus and Democritus; 1815), *El Conductor Eléctrico* (The electric conductor; 1820), and *El Payaso de los Periódicos* (The clown of the newspapers; 1823).
12. Lizardi, *Mangy Parrot*, 541.
13. Lizardi, *Don Catrín*, 63–64.
14. My précis about *costumbrismo* is based on Pupo-Walker, "Brief Narrative," and Pérez Salas, *Costumbrismo y litografía*, 62.
15. Aguilar Ochoa, "La influencia."
16. Frías y Soto et al., *Los mexicanos pintados*, 1–6.
17. De Cárdenas y Rodríguez, "¡Educado Fuera!," 77. My translation.
18. For an overview of Palma's *Peruvian Traditions*, see Conway, "Introduction."
19. For Jerónimo de la Ossa, see "Advertencia" in the first Argentinian edition of *María* by Jorge Isaacs, published in Buenos Aires in 1870 by the Imprenta Americana. For the novel's Mexican publishing history, see Dumas, *Justo Sierra*, 528.
20. Laera, "Cronistas," 496.
21. Arcos, "Novelas-folletín," 37; see also Castro and Curiel, *Publicaciones periódicas*, 517.
22. In 1844, a bookstore published an advertisement in the Peruvian newspaper *El Comercio* announcing subscriptions for scientific and literary books, including the poetry of the Spanish writers José Zorrilla and José de Espronceda ("Aviso al público," 8). Also, see Guiot de la Garza, "Las librerías," 39–40.
23. Ignacio Manuel Altamirano, "Honra y provecho," 321–25.
24. My account of this shop is drawn from Guiot de la Garza, "Las librerias," 41.
25. Staples, "La lectura," 95–96.
26. See Castro and Curiel, *Publicaciones periódicas*, 518.
27. Rivera, "Ingreso, difusión e instalación," 551.
28. Parada, "El orden," 21–26.
29. Subercaseaux, *Historia del libro*, 71.
30. For US and European print runs, see Lyons, *Reading Culture*, 47; and Michelson, *Printer's Devil*, 253. For the publishing history of *María*, see Isaacs, *Obras completas*, xxxi and xxxvi–xxxvii.
31. My numeration and classification of editions is based on a search on the WorldCat database. Estimates on print runs for French editions of books for the Spanish-speaking market are based on the examples of *Curso metódico de dibujo lineal* (1880) by Francisco Canale (five thousand copies) and *La historia patria* (1912) by Justo Sierra (ten thousand copies). See Alberto Navarro Viola, *Anuario bibliográfico*, 152; and Millares Carlo, *Repertorio bibliográfico*, 128.
32. Quoted in Ramos, *Divergent Modernities*, 92. Translation by Ramos.
33. Quoted in ibid., 99. Translation by Ramos.
34. Ibid., 97. Also, see Aníbal González, "Cultural Journalism," 88.
35. Zaragoza, *Anarquismo argentino*, 390. For information on the Peruvian anarchist press, see Beigel, *La epopeya*, 49–50; and Armas Asin, *Liberales, protestantes, y masones*, 118–19.

36. Buffington, "Homophobia," 196.
37. The treatise has also been published with the title *The Influence of Literature upon Society*.
38. See Staël, *Influence of Literature*, 101–2.
39. See Kale, *French Salons*, 42.
40. For the reading room of the Bolsa de Comercio (Business Owner's Association) of Lima, see de la Lama, *Código de comercio*, 376–77. For the reading room as a civilizing mechanism in Guatemala, see Sociedad Económica de Amigos del País, *Memoria*, 6.
41. Lafragua, *Memoria*, 120. My translation.
42. For a biography of Gorriti, see Masiello, "Introduction."
43. Quoted in Gorriti, *Veladas literarias*, 172. My translation.
44. Ibid., 7.
45. Gamarra, "Apuntes de viaje," 6. My translation.
46. The names, occupations, and addresses of some of Gorriti's neighbors are drawn from Atanasio Fuentes, *Guía de domicilio*.
47. García Márquez, *One Hundred Years*, 50.
48. Shumway, *Invention of Argentina*, 69, 79.
49. See ibid., 75, for the piece titled "Interesting Patriotic Dialogue between Jacinto Chano and the Gaucho of the Mountain Guard," in which Hidalgo decries the corruption and classism plaguing independent Argentina.
50. Rivera, "Ingreso, difusión e instalación," 552.
51. Acree, *Everyday Reading*, 57.
52. Lizardi, *Mangy Parrot*, 6.
53. Forment, *Democracy in Latin America*, 198.
54. For a discussion of Ventura de Molina and his context, see Acree, "Jacinto Ventura de Molina"; Borucki, "Tensiones raciales"; and Ventura de Molina, *Los caminos*.
55. Tinajero, *El Lector*, 35.
56. Ibid., 143–53.
57. Rodríguez Castro, "Oír y leer," 234.
58. Sosa, *Escritores y poetas*, 225.
59. Berisso, *El pensamiento de América*, 107.
60. María is thirteen years old in the first edition of the novel. Isaacs made her fifteen years old for the second edition of the novel. See McGrady, "Introducción," 67.
61. Mejías-López, *Inverted Conquest*, 63–64.
62. Vergara y Vergara, "Juicio Crítico," 4.
63. For judgments that align with Vergara y Vergara's, see Páez, "Crítica de *María*," 252; Ignacio Manuel Altamirano, "*María*," xx; Prieto, "*María*," 420; and Gutiérrez Nájera, "Una edición mexicana," 216–17.
64. Quoted in Pastor Ríos, "*María* y Jorge Isaacs," 12. My translation.
65. Prieto, "*María*," 420; Enríquez y Terrazas, *Alfredo*, 78; and Esguerra, "*María*," 8–11.
66. Pinch, "Sensibility," 49–50; and Stabler, "Literary Background," 30.
67. Ignacio Manuel Altamirano said that the novel was a powerful and much-needed spiritual rejoinder to French realist and naturalist writers like Balzac and Zola, whose novels channel the detritus of a civilization defined by a diseased sensuality ("*María*," 418). For similar assessments, see Berisso, *El pensamiento de América*, 106; Páez,

"Crítica de *María*," 257; and the anonymously authored "Meditación sobre *María*," 10–11.

68. Lizardi, *Mangy Parrot*, 292. Translation by Frye.

69. Ibid., 291–92. Also, see Beezley, *Mexican National Identity*, 3–18.

70. Speckman Guerra, "Cuadernillos," 393.

71. In June 1901 alone, he sent out more than twenty-one thousand sheets of print to Mexico's provinces, to cities such as Querétaro and Chihuahua. See Speckman Guerra, "Cuadernillos," 395.

72. The cries of the *listín* sellers are described in several sources: Prince, *Lima antigua*, 28; Atanasio Fuentes, *Lima*, 138; and Ultimo Harabica, *Algo de Perú*, 167. The precise meaning of *Y á claaa ri táaa* is not reported, but it served to announce the availability of *listines*.

73. In 1810, such *listines* doubled as political propaganda; see Palma, "Tauromaquia," 235–36.

74. Quoted in López Martínez, *Plaza de Acho*, 62. My translation.

75. See Lois and Núñez, "Advertencia editorial," vi–vii.

76. Silva Valdés, "Recuerdos,'" 175–80.

77. Hernández, *Gaucho Martín Fierro*, 49.

78. Hernández, *El gaucho Martín Fierro/La vuelta de Martín Fierro*, 105–7.

79. Quoted in Hernández, *El gaucho Martín Fierro* (1894 edition), xi.

80. Josefina Ludmer calls *The Gaucho Martín Fierro* an antijuridical and antimilitary poem, but also describes it as "a defense of landholders' interests, who sought to protect the available labor force from indiscriminate conscription" ("Gaucho Genre," 628).

81. Ibid., 629.

82. Ludmer, *Gaucho Genre: A Treatise*, 28.

83. Dabove, *Nightmares*, 179.

84. Mejías-López, *Inverted Conquest*, 68.

85. Acree, *Everyday Reading*, 182.

CHAPTER 3 *Theatricality*

1. This definition is based on the entry for "theatricality" in the *Oxford English Dictionary* (2nd ed., online version, June 2012).

2. Salvador, *Efímeras efemérides*, 9–105. See also Ortemberg, "La entrada," 70–73, 81; and Silva Hernández, "Las fiestas," 35.

3. Will Fowler, "Fiestas Santanistas," 410; and Silva Hernández, "Las fiestas," 33–34. For an excellent analysis and vivid recreation of Republican fanfare, see Santoni, "Salvas," 130–35.

4. See Acree, *Everyday Reading*, 29–30; Salvador, *Efímeras efemérides*, 399–400; and Silva Hernández, "Las fiestas," 36.

5. Silva Hernández, "Las fiestas," 37.

6. The account of the fiesta of July 20, 1849, is here drawn from González Pérez, *Fiesta y nación*, 62–70.

7. Red Phrygian caps were associated with liberty and Republicans, and were worn by

revolutionaries in both the American and French Revolutions. See Nabarz, *Mysteries of Mithras*, 55. Also, see Acree, *Everyday Reading*, 35–36.

8. See Lasso, *Myths of Harmony*, 59.

9. Conway, "El aparecido azteca," 125–26. Also, for martial hero worship in nineteenth-century Spanish America, see González Stephan, "Narrativas duras," 111–12 and 125.

10. For an account of Bolívar's final years and afterlife, see Conway, *Cult of Bolívar*, 29–37. For further examples of the nationalism of funerary rites, see Will Fowler, "Fiestas santanistas," 427; and Esposito, *Funerals*.

11. My description of Bolívar's funeral is drawn from Toro, *Descripción*, 22–50.

12. "Deberes morales del hombre," in Carreño, *Manual de urbanidad*, 11–37.

13. "Del acto de levantarnos," in Carreño, *Manual de urbanidad*, 85–89.

14. "Del aseo," in Carreño, *Manual de urbanidad*, 53–75.

15. "Del aseo en nuestros vestidos," in Carreño, *Manual de urbanidad*, 60–62.

16. "Del aseo," 53–60.

17. "Del modo de conducirnos en la calle," in Carreño, *Manual de urbanidad*, 126–37.

18. "De las visitas," in Carreño, *Manual de urbanidad*, 206–54.

19. "De los festines en general," in Carreño, *Manual de urbanidad*, 263–71.

20. "De la conversación," in Carreño, *Manual de urbanidad*, 157–90.

21. "De la mesa en general," in Carreño, *Manual de urbanidad*, 299–313; and "Del modo de trinchar . . ." in Carreño, *Manual de urbanidad*, 313–18.

22. Burke, *Popular Culture*, 191–204; and Chasteen, "Anything Goes," 135–37.

23. Chasteen, "Anything Goes," 137. See also Viqueira Albán, *Propriety and Permissiveness*, 104–10. The reference to sugar plums is from Segur, *Memoirs*, 418–19.

24. Bibliófilo, "Apuntes de un cronista," 4.

25. Gerstaecker, "Tres días de carnaval," 169–86.

26. Hall, *Across Mexico*, 327–37.

27. For elite resistance and flight from Carnival, see Rojas Rojas, *Tiempos de carnaval*, 77–84; 87. See also Bibliófilo, "Apuntes de un cronista." Regarding social and gendered transgressions, see Chasteen, "Anything Goes," 143, and Rojas Rojas, *Tiempos de carnaval*, 77–84.

28. See Rojas Rojas, *Tiempos de carnaval*, 87.

29. My account of the historical meanings of the Oruro carnival is drawn primarily from Harris, *Carnival*, 213, 218, and 220. I also utilized Lecount's "Carnival in Bolivia," 231–52.

30. My account is drawn from Oehmichen, "El carnaval de Culhuacán," 163–80.

31. My account of ethnic groups in Cuba and the *cabildo* system is drawn from Brown, *Santería Enthroned*, 26–35.

32. For the cult of the magus Melchior, see ibid., 43–44, and Ortiz, "Afro-Cuban Festival," in Bettelheim, *Cuban Festivals*, 21 (hereafter "Ortiz, in *Cuban Festivals*"). For *aguinaldos* in relation to military service and African traditions, see Ortiz, in *Cuban Festivals*, 22–28.

33. My description of the Day of the Kings is drawn from Ortiz, in *Cuban Festivals*, 8–20.

34. Ortiz, in *Cuban Festivals*, 33 (quoting a chant collected by Antonio Bachiller y Morales).

35. My account of the Day of the Kings is drawn from Brown, *Santería Enthroned*, 35–51, as well as from the *Inter-America* version of Ortiz's "The Afro-Cuban Festival of the 'Day of the Kings,'" 323–25. Ortiz's revised account, published in *Cuban Festivals*, does not include some of the details from this earlier article. The 1866 quote in this paragraph is from the *Inter-America* account, 326.

36. Sarmiento, "El teatro," 274. For similar views from Mexico, see Conway, "Próspero," 155.

37. A review of Enrique de Olavarría y Ferrari's encyclopedic history of the Mexican theater, *Reseña histórica del teatro mexicano*, reveals that *La pata de cabra* was staged in 1841, 1848, 1853, 1854, 1887, and 1894. For the popularity of the play in Buenos Aires, see Rosenblat and Blanco Amores, "Diez años de actividad," 159. Also, see Gies, *Theatre*, 73.

38. As per Olavarría y Ferrari's chronicle, *The Lady of the Camellias* was staged practically every year in Mexico between 1867 and 1900. For the popularity of Dumas in nineteenth-century Argentina, see Dubatti, "El teatro francés," 17–18. If we take into account the popularity of the opera *La traviata*, we can conclude that Spanish American audiences in the second half of the century were completely awash in the story of Armand and Marguerite.

39. For criticisms of *The Lady of the Camellias* on moral grounds, see Vicuña Mackenna, *Pájinas de mi diario*, 145; Céspedes y Santa Cruz, *La prostitución*, vii; Anonymous, "Alejandro Dumás," 762; and Valero de Tornos, "Zola," 307. For defenses of the same play, see Giralt, *El amor*, 115 (a direct reply to Céspedes); Zamacois, *Tipos de café*, 63; and Picón Febres, *La literatura venezolana*, 44.

40. *Costumbrista* comedies were also known in Spain as *alta comedia* (high comedy). My definition of the *costumbrista* comedies of Latin America is indebted to Gies, *Theatre*, 231.

41. Ascencio Segura, *Ña Catita*, 92–93. My translation.

42. There are too many *costumbrista* plays from this period to mention here, even in passing, but three that are similar to Ascencio Segura's *Ña Catita* are *El jefe de la familia* (1858) by the Chilean Alberto Blest Gana, *Un alcalde a la antigua* (1856) by the Colombian José María Samper, and *Fabricar sobre la arena* (1873) by the Venezuelan Heraclio Martín de la Guardia. All three deal with marriage plots or married life, suitors, *enredos*, and the contrast between truth and illusion. For a list of other *costumbrista* plays, see Carrilla, "Romantic Theater," 374.

43. My evocation of Don Chole's establishment and its audiences is based on García Cubas, *El libro*, 255–58.

44. Ibid., 256. My translation.

45. Seibel, *Historia del teatro argentino*, 64, 70, and 78.

46. Golluscio de Montoya, "Del circo colonial," 142–43.

47. For a brief overview of Pepe Podestá's life, see Seibel, *Historia del circo*, 32–50. Pepe Podestá's invaluable memoirs may be found in José J. Podestá, *Medio siglo de farándulas*. Also, see Cilento, "Pepe Podestá," 25–33.

48. José J. Podestá, *Medio siglo de farándulas*, 41.

49. Ibid., 46.

50. All three of these songs are excerpted in the original Spanish by Seibel, *Historia del circo*, 46–47. Translations mine.

51. Lafforgue, *Teatro rioplatense*, 16 (my translation). A later version of the play that differs from the one collected by Lafforgue may be found in Bierstadt, *Three Plays*, 1–20.

52. For a discussion of *moreirismo*, see Guido A. Podestá, "La reescritura," 10–11; and Dabove, *Nightmares*, 190–92 and 230–34. See also Ludmer, *Corpus Delicti*, 96–97.

53. Agustín Alvarez, *Manual de patología política*, 139. My translation.

54. This anecdote is much retold in histories of the Argentine theater and the circus. Two of the best English-language studies of Cocoliche are Ana C. Cara's "Cocoliche: The Art of Assimilation and Dissimulation among Italians and Argentines," from which I take the English translation of Petray's declaration; and Seigel's "Cocoliche's Romp."

55. Meza, "José," 511–14.

56. My account of Valdivieso is drawn from Gamarra, "El Maestro Valdivieso," 182–93. Valdivieso is also lovingly mentioned by Ricardo Palma in his *tradición* "Santiago el volador" (Santiago the flier). Also, see Basadre, *Historia*, 7:2164–65.

57. Gamarra, "El Maestro Valdivieso," 192–93.

58. My account of Cayetano Vallejo is drawn from a collection of oral histories collected at the beginning of the twentieth history. See Zañartu, *El Tile Vallejo*, 37–41. My translation.

59. Basadre, *Historia*, 4:1908.

60. Beezley, *Mexican National Identity*, 3–18 and 111–32.

61. Cordovez Moure, *Reminiscencias*, 1899.

62. See Davey, "Havana and the Havanese," 698.

63. Madden, *Island of Cuba*, 64.

64. See Iglesias Utset, *Cultural History*, 50–53.

65. Vidriera, "El gallero," 230. The pseudonym "Licentiate Vidriera" is inspired by the titular protagonist of a 1613 tale by Miguel de Cervantes, who is afflicted by the belief that his whole body is made of glass.

66. Quoted in Louis A. Pérez Jr., "Between Baseball and Bullfighting," 506.

67. My evocation of a bullfight in mid-nineteenth-century Lima is primarily from Ruschenberger, *Three Years*, 129–44; and from Proctor, *Narrative of a Journey*, 248–58.

68. Lastarria, *Miscelanea literaria*, 250. My translation.

69. Ruschenberger, *Three Years*, 132.

70. López Martínez, *Plaza de Acho*, 64–65.

71. Ibid., 20.

72. See Proctor, *Narrative of a Journey*, 253; Ruschenberger, *Three Years*, 133; and Atanasio Fuentes, *Lima*, 139.

73. Ruschenberger, *Three Years*, 287.

74. López Martínez, *Plaza de Acho*, 45.

75. Ibid., 48–50.

76. Palma, *Tradiciones peruanas*, 143.

77. See Ruschenberger, *Three Years*, 142; and Atanasio Fuentes, *Lima*, 141. My description of the *mojarreros* as drunk is not meant to disparage these men. This detail is drawn from the eyewitness accounts of Ruschenberger and Atanasio Fuentes, as well as from Belgrano Rawson, *Noticias secretas*, 321. Being a *mojarrero* required tremendous valor, and being drunk was undoubtedly a good way to get into that spirit.

78. López Martínez, *Plaza de Acho*, 79.
79. My account of Valdez is drawn from ibid., 122–28.
80. Quoted in ibid., 108. My translation.
81. Quoted in López Martínez, *Plaza de Acho*, 109. My translation.
82. Beezley, *Judas*, 212.
83. Quoted in Frank, *Posada's Broadsheets*, 137.
84. The literature on the *velorio del angelito* in colonial and nineteenth-century Spanish America is ample. A few sources include: Marco Antonio León León's *La cultura de la muerte en Chiloé* (Chile), Luis Mario Schneider's "La muerte angelical, el velorio de los angelitos en Malinalco" (Mexico), John Mendell Schechter's *The Indispensable Harp* (Ecuador), and Luis Alfredo López Rojas's *Historiar la muerte (1508–1920)* (Puerto Rico). The *velorio* tradition originated in the Arab world, and it spread to Spain in the medieval period. After the Conquest of America, the tradition became common among the humbler classes across Spanish America.
85. Schechter, *Indispensable Harp*, 60. Schechter bases his claim on a nineteenth-century Ecuadorian painting by Joaquin Pinto (1842–1906), who belonged to the Cuzco school.

CHAPTER 4 *Image*

1. My account of the Ávila exhibit from inception to execution, as well as its reception by the local Caracas press, is drawn from Spence's memoir of his Venezuelan experiences, *Land of Bolívar*, 127–30 and 245–49.
2. Eastwick, *Venezuela*, 41.
3. Amunátegui, "Apuntes" 44–45 (my translation). Also, see Ripamonti Montt, "Academia de pintura," 137–41; and Ignacio Manuel Altamirano, "La semana santa," 62–63, 70–73.
4. Scavizzi, "Institutes and Associations," 151; and Chu, *Nineteenth-Century European Art*, 33. Also, see "Academies," in Osborn, *Oxford Companion to Art*, 4.
5. Osborn, *Oxford Companion to Art*, 5.
6. Boime, *Academy and French Painting*, 10.
7. For Chile, see Ripamonti Montt, "Academia de pintura," 130–35; for Peru, see Cárdenas, "Academias y academicismos," 80–82; and for Venezuela, see Boulton, *Historia de la pintura*, 1:11–12.
8. The first academic-style school in Republican Argentina was the school of drawing of the Consulado of Buenos Aires (1815–1821), followed by the school of drawing at the University of Buenos Aires in 1822 and a government-sponsored school of drawing founded in 1870 by President Sarmiento. See Ribera, "La pintura"; and López Anaya, *Arte argentino*, 54–58 and 78–81.
9. Before 1886, Colombian painters could exhibit their works in public only under the category of miscellany or "other objects" in national expositions (that is, fairs of industry and agriculture). See Garay Celeita, "El campo artístico colombiano," 305.
10. The author of the 1852 city guide to Lima wrote that coursework was free and that the only staff member to receive remuneration was the director, who earned six hundred pesos a year. See Carrasco, *Calendario y guía*, 76. Carrasco's entry establishes that Laso was acting director during Merino's European travels.

11. See Charlot, *Mexican Art*, 35, 56–58; Boulton, *Historia de la pintura*, 1:32–33; and Galaz and Ivelic, *La pintura en Chile*, 90. To understand the pedagogical culture of the copy in developing art skills, see the selections from Anton Raphael Mengs's *Thoughts on Beauty and Taste in Painting* (1762), in Eitner, *Neoclassicism and Romanticism*, 31–33.

12. Quoted in Francisco Zarco, "Don Juan Cordero."

13. Charlot, *Mexican Art*, 54–65.

14. Uribe, "1843–1860," 74 and 92.

15. For artisans in Chile's Academy of Painting, see "Memorias científicas y literarias," 78. The decree founding the school of Chimba is in "Leyes i decretos," 571. For Sarmiento, see his "Escuelas nocturnas," 209–10 (my translation).

16. For an equivalent Ecuadorian example, see Pallares Peñafiel and Trajano Mera, "Notas literarias y bibliográficas," 79.

17. Quoted in Martínez Silva, *Arte americano*, 170. My translation.

18. Rodríguez Prampolini, *La crítica de arte*, 153.

19. For approximate salaries of Mexican artisans in 1893, see Peñafiel, *Anuario estadístico*, 372–430. For Colombian salaries, see Londoño Vélez, *Historia de la pintura*, 82.

20. My précis of Paul Marcoy's observations about devotional art is from his *Travels in South America*, 1:269–71.

21. The painting is difficult to discern but shows a friar with a baby. In the Catholic iconographic tradition, Saint Anthony of Padua is often represented with the baby Jesus.

22. To this day, the Holy Child of Atocha is widely available in Spanish America as an object of pictorial or sculptural devotion, as well as in *botánicas* or religious shops in the United States.

23. This material is drawn from Macera, *Pintores populares andinos*, xxv–xxvi, xxxix, xl–xlv.

24. My account of *retablos* is drawn from Giffords, *Mexican Folk Retablos*, 4–5 and 143–47.

25. Both *retablos* described here are from ibid., 68, 72.

26. Baralt, *Resumen de la historia*, 596. My translation.

27. Serrano Barquín, *Imagen y representación*, 180.

28. Rojas Líbano, "Estudio de las percepciones," 40. The quoted passage is from the Chilean newspaper *La Época* and is dated September 1883.

29. Gasso y Vidal, "La mujer artista," 189–93. My translation.

30. Pachas Macedo, *Las artistas plásticas*, 26.

31. The Mira sisters won gold medals in Chilean salons, and had their work exhibited at the world's fairs of 1889 (Paris) and 1901 (Buffalo, NY), alongside the paintings of other Chilean women, including Celia Castro. Rebeca Oquendo Díaz exhibited at more than one Parisian salon, as well as the world's fair of 1878 (Paris), and several Mexican women artists had work exhibited at the world's fairs of 1876 (Philadelphia), 1889 (Paris), and 1893 (Chicago).

32. For an overview of pictorial *costumbrismo* and its relationship to Spanish American art, see Ades, *Art in Latin America*, 65–85.

33. For quality reproductions of the *Gauchitos*, see Manthorne, "Brothers under the Skin," 151–212.

34. For sale of wax figurines on the streets of nineteenth-century Mexico City, see Pérez Salas, *Costumbrismo y litografía*, 139. For traces of *costumbrista* influences in Andean folk art, see Macera, *Pintores populares andinos*, liv–lvi.
35. For Fierro's father, see Majluf, "Pancho Fierro," 19; see also Durán, *Apuntes históricos genealógicos*, 85.
36. For Alleguez's friendship with Fierro and the Escribanos location, see Portal, *Cosas limeñas*, 188–89. A reference to Fierro's brother can be found in Stastny, "Pancho Fierro," 21.
37. Stastny, "Pancho Fierro," 21.
38. Ibid., 21–22. Background details about the Cercada neighborhood are drawn from Cobo, *Historia de la fundación* 136–37.
39. Portal, *Cosas limeñas*, 185–86.
40. For Palma and muralism, see his *tradición* "De esta capa."
41. Portal, *Cosas limeñas*, 189.
42. All the watercolors cited here are beautifully reproduced in Colección Ricardo Palma, *Acuarelas de Pancho Fierro*. The volume also contains annotations by Ricardo Palma, identifying and expanding on some of the characters represented in many watercolors.
43. My framework for reading Fierro as a commercial artist is drawn from Majluf's excellent and indispensable analysis, "Pancho Fierro," 17–50. Majluf also explores the circulation and reproduction of his art.
44. My references to the artist's buyers are common to much Fierro scholarship, but Majluf traces the China connection in outstanding detail and alerts us to the resale of at least one Chinese album in the Peruvian port of Callao ("Pancho Fierro," 34–35).
45. Taft, *Photography*, 14–15; and Debroise, *Mexican Suite*, 20.
46. The best study of *L'Orientale* is Wood's "Voyage of Captain Lucas."
47. McElroy, *Early Peruvian Photography*, 6–7.
48. Ibid., 6; and Debroise, *Mexican Suite*, 22.
49. Londoño Vélez, *Testigo ocular*, 30–31; and McElroy, *Early Peruvian Photography*, 8.
50. Londoño Vélez, *Testigo ocular*, 33–34. My translation.
51. McElroy, *Early Peruvian Photography*, 8. Moreover, a review of early daguerreotype artists active in Colombia and Mexico underline that most were from abroad.
52. Debroise, *Mexican Suite*, 20–22; and McElroy, *Early Peruvian Photography*, 7–8.
53. Londoño Vélez, *Testigo ocular*, 90.
54. Debroise, *Mexican Suite*, 22.
55. McElroy, *Early Peruvian Photography*, 58.
56. These reflections are inspired by the discussion of two different nineteenth-century Colombian photo albums in Londoño Vélez, *Testigo ocular*, 80–83.
57. Mraz, *Looking for Mexico*, 40.
58. Hutchinson, *Two Years in Peru*, 322.
59. This list is a composite of samples drawn from the *cartes de visite* of Cruces y Campa in Mexico and E. Courret y Manoury of Peru.
60. McElroy, *Early Peruvian Photography*, 79 (figure 65 in his appendices).
61. For Mexico, see Aceves, "Images," 84–85. There are indications that analogous practices were common in Colombia as well; see Tiberio Alvarez, "El arte ritual,"

381; and Londoño Vélez, *Testigo ocular*, 70 and 161. For Costa Rica, see Corella V., "Retratos eternos." We need more original research in this area.

62. The murders took place in December 1783; see Londoño Vélez, *Testigo ocular*, 49. For a Mexican example of this kind of photography, see Debroise's discussion of Chucho el Roto (*Mexican Suite*, 43). *Carte de visite* collectible photographs related to the famous murder of a young man named Betancourt in Montevideo also circulated in 1882. To see one of the photographs, see Broquetas, *Fotografía en Uruguay*. For an overview of the famous case, called "El Caso Volpi," see Olaechéa, *Cuestiones prácticas*, 208–11.

63. Several of these posed photographs are reproduced in Broquetas, *Fotografía en Uruguay*.

64. See Puebla, *Código de procedimientos*, 638–39.

65. See *Historias de la ciudad: Una revista de Buenos Aires*, nos. 31–35 and 50.

66. See Debroise, *Mexican Suite*, 169–70. The French writer Marguerite Cunliffe-Owen, an unabashed defender of European royalty, once found one of the photographs of the bullet-ridden body of Maximilian, stood upright and nearly naked in a coffin, on display at the office of a New York historical society. She was outraged that someone as honorable, chivalrous, and "high-souled" as Maximilian had been killed by a barbarous people and "dishonored in his death that the curiosity of the many might be cheaply satisfied" (*Keystone of Empire*, 241–42).

67. López Casillas, *José Guadalupe Posada*, 207. For a different image that shows only a gentleman customer, see 208.

68. Such vocational schools were common in nineteenth-century Mexico and Spanish America. For one program of study in Aguascalientes, see "Escuela de artes," lxxvii–lxxx. See also Bazant de Saldaña, *Historia de la educación*, 117.

69. My account of Posada's technique is drawn from the indispensable and groundbreaking study by Thomas Gretton, "Posada's Prints as Photomechanical Artefacts," which presents a rigorous, persuasive, and detailed case for Posada's use of photomechanical techniques. Gretton's account cuts against the grain of the traditionalist view of Posada as a more primitive artisan who worked outside of some of the major printing advances of his day. For a dissenting view, see Frank, *Posada's Broadsheets*, 6 and 239–40.

70. For the mixing of hand work and photomechanical etching, see Gretton, "Posada's Prints," 346–47. For Posada's stylistic choices for Vanegas Arroyo versus the style he elected for other publications, see 354.

71. Some of the images produced by Posada are clearly copies of photographs, as indicated by the poses of his subjects and the backgrounds used. See, for example, *M. Acuña* (37), *Los parranderos* (77), and *Los amores de un duende* (111), in López Casillas, *José Guadalupe Posada*.

72. Carmichael and Sayer, *Skeleton at the Feast*, 18–20 and 52–55.

73. Ibid., 24.

74. In the 1729 *Diccionario de autoridades*, *calavera* is not explicitly associated with foolishness, although the dictionary indicates it is a jocular term and that it is associated with men with small or upturned noses. In the 1780 *Diccionario de autoridades*, *calavera* contains an entry stating that it is a nickname for a fool.

75. Gutiérrez Nájera, *La música*, 50.

CHAPTER 5 *Musicality*

1. Sarmiento, *Facundo*, 63–64.
2. Sarmiento, "Lucía de Lamermoor," 202.
3. Reyes Carballido, "Las sociedades e instituciones," 11. My translation.
4. Merino Montero, "La Sociedad Filarmónica," 9 and 13.
5. Siliceo, "La Sociedad Filarmónica Mexicana," 2. For more on the exclusivity of the Sociedad Filarmónica Mexicana, see the distribution of performances (two public, ten for fee-paying members) and references to attendance by foreign diplomats as listed in *Memoria en que el secretario*, 5, 8; and Olavarría y Ferrari's reference to eminent aficionados and "brilliant" performances in 1867, in *Reseña histórica del teatro*, 3:12. For an account that emphasizes the ethnic diversity of the *filarmónica*, see Forment, *Democracy in Latin America*, 264.
6. Duque, "Presentación," 243. The price of joining the *sociedad filarmónica* of Buenos Aires in 1823 was a twelve-peso sign-up fee, plus four pesos per month. See Gómez, *Proyecto de reglamento*, 4.
7. See articles 19 and 21 of "De los socios," in Gómez, *Proyecto de reglamento*; article 7 of Sociedad Filarmónica de Bogotá, *Reglamento*; article 2 of "Estatutos de la Sociedad Filarmónica de Guatemala" (1883); article 12 of "Socios activos," in Sociedad Unión, *Reglamento interior*; and chapter 2 of Legislatura de la provincia de Córdoba, *Estatutos*.
8. Zapiola, *Recuerdos de treinta años*, 62; and Raygada, *Guía musical del Perú*, 30.
9. Calderón de la Barca, *Life in Mexico*, 24.
10. García Cubas, *El libro*, 523.
11. Mendoza Arce, *Music in Ibero-America*, 372; Duque, "Presentación," 244; Tovey, "José Mariano Elizaga," 133; and García Cubas, *El libro*, 522–23.
12. Merino Montero, "La Sociedad Filarmónica," 10.
13. See Merino Montero, "La Sociedad Filarmónica," for a list of Chilean programs. See multiple issues of *La Armonía: Organo de la Sociedad Filarmónica Mexicana* (1866), for a list of Mexican programs.
14. Mendoza Arce, *Music in Ibero-America*, 373; Duque, "Presentación," 238–39.
15. Weber, *Music*, 22–23; Mendoza Arce, *Music in Ibero-America*, 374; Iturriaga and Estenssoro, "Música y sociedad peruana," 64–65; Duque, "Presentación," 237; and Merino Montero, "La Sociedad Filarmónica," 9.
16. Nolasco Cruz, "La música," 108; and Dupanloup, "Mujeres sabias," 176.
17. Grez Toso, *De la "regeneración,"* 454.
18. Bórquez Solar, *Dilectos decires*, 165–66. My translation.
19. Cuéllar, *Ensalada de pollos*, 181.
20. In Mexico City, the Filarmónica de Auxilios Mutuos (Mutual Aid Philharmonic), over six hundred strong in 1875, supported musical performers in good times and bad, as well as providing them with dances, lectures, and concerts. See Juan E. Pérez, *Almanaque estadístico*, 700.
21. Raygada, *Guía musical del Perú*, 26. My translation.
22. My account of Mexican village bands in the nineteenth-century is drawn from Thompson, "Ceremonial and Political Roles," 318.
23. Louis A. Pérez Jr., *Structure of Cuban History*, 124.

24. See Díaz Seijas, *Caracas*, 67–68; and Curtis, *Venezuela*, 152–53.
25. Rosselli, "Latin America," 140–42.
26. On the popularity of these composers, see Peter Manuel on Cuba, in *Caribbean Currents*, 37; George Torres on Mexico, in *Encyclopedia*, 71; and Domingo Faustino Sarmiento's extensive 1844 review of these composers in "La opera italiana en Santiago," 187–94.
27. Clemente Althaus, "A Rossini," 21; Sarmiento, "La opera italiana," 191; and Nemoat, "Rossini," 138.
28. Toft, *Bel Canto*, 4.
29. Anonymous, "Noticias: José Verdi," 943.
30. My account of the zarzuela is drawn from Mikkelsen, *Spanish Theater Songs*, 5–6; and Sturman, *Zarzuela*, 36–38.
31. Webber, *Zarzuela Companion*, 5.
32. On *La verbena de la Paloma* in Buenos Aires, see Doppelbauer and Sartingen, *De la zarzuela*, 53. On its popularity in Mexico, and *La verbena de la Guadalupe*, see Olavarría y Ferrari, *Reseña histórica del teatro* 4:560 and 614.
33. Sturman, *Zarzuela*, 41.
34. Prieto, *Memorias de mis tiempos*, 146–50.
35. See "Del modo de conducirnos en sociedad, artículo IV, Sección Segunda, De los bailes," in Carreño, *Manual de urbanidad*, 271–76.
36. Amunátegui, *Las primeras representaciones*, 97–99.
37. Anonymous, "Letter from a Resident," 173.
38. My précis of the contradance is indebted to Sachs, *World History*, 416–21; and Manuel, *Creolizing Contradance*, 63-66. The *cedazo* has been described as a closed-couple, waltz-like dance, or as "passing through." For closed-couple references, see Manuel, *Creolizing Contradance*, 66; and Chasteen, *National Rhythms, African Roots*, 158. For a definition of "passing through," see Rodríguez, "Cuba," 118. Both definitions can be reconciled through the idea of "twirling" or "spinning" your partner under or through your raised arm. This is supported by a pseudonymous 1795 article in the *Diario de Madrid* that refers to the *cedazo* as "spinning around" (my translation). See Muchitango, "Ordenanzas," 2112.
39. For a genealogical account of these dances, see Sachs, *World History*, 421–24.
40. The figures and sequence of the quadrille were set as: *le pantalon, l'été, la poule, la trénis, la pastourelle*, and *le finale*. See Sachs, *World History*, 423–24.
41. For a nineteenth-century list of cotillion choreographies, see de Garmo, *Dance of Society*, 114–21. For a period account from Cuba, see H., "Crónica del buen tono." For Mexico, see Díaz y de Ovando, *Invitación al baile*, 215; and Anonymous, "Un baile nuevo."
42. Anonymous, "El baile."
43. Ibarra, *Colección de bailes*, 14–15. Ibarra also makes a few cameos as a dance master and personality in Guillermo Prieto's *Memorias de mis tiempos*, 147.
44. For an overview of this theme, see Chasteen, *National Rhythms, African Roots*, 122–23.
45. My overview of the nineteenth-century polka is informed by the summary provided by Giordano, *Social Dancing in America*, 169–71.
46. Will Fowler, *Santa Anna of Mexico*, 264.

47. My characterization of the *pericón* and its relationship to the contradance is based on Vega, "Contradanza y pericón," 4. For more on this relationship, see Sánchez Zinny, *Integración del folklore argentino*, 138; and Berruti, *Manual de danzas nativas*, 203.
48. The scene featuring Chiclina is drawn from Palomeque, *Mi año político*, 3:756. Palomeque quotes from an observer named Manuel Bernárdez and seems to take it for granted that the reader would recognize Chiclina's name. We don't know if the singer might be related, symbolically or literally, to the "Jacinto Chiclana" immortalized in the poem "Milonga for Jacinto Chiclana" by Jorge Luis Borges.
49. Manuel, *Creolizing Contradance*, 66.
50. Quoted in Díaz Díaz and Manuel, "Puerto Rico," 130.
51. Quoted in Chasteen, "National Rhythm," 74.
52. My sketch of the tango is drawn from Collier, "Birth of the Tango," 197–200; and Chasteen, *National Rhythms, African Roots*, 66. Another useful source for the influence of Afro-Argentines on the *milonga* and the tango is Rossi, *Cosas de negros*.
53. Quoted in Spencer Espinosa, "Imaginario nacional," 160 (my translation). Spencer Espinosa also explains how the *zamacueca* was nationalized in Chile (160–62).
54. The Mexican account is drawn from Carson, *Mexico*, 293. The Bolivian dance is from Squier, *Peru*, 305–6.
55. For sample lists of trumpet and cornet calls, see "Aplicación de los toques," in Mansilla, *Reglamento*, 3–5; and "Toques de la marcha," in Manuel González, *Ordenanza general*, 1:230–32.
56. Fernández Calvo, "La música militar," 32.
57. Zapiola, *Recuerdos de treinta años*, 69–70.
58. Claro Valdés, "La vida musical," 7.
59. Spencer Espinosa, "Imaginario nacional," 150–51; and Fernández Calvo, "La música militar," 40.
60. Díaz Díaz, "Danza antillana," 239–40.
61. Transcripts of various Spanish American national anthems may be found in Oscar Galeno's *Las Tres Américas (A Spanish Reader)*, as well as on the Internet.
62. My précis of the *romance* is drawn from Díaz-Mas, *Romancero*, 3–29. Also, see Lozano, *Cantemos al Alba*, 432–40.
63. Lozano, *Cantemos al Alba*, 447; Menéndez Pidal, *Los romances de América*, 32–34; Fernández Latour de Botas, *Folklore y poesía argentina*, 54; and Paredes, *Texas-Mexican Cancionero*, 5–6.
64. Lozano, *Cantemos al Alba*, 451.
65. Ibid., 475. Castellanos, "El tema de Delgadina," 44.
66. López Tamés, *Introducción*, 201–2; Menéndez Pidal, *Romancero hispánico*, 385; and Castellanos, "El tema de Delgadina," 43–44. For children's games in general, see Solís Miranda, *El libro*, 44–45; and Marco and Ochoa, *Repertorio completo*, 856–57.
67. The standard work comparing the *corrido* to romances and linking them together is Vicente Mendoza's *El romance español y el corrido mexicano*; see especially 217–18. For some non-Mexican examples of nineteenth-century *corridos* in Spanish America, see Fernández Latour de Botas, *Cantares históricos*, xxxi–xxxii, 41–50; and 104–6. Also, see Álvarez Mendoza, *Presencia de la música*, 53–54; Vicuña Cifuentes, *Romances populares y vulgares*, xxi–xxii; and Navarrete, *El romance tradicional*, 77–87.

68. Simmons, *Mexican Corrido*, 8–10; Mendoza, *El romance español*, 132–33; and Santa Cruz, *Obras completas*, 2:xx.
69. My bird's-eye definition of the *corrido* draws from Mendoza, *El romance español*, 132–33; Paredes, *With His Pistol*, 206–7, 219–24, 227–40; and Simmons, *Mexican Corrido*, 16–20.
70. There are many variants and transcriptions of the "Corrido of Heraclio Bernal." The one I quote is drawn from Custodio, *El corrido popular mexicano*, 136–39 (my translation).
71. My definition of the *copla* is drawn from Pinto Espinosa, "La apropiación," and Acaso, "Aproximación al fenómeno."
72. Kofman, "La copla española," 66–68.
73. The *coplas* I've translated here are from more than one source. "Jacinta me dio una cinta" (Jacinta gave me a piece of ribbon) is from Pérez Bugallo, *Cancionero popular de Corrientes*, 36, among other sources; "Mariquita" is from Palau, *Cantares populares y literarios*, 281, among other sources; "Una novia" (One of the girlfriends) is from Mendoza and Mendoza, *Folklore de la región*, 70, among other sources; "Desde el llano abajo vengo" (I ride down from the plains) is from Carrizo and Fernández Latour de Botas, *Cantares hispanoamericanos*, 439, among other sources; and "Yo soy como ají" (I am like a hot green pepper) is from Kofman, "La copla española," 77.
74. My précis of the *décima* is informed by Santa Cruz, *La décima*, 28–37; and Tala, *La cultura popular*, 3–7.
75. Paredes, "Décima," 156–58.
76. Carrizo and Universidad Nacional de Tucumán, *Cancionero popular de Salta*, 53–54. My translation.

AFTERWORD *Change*

1. Singhal, Obregon, and Rogers, "Reconstructing the Story," 8.
2. Ibid., 5, 10.
3. For some statistics on television coverage in Latin America, see Menéndez Alarcón, *Power and Television*, 18–22; and Forero, Gutiérrez Coba, et al, "Media in Colombia," 67.
4. For the ubiquity of tango on Argentinian radio, see Adamovsky, *Historia*; in Mexico, see Buffington, "Radio," 427.
5. For the political uses of television in Colombia, see Fox, *Latin American Broadcasting*, 91; in the Dominican Republic, see Menéndez Alarcón, *Power and Television*, 16–19; and in Argentina, see Karush and Chamosa, *New Cultural History*, 30–31 and 115.

BIBLIOGRAPHY

Acaso, Francisco. "Aproximación al fenómeno de la poesía popular." In Acaso, *Diccionario de coplas populares*, 19–61.

———, ed. *Diccionario de coplas populares anónimas: Ordenación, ideológica; Aproximación al fenómeno de la poesía popular anónima*. Madrid: Doraprint, 1991.

Aceves, Gutierre, ed. "El arte ritual de la muerte niña." Special issue, *Artes de México*, no. 15 (1998).

———. "Images of an Eternal Innocence." *Artes de México* 15 (1992): 84–89.

Acree, William G., Jr. *Everyday Reading: Print Culture and Collective Identity in the Río de la Plata, 1780–1910*. Nashville: Vanderbilt University Press, 2011.

———. "Jacinto Ventura de Molina: A Black *Letrado* in a White World of Letters, 1766–1841." *Latin American Research Review* 44, no. 2 (Spring 2009): 37–58.

Acree, William G., Jr., and Juan Carlos González Espitia, eds. *Building Nineteenth-Century Latin America: Re-Rooted Cultures, Identities, and Nations*. Nashville: Vanderbilt University Press, 2009.

Adamovsky, Ezequiel. *Historia de las clases populares en la Argentina: Desde 1880 hasta 2003*. Buenos Aires: Editorial Sudamericana, 2012.

Ades, Dawn. *Art in Latin America: The Modern Era, 1820–1980*. New Haven, CT: Yale University Press, 1989.

Aguila Peralta, Alicia del. *Callejones y mansiones: Espacios de opinión pública y redes sociales y políticas en la Lima del 900* [i.e., 1900]. Lima: Pontificia Universidad Católica del Perú, Fondo Editorial, 1997.

Aguilar Ochoa, Arturo. "La influencia de los artistas viajeros en la litografía mexicana (1837–1849)." *Anales del Instituto de Investigaciones Estéticas*, no. 76 (2000): 113–41.

Albarran, Alan B., ed. *The Handbook of Spanish Language Media*. New York: Routledge, 2009.

Albes, Edward. *Viajando por Sud América*. New York: Holt, 1917.

Almandoz Marte, Arturo, ed. *Planning Latin America's Capital Cities, 1850–1950*. London: Routledge, 2002.

———. "Urbanization and Urbanism in Latin America: From Haussmann to CIAM." In Almandoz Marte, *Planning*, 13–43.

Altamirano, Carlos, dir. *Historia de los intelectuales en América Latina*. Buenos Aires: Katz, 2008.

Altamirano, Ignacio Manuel. "Crónica de la semana." *El Renacimiento: Periódico Literario* 2 (1869): 97–101.

———. "Honra y provecho de un autor de libros en México." In *Obras completas*, vol. 2: *Escritos de literatura y arte*, 90–93. Edited by José Joaquín Blanco. Mexico City:

Dirección General de Publicaciones y Medios de la Secretaría de Educación Pública, 1986.

———. *"María*: Novela americana por Jorge Isaacs." In Isaacs, *María* [Garnier], 411–18.

———. *Obras completas*. Vol. 5, *Textos costumbristas*. Edited by José Joaquín Blanco. Mexico City: Dirección General de Publicaciones y Medios de la Secretaría de Educación Pública, 1986.

———. *Para leer la patria diamantina: Una antologia general*. Biblioteca Americana. Viajes al Siglo XIX. Mexico City: Fondo de Cultura Económica, Fundación Para las Letras Mexicanas, Universidad Nacional Autónoma de México, 2006.

———. *Revistas literarias de México*. Mexico City: F. Diaz de Leon y S. White, 1868.

———. "La semana santa en mi pueblo." In Ignacio Manuel Altamirano, *Obras completas*, 5:37–55.

Althaus, Clemente. "A Rossini." In *Obras poéticas de Clemente Althaus (1852–1871)*, 21–22. Lima: Imprenta del Universo, de Carlos Prince, 1872.

Alvarez, Agustín. *Manual de patología política*. Buenos Aires: La Cultura Argentina, 1916.

Alvarez, Tiberio. "El arte ritual de la muerte niña." *Revista Colombiana de Anestesiología* 26, no. 377 (1998): 377–82.

Álvarez Mendoza, Carlos Luis. *Presencia de la música en los relatos sobre Venezuela de los viajeros de la primera mitad del siglo XX*. Caracas: Fondo Editorial de Humanidades y Educación, Universidad Central de Venezuela, 2002.

Amorena, José Antonio. *Memorandum enciclopédico administrativo y comercial: Descriptivo de Buenos Aires, capital de la República Argentina*. Buenos Aires: J. Mackern, 1885.

Amunátegui, Miguel Luis. "Apuntes sobre lo que han sido las bellas artes en Chile." *Revista de Santiago* 3, no. 21 (April 1849): 37–47.

———. *Las primeras representaciones dramáticas en Chile*. Ed. oficial. Santiago: Imprenta Nacional, 1888.

Anderson, Benedict. *Imagined Communities: Reflections on the Origin and Spread of Nationalism*. Rev. ed. London: Verso, 2006.

Anonymous. "Alejandro Dumás." *La Semana Católica* 14, no. 24 (December 15, 1895): 762.

Anonymous. "El baile del club hípico aleman." *El Mundo Ilustrado* 2, no. 10 (September 2, 1900): 4.

Anonymous. "Un baile nuevo: La ola." *El Mundo Ilustrado* year 15, vol. 1, no. 12 (March 22, 1908): 15.

Anonymous. "Letter from a Resident at Cuba." *New Monthly Magazine and Universal Register* 14, no. 79 (August 1, 1820): 168–74.

Anonymous. "Meditación sobre *María*." *La Revista Uruguaya* 2, no. 39 (December 1, 1906): 7–11.

Anonymous. "Noticias: José Verdi." *El Monitor de la Educación Común* 12, no. 336 (February 28, 1901): 943.

Arcos, Carol. "Novelas-folletín y la autoría femenina en la segunda mitad del siglo XIX en Chile." *Revista Chilena de Literatura*, no. 76 (April 2010): 27–42.

Armas Asin, Fernando. *Liberales, protestantes y masones: Modernidad y tolerancia religiosa; Perú siglo XIX*. Archivos de Historia Andina 29. Lima: Fondo Editorial de la Pontificia Universidad Católica del Perú; Cusco: Centro de Estudios Regionales Andinos "Bartolomé de Las Casas," 1998.

Arteaga y Alemparte, Justo. "Sociabilidad y progreso." *La Semana, Periódico Noticioso, Literario y Científico*, September 3, 1859, 241–43.

Ascencio Segura, Manuel. *Ña Catita / Las tres viudas*. Lima: Editorial Mercurio, 1976.

Astete, Francisco Hernández, coord. *100 años, Sociedad Filarmónica de Lima*. Lima: Sociedad Filarmónica de Lima, 2006.

Atanasio Fuentes, Manuel. *Guía de domicilio de Lima para el año de 1864*. Self-published, 1863.

———. *Lima; or, Sketches of the Capital of Peru, Historical, Statistical, Administrative, Commercial and Moral*. London: Trübner, 1866.

"Aviso al público." *El Comercio* (Lima), September 21, 1844, 8.

Ayala Mora, Enrique, and Eduardo Posada Carbo, eds. *Historia general de América Latina*. Madrid: Editorial Trotta; Paris: Ediciones UNESCO, 1999.

Baralt, Rafael María. *Resumen de la historia de Venezuela desde el descubrimiento de su territorio por los castellanos en el siglo XV, hasta el año de 1797*. Curazao: Imprenta de la Librería de A Bethencourt e Hijos, 1887.

Baranda, Joaquín. *Memoria que el secretario de justicia e instrucción pública presenta al Congreso de la Unión (1888–1892)*. Mexico City: Imprenta del Gobierno Federal, en el ex-Arzobispado, 1892.

Basadre, Jorge. *Historia de la República del Perú*. 5th ed. Lima: Editorial Peruamérica, 1963.

Bazant de Saldaña, Mílada. *Historia de la educación durante el Porfiriato*. Serie Historia de La Educación. Mexico City: Colegio de México, Centro de Estudios Históricos, 1993.

Beezley, William H. *Judas at the Jockey Club and Other Episodes of Porfirian Mexico*. Lincoln: University of Nebraska Press, 1987.

———. *Mexican National Identity: Memory, Innuendo, and Popular Culture*. Tucson: University of Arizona Press, 2008.

Beezley, William H., Cheryl English Martin, and William E. French, eds. *Rituals of Rule, Rituals of Resistance: Public Celebration and Popular Culture in Mexico*. Wilmington, DE.: Scholarly Resources, 1994.

Beigel, Fernanda. *La epopeya de una generación y una revista: Las redes editoriales de José Carlos Mariátegui en América Latina*. Sociedad. Buenos Aires: Editorial Biblos, 2006.

Belgrano Rawson, Eduardo. *Noticias secretas de América*. 4th ed. Seix Barral Biblioteca Breve. Buenos Aires: Seix Barral, 2008.

Berisso, Luis. *El pensamiento de América*. Buenos Aires: F. Lajouane, 1898.

Berruti, P. *Manual de danzas nativas: Coreografías, historia y texto poético de las danzas*. 4th ed. Buenos Aires: Editorial Escolar, 1961.

Betancourt, Luis Victoriano. *Artículos de costumbres y poesías*. Guanabacoa, Cuba: La Revista de Almacenes, 1867.

Bettelheim, Judith, ed. *Cuban Festivals: A Century of Afro-Cuban Culture*. Princeton, NJ: Markus Wiener, 2001.

Bibliófilo [pseud.]. "Apuntes de un cronista." *Fígaro: Periódico de Literatura, Bellas Artes y Modas*, no. 22 (March 5, 1865): 163–65.

Bierstadt, Edward Hale. *Three Plays of the Argentine: Juan Moreira, Santos Vega, The Witches' Mountain*. New York: Duffield, 1920.

Bilbao, Francisco. *El evangelio americano*. Caracas: Biblioteca Ayacucho, 1988.

Boime, Albert. *The Academy and French Painting in the Nineteenth Century.* New Haven, CT: Yale University Press, 1986.

Bórquez Solar, Antonio. *Dilectos decires.* Paris: P. Ollendorff, 1911.

Borucki, Alex. "Tensiones raciales en el juego de la representación: Actores afro en Montevideo tras la fundación republicana (1830–1840)." *Gestos* 21, no. 42 (November 2006): 33–56.

Botana, Natalio R. "Sarmiento and Political Order: Liberty, Power, and Virtue." In Halperín Donghi et al., *Sarmiento: Author of a Nation,* 101–13.

Boulton, Alfredo. *Historia de la pintura en Venezuela.* Caracas: E. Armitano, 1964.

Briggs, Ronald. *Tropes of Enlightenment in the Age of Bolívar: Simón Rodríguez and the American Essay at Revolution.* Nashville: Vanderbilt University Press, 2010.

Broquetas, Magdalena, coord. *Fotografía en Uruguay: Historia y usos sociales, 1840–1930.* Montevideo: Centro de Fotografía (Intendencia de Montevideo), 2011.

Brown, David H. *Santería Enthroned: Art, Ritual, and Innovation in an Afro-Cuban Religion.* Chicago: University of Chicago Press, 2003.

Bueno, Salvador, coord. *Costumbristas cubanos del siglo XIX.* Caracas: Biblioteca Ayacucho, 1985.

Buenos Aires. *Digesto de ordenanzas, reglamentos, acuerdos y disposiciones de la municipalidad de la ciudad de Buenos Aires.* 2nd rev. ed. Buenos Aires: Imprenta y Lit. La Tribuna Nacional, 1884.

Buffington, Robert. "Homophobia and the Mexican Working Class, 1900–1910." In Irwin, McCaughan, and Nasser, *Famous 41,* 196–206.

———. "Radio." In Coerver, Pasztor, and Buffington, *Mexico,* 425–29.

Bulmer-Thomas, Victor. *The Economic History of Latin America since Independence.* 2nd ed. Cambridge Latin American Studies 77. Cambridge: Cambridge University Press, 2003.

Burke, Peter. *Popular Culture in Early Modern Europe.* 3rd ed. Farnham, England: Ashgate, 2009.

Burns, E. Bradford. *The Poverty of Progress: Latin America in the Nineteenth Century.* Berkeley: University of California Press, 1980.

Cabello de Carbonera, Mercedes. *Blanca Sol: Novela social.* 1st American critical ed. Miami: Stockcero, 2007.

Calderón de la Barca, Fanny. *Life in Mexico during a Residence of Two Years in That Country.* Boston: Charles C. Little and James Brown, 1843.

Calvo, Hortensia. "Latin America." In Eliot and Rose, *Companion,* 138–52.

Cámara de la Asamblea General. *Diario de sesiones de H. Cámara de Representantes: Sesiones ordinarias del 2do. período de la XXII legislatura.* Montevideo: Imprenta El Siglo Ilustrado, de Mariño y Caballero, 1907.

Cara, Ana C. "Cocoliche: The Art of Assimilation and Dissimulation among Italians and Argentines." *Latin American Research Review* 22, no. 3 (1987): 37–67.

Cárdenas, Ricardo Estabridis. "Academias y academicismos en Lima decimonónica." *Tiempos de América: Revista de Historia, Cultura y Territorio,* no. 11 (2004): 77–90.

Carilla, Emilio. "The Romantic Theater in Hispanic America." In Gillespie, *Romantic Drama,* 359–75.

Carmichael, Elizabeth, and Chloë Sayer. *The Skeleton at the Feast: The Day of the Dead in Mexico.* Austin: University of Texas Press, 1992.

Carpenter, Frank G. *South America, Social, Industrial, and Political: A Twenty-Five-Thousand-Mile Journey in Search of Information*. Akron, OH: Saalfield, 1900.

Carrasco, Eduardo. *Calendario y guía de forasteros de la república peruana para el año de 1852*. Lima: Imprenta de Instrucción Primaria, 1851.

Carreño, Manuel Antonio. *Manual de urbanidad y buenas maneras para uso de la juventud de ambos sexos . . . precedido de un breve tratado sobre los deberes morales del hombre*. New York: Appleton, 1859.

Carrizo, Juan Alfonso. "Del cantar popular a la prosa de Sarmiento." In Zárate, *Facundo Quiroga*, 231–42.

Carrizo, Juan Alfonso, and Olga Fernández Latour de Botas. *Cantares hispanoamericanos*. San Isidro, Argentina: Academia de Ciencias y Artes de San Isidro, 2002.

Carrizo, Juan Alfonso, and Universidad Nacional de Tucumán. *Cancionero popular de Salta*. Buenos Aires: A. Baiocco, 1933.

Carson, William English. *Mexico: The Wonderland of the South*. New York: Macmillan, 1909.

Castañeda, Carmen, coord. *Del autor al lector: Libros y libreros en la historia*. Mexico City: Centro de Investigaciones y Estudios Superiores en Antropología Social; Consejo Nacional de Ciencia y Tecnología, 2002.

Castellanos, Carlos. "El tema de Delgadina en el folklore de Santiago de Cuba." *Journal of American Folklore* 33, no. 127, Hispanic Number (January–March 1920): 43–46.

Castro, Miguel Ángel, ed. *Tipos y carácteres: La prensa mexicana (1822–1855); Memoria del coloquio celebrado los días 23, 24 y 25 septiembre de 1998*. Mexico City: Universidad Nacional Autónoma de México, Instituto de Investigaciones Bibliográficas, Seminario de Bibliografía Mexicana del Siglo XIX, 2001.

Castro, Miguel Ángel, and Guadalupe Curiel, coords. *Publicaciones periódicas mexicanas del siglo XIX, 1856–1876: Fondo antiguo de la Hemeroteca Nacional de México, parte 1*. Mexico City: Universidad Nacional Autónoma de México, Coordinación de Humanidades, Instituto de Investigaciones Bibliográficas, 2003.

Caveda Romani, María, ed., *Las sociedades filarmónicas habaneras (1824–1844)*. Havana: Instituto Cubano de Investigación Cultural Juan Marinello, 2009.

Céspedes y Santa Cruz, Benjamín de. *La prostitución en la ciudad de la Habana*. Havana: Establecimiento Tipográfico O'Reilly, 1888.

Charlot, Jean. *Mexican Art and the Academy of San Carlos, 1785–1945*. Austin: University of Texas Press, 1962.

Chasteen, John Charles. "Anything Goes: Carnivalesque Transgressions in Nineteenth-Century Latin America." In Acree and González Espitia, *Building Nineteenth-Century Latin America*, 133–49.

———. *Born in Blood and Fire: A Concise History of Latin America*. New York: Norton, 2001.

———. "A National Rhythm: Social Dance and Elite Identity in Nineteenth-Century Havana." In Young, *Music, Popular Culture, Identities*, 65–84.

———. *National Rhythms, African Roots: The Deep History of Latin American Popular Dance*. Albuquerque: University of New Mexico Press, 2004.

Child, Theodore. *The Spanish-American Republics*. New York: Harper, 1892.

Chu, Petra ten-Doesschate. *Nineteenth-Century European Art*. Boston: Prentice Hall, 2011.

Cilento, Laura. "Pepe Podestá: Medio siglo de (supervivencia en la) farándula." In Pellettieri, *De Eduardo de Filippo*, 25–39.

Clark, Peter, ed. *The Oxford Handbook of Cities in World History*. Oxford: Oxford University Press, 2013.

Clark de Lara, Belem, and Elisa Speckman Guerra, coords. *La república de las letras: Publicaciones periódicas y otros empresos*. Mexico City: Universidad Nacional Autónoma de México, 2005.

Claro Valdés, Samuel. "La vida musical en Chile durante el gobierno de don Bernardo O'Higgins." *Revista Musical Chilena* 33, no. 145 (January–March, 1979): 5–24.

Clemente Travieso, Carmen. *Las esquinas de Caracas: Sus leyendas, sus recuerdos*. Caracas: Editorial "Ancora," 1956.

Club del Progreso. *Club del progreso: Datos históricos sobre su origen y desenvolvimiento; Apuntes coleccionados por la comisión directiva de este centro con motivo del 50 aniversario de su fundación*. Buenos Aires: Club del Progreso, 1902.

Cobo, Bernabé. *Historia de la fundación de Lima*. Coleccion de Historiadores del Perú. Vol. 1. Lima: Imprenta Liberal, 1882.

Coerver, Don, Suzanne Pasztor, and Robert Buffington, eds. *Mexico: An Encyclopedia of Contemporary Culture and History*. Santa Barbara, CA: ABC-CLIO, 2004.

Colegio de México. *Historia de la lectura en México*. Mexico City: Ediciones del Ermitaño: Colegio de México, Centro de Estudios Históricos, 1988.

Collier, Simon. "The Birth of the Tango." In Nouzeilles and Montaldo, *Argentine Reader*, 196–202.

Congreso de la Nación Argentina. *Diario de sesiones de la Cámara de Diputados*. Buenos Aires: Imprenta de "La Universidad," 1883.

——. *Diario de sesiones de la Cámara de Diputados*. Buenos Aires: Establecimiento Tipográfico "El Comercio," 1908.

Conway, Christopher. "El aparecido azteca: Ignacio Manuel Altamirano en el necronacionalismo mexicano, 1893." *Revista de Crítica Literaria Latinoamericana* 31, no. 62 (2nd semester 2005): 125–42.

——. *The Cult of Bolívar in Latin American Literature*. Gainesville: University Press of Florida, 2003.

——. "Introduction." In Palma, *Peruvian Traditions*, xix–xlv.

——. "Próspero y el teatro nacional: Encuentros trasatlánticos en las revistas teatrales de Ignacio Manuel Altamirano, 1867–1876." In Ortega and del Palacios, *México trasatlántico*, 132–57.

——, ed. *The U.S.-Mexican War: A Binational Reader*. Indianapolis: Hackett, 2010.

Cordovez Moure, J. M. *Reminiscencias de Santafé y Bogotá*. Biblioteca Básica Colombiana 35. Bogotá: Instituto Colombiano de Cultura, Subdirección de Comunicaciones Culturales, División de Publicaciones, Biblioteca Básica Colombiana, 1978.

Corella V., Randall. "Retratos eternos." *La Nación* (Costa Rica), November 28, 2010.

"Correspondencia." *El Mercurio*, November 5, 1850, 2.

Cortés, Hernán. *Escritos sueltos de Hernan Cortés: Coleccion formada para servir de complemento a las "cartas de relación" publicadas en el tomo I de la biblioteca*. Mexico City: I. Escalante, 1871.

Costa Rica. *Colección de leyes, decretos, acuerdos y resoluciones*. Vol. 2. San José: Imprenta Nacional, 1894.

Cuéllar, José Tomás de. *Ensalada de pollos y baile y cochino*. Edited by Antonio Castro Leal. Mexico City: Editorial Porrúa, 1982.

———*La linterna mágica*. . . . Mexico City: Ignacio Cumplido, 1871.

Cunliffe-Owen, Marguerite. *A Keystone of Empire: Francis Joseph of Austria*. London: Harper, 1903.

Curtis, William Eleroy. *Venezuela: A Land Where It's Always Summer*. New York: Harper, 1896.

Custodio, Álvaro. *El corrido popular mexicano: Su historia, sus temas, sus intérpretes*. Madrid: Ediciones Júcar, 1975.

Dabove, Juan Pablo. *Nightmares of the Lettered City: Banditry and Literature in Latin America, 1816–1929*. Illuminations: Cultural Formations of the Americas. Pittsburgh: University of Pittsburgh Press, 2007.

Darío, Rubén. "The Bourgeois King." In *Rubén Darío: Selected Writings*. Translated by Andrew Hurley, Greg Simon, and Steven F. White. Edited by Ilan Stavans. New York: Penguin, 2007.

Dauster, Frank. "The Spanish American Theater of the Nineteenth Century." In González Echevarría and Pupo-Walker, *Cambridge History*, 536–55.

Davey, Richard. "Havana and the Havanese." In *Living Age* 217, no. 2814 (June 11, 1898): 691–703.

Dávila, Francisco. *La babel argentina: Pálido bosquejo de la Ciudad de Buenos Aires en su triple aspecto material, moral y artístico*. Buenos Aires: El Correo Español, 1886.

Debroise, Olivier. *Mexican Suite: A History of Photography in Mexico*. Austin: University of Texas Press, 2001.

de Cárdenas y Rodríguez, José María. "¡Educado fuera!" In Bueno, *Costumbristas*, 75–79.

"Decreto #1 de 7 de agosto, reglamento de profilaxis venérea." In Costa Rica, *Colección de leyes*, 83–84.

de Gandía, Enrique. *Historia de la república argentina en el siglo XIX*. Buenos Aires: A. Estrada, 1940.

de Garmo, William. *The Dance of Society: A Critical Analysis of All of the Standard Quadrilles, Round Dances, 102 Figures of Le Cotillon*. . . . New York: W. A. Pond, 1875.

de la Fuente, Ariel. *Children of Facundo: Caudillo and Gaucho Insurgency during the Argentine State-Formation Process (La Rioja, 1853–1870)*. Durham, NC: Duke University Press, 2000.

de la Lama, Miguel Antonio. *Código del comercio del Perú con citas, notas, concordancias y un apéndice de leyes, decretos, resoluciones, reglamentos, etc. hasta el 30 de diciembre de 1895*. Lima: Librería, Imprenta y Encuadernación Gil, 1897.

de Landaluze, Victor Patricio. *Los cubanos pintados por sí mismos*. Havana: Imprenta y papelería de Barcina, 1852.

de Sales Pérez, Francisco. *Costumbres venezolanas*. New York: Imprenta y Librería de N. Ponce de Leon, 1877.

Díaz Díaz, Edgardo. "Danza antillana, conjuntos militares, nacionalismo musical e identidad dominicana: retomando los pasos perdidos del merengue." *Latin American Music Review/Revista de Música Latinoamericana* 29, no. 2 (Fall–Winter 2008): 232–62.

Díaz Díaz, Edgardo, and Peter Manuel. "Puerto Rico: The Rise and Fall of the Danza as National Music." In Manuel, *Creolizing Contradance*, 113–54.

Díaz-Mas, Paloma. *Romancero*. Barcelona: Crítica, 2000.

Díaz Seijas, Pedro. *Caracas, la gentil: Biografía de una ciudad*. Colección Ares 51. Caracas: Libros de El Nacional, 2005.

Díaz y de Ovando, Clementina. *Invitación al baile: Arte, espectáculo y rito en la sociedad mexicana (1825–1910)*. Mexico City: Universidad Nacional Autónoma de México, 2006.

Doppelbauer, Max, and Kathrin Sartingen, eds. *De la zarzuela al cine: Los medios de comunicación populares y su traducción de la voz marginal*. Munich: Martin Meidenbauer, 2010.

Dubatti, Jorge. "El teatro francés en la Argentina (1880–1900)." In Pellettieri, *De Sarah Bernhardt*, 13–20.

Dumas, Claude. *Justo Sierra y el México de su tiempo, 1848–1912*. Mexico City: Universidad Nacional Autónoma de México, 1986.

Dunkerley, James. *Americana: The Americas in the World around 1850 (or "Seeing the Elephant" as the Theme for an Imaginary Western)*. New York: Verso, 2000.

Dupanloup, Mons. "Mujeres sabias y mujeres estudiosas." In Miguel Navarro Viola, *La biblioteca popular*, 1:139–212.

Duque, Ellie Anne. "Presentación del documento: Reglamento de la Sociedad Filarmónica." *Ensayos, Historia y Teoría del Arte* 9, no. 9 (2004): 237–46.

Durán, Gustavo León y León. *Apuntes históricos genealógicos de Francisco Fierro: Pancho Fierro*. Lima: Biblioteca Nacional del Perú, Fondo Editorial, 2004.

Eastwick, Edward Backhouse. *Venezuela*. 2nd ed. London: Chapman and Hall, 1868.

Eitner, Lorenz, comp. *Neoclassicism and Romanticism, 1750–1850: Sources and Documents*. Sources and Documents in the History of Art Series. Englewood Cliffs, NJ: Prentice Hall, 1970.

Eliot, Simon, and Jonathan Rose, eds. *A Companion to the History of the Book*. Malden, MA: Blackwell, 2007.

Engerman, Stanley L., and Kenneth L. Sokoloff. *Economic Development in the Americas since 1500: Endowments and Institutions*. NBER Series on Long-Term Factors in Economic Development. New York: Cambridge University Press, 2012.

Enríquez y Terrazas, J. *Alfredo: Preludio literario*. Mexico: E. Orozco, 1892.

"Escuela de artes y oficios para hombres." In Baranda, *Memoria*, lxxvii–lxxx.

Esguerra, Arsenio. "*María*: A Jorge Isaacs." In Esguerra, *Poesías y artículos*, 8–11.

———. *Poesias y articulos en prosa de Arsenio Esguerra*. Bogotá: Imprenta de Medardo Rivas, 1880.

Esherick, Joseph, Hasan Kayali, and Eric Van Young, eds. *Empire to Nation: Historical Perspectives on the Making of the Modern World*. Lanham, MD.: Rowman and Littlefeld, 2006.

Espinosa, Roberto. *La reforma de la lejislación: Idea jeneral de un estudio que hace actualmente el autor*. Concepción, Chile: Imprenta de "El sur," 1899.

Esposito, Matthew. *Funerals, Festivals, and Cultural Politics in Porfirian Mexico*. Albuquerque: University of New Mexico Press, 2010.

"Estatutos de la Sociedad Filarmónica de Guatemala." In Viviano Guerra, *Leyes emitidas*, 97–99.

Estrada y Zenea, Ildefonso. "La concurrenta a Escauriza." *El Almandares: Periódico Semanal, Literario y de Modas* 1 (1852): 69–75.

———. "El concurrente a Escauriza." *El Almandares: Periódico Semanal, Literario y de Modas* 1 (1852): 88–92.

Fernández Armesto, Felipe. "Latin America." In Clark, *Oxford Handbook of Cities*, 364–84.

Fernández Calvo, Diana. "La música militar en la Argentina durante la primera mitad del siglo XIX." *Revista Digital del Instituto Universitario Naval*, no. 1 (2009): 29–54.

Fernández Latour de Botas, Olga. *Cantares históricos de la tradición argentina*. Buenos Aires: Instituto Nacional de Investigaciones Folklóricas, 1960.

———. *Folklore y poesía argentina*. Buenos Aires: Editorial Guadalupe, 1969.

Fierro, Pancho. *Acuarelas de Pancho Fierro y seguidores*. Lima: Municipalidad Metropolitana de Lima, 2007.

Forero, Germán Arango, Liliana Gutiérrez Coba, et al. "The Media in Colombia." In Albarran, *Handbook*, 63-76.

Forment, Carlos A. *Democracy in Latin America, 1760–1900*. Morality and Society Series. Chicago: University of Chicago Press, 2003.

Foucrier, Annick, ed. *The French and the Pacific World, 17th–19th Centuries: Discoveries, Migrations and Cultural Exchanges*. The Pacific World. Aldershot: Ashgate Variorum, 2003.

Fowler, Elizabeth. "The Mexican Revolt against Positivism." *Journal of the History of Ideas* 10, no. 1 (January 1949): 115–49.

Fowler, Will, ed. *Celebrating Insurrection: The Commemoration and Representation of the Nineteenth-Century Mexican Pronunciamiento*. Lincoln: University of Nebraska Press, 2013.

———. "Fiestas santanistas: La celebración de Santa Anna en la Villa de Xalapa, 1821–1855." *Historia Mexicana* 52, no. 2 (October–December 2002): 391–447.

———. *Santa Anna of Mexico*. Lincoln: University of Nebraska Press, 2007.

Fox, Elizabeth. *Latin American Broadcasting: From Tango to Telenovela*. Luton, UK: University of Luton Press, 1997.

Frank, Patrick. *Posada's Broadsheets: Mexican Popular Imagery, 1890–1910*. Albuquerque: University of New Mexico Press, 1998.

Frías y Soto, Hilarion, Niceto de Zamacois, Juan de Dios Arias, José María Rivera, Pantaleón Tovar, and Ignacio Ramírez. *Los mexicanos pintados por sí mismos*. Mexico City: Librería de Manuel Porrúa, 1974.

Fundación Bunge y Born. *The Art of Juan Manuel Blanes*. Buenos Aires: Fundación Bunge y Born, 1994.

Galaz, Gaspar, and Milan Ivelic. *La pintura en Chile desde la colonia hasta 1981*. El Rescate. Valparaíso: Universidad Católica de Valparaíso, Ediciones Universitarias de Valparaíso, 1981.

Galeno, Oscar. *Las Tres Américas (A Spanish Reader)*. New York: Gregg, 1921.

Gamarra, Abelardo. "Apuntes de viaje: Clorinda Matto de Turner." In Matto de Turner, *Tradiciones cuzqueñas*, 187–91.

———. *Lima: Unos cuantos barrios y unos cuantos tipos, al comenzar el siglo XX*. Lima: Pedro Barrio, 1907.

———. *El maestro valdivieso*. Lima: Servicio de Publicaciones, 1968.

Garay Celeita, Alejandro. "El campo artístico colombiano en el salón de arte de 1910." *Historia Crítica*, no. 32 (July–December 2006): 302–33.

García Cubas, Antonío. *El libro de mis recuerdos: Narraciones históricas*. Mexico City: Imprenta de Arturo García Cubas, 1904.

García Marquez, Gabriel. *A Hundred Years of Solitude*. New York: HarperCollins, 2003.

Gasso y Vidal, Leopolda. "La mujer artista." In Rodríguez Prampolini, *La crítica de arte*, 188–93.

Gay, Claudio. *Atlas de la historia física y política de Chile*. 2 vols. Paris: Paris: Imprenta de E. Thunot, 1854.

Gayol, Sandra. *Sociabilidad en Buenos Aires: Hombres, honor y cafés, 1862–1910*. Colección Plural. Buenos Aires: Ediciones del Signo, 2000.

Gerstaecker, Friedrich. "Tres días de carnaval en Lima." In Núñez, *Cuatro viajeros*, 169–86.

Gies, David Thatcher. *The Theatre in Nineteenth-Century Spain*. New York: Cambridge University Press, 1994.

Giffords, Gloria Fraser. *Mexican Folk Retablos*. Rev. ed. Albuquerque: University of New Mexico Press, 1992.

Gillespie, Gerald, ed. *Romantic Drama*. Philadelphia: John Benjamins, 1994.

Giordano, Ralph G. *Social Dancing in America: A History and Reference*. Westport, CT: Greenwood Press, 2007.

Giralt, Pedro. *El amor y la prostitución replica a un libro del Dr. Céspedes*. Havana: Ruiz y Hermano, 1889.

Golluscio de Montoya, Eva. "Del circo colonial a los teatros ciudadanos: Proceso de urbanización de la actividad dramática rioplatense." *Cahiers du Monde Hispanique et Luso-Brésilien, Littérature et Société en Amérique Latine*, no. 42 (1984): 141–49.

Gómez, José Valentín. *Proyecto de reglamento de la Sociedad Filarmónica de Buenos Aires*. Buenos Aires: Imprenta de Expósitos, 1823.

González, Aníbal. "Cultural Journalism in Spanish America: An Overview." In Valdés and Kadir, *Literary Cultures*, 87–91.

González, Manuel. *Ordenanza general para el ejército de la República Mexicana*. Mexico City: Ignacio Cumplido, 1882.

González Echevarría, Roberto, and Enrique Pupo-Walker, eds. *The Cambridge History of Latin American Literature*. Vol. 1, *Discovery to Modernism*. New York: Cambridge University Press, 1996.

González Pérez, Marcos. *Fiesta y nación en Colombia*. Aula Abierta. Bogotá: Cooperativa Editorial Magisterio, 1998.

González Stephan, Beatriz. "Narrativas duras en tiempos blandos: Sensibilidades amenazadas de los hombres de letras." *Revista de Crítica Literaria Latinoamericana* 26, no. 52 (2nd semester 2000): 107–34.

Gorriti, Juana Manuela. *Dreams and Realities: Selected Fictions of Juana Manuela Gorriti*. Translated by Sergio Waisman. Edited by Francine Masiello. New York: Oxford University Press, 2003.

———. *Veladas literarias de Lima, 1876–1877*. Buenos Aires: Imprenta Europea, 1892.

Goyena, Pablo. *La legislación vigente de la república del Uruguay*. Montevideo: Tipografía á Vapor de "La Nación," 1888.

———. "Reglamento de la prostitución aprobado por decreto de 4 de setiembre de 1883." In Goyena, *La legislación vigente*, 701–4.

Gretton, Thomas. "Posada's Prints as Photomechanical Artefacts." *Print Quarterly* 9, no. 4 (December 1992): 335–56.

Grez Toso, Sergio. *De la "regeneración del pueblo" a la huelga general: Génesis y evolución histórica del movimiento popular en Chile (1810–1890).* Colección Sociedad y Cultura. Santiago: Dirección de Bibliotecas, Archivos y Museos, 1997.

Guerra, François-Xavier, ed. *Los espacios públicos en Iberoamérica: Ambigüedades y problemas, siglos XVIII y XIX.* Sección de Obras de Historia. Mexico City: Centro Francés de Estudios Mexicanos y Centroamericanos, Fondo de Cultura Económica, 1998.

Guerra, Viviano, ed. *Leyes emitidas por el gobierno democrático de la república de Guatemala y por la asamblea nacional constituyente y lejislativa desde 1 de julio de 1883 a 31 diciembre de 1885.* Vol. 4. Guatemala City: Tipografía de Pedro Arenales, 1886.

Guiot de la Garza, Lilia. "Las librerías en la Ciudad de México: Primera mitad del siglo XIX." In Castro, *Tipos y carácteres,* 31–57.

Gutiérrez Nájera, Manuel. "Una edición mexicana de *María.*" In *Obras I: Crítica literaria, ideas y temas literarios, literatura mexicana.* Mexico City: Universidad Nacional Autonoma de México, 1995.

———. *La música y el instante: Crónicas.* Edited by Oscar Rodríguez Ortiz. Mexico City: Fundación Biblioteca Ayacucho, 2003.

Guy, Donna J. *Sex and Danger in Buenos Aires: Prostitution, Family, and Nation in Argentina.* Engendering Latin America, vol. 1. Lincoln: University of Nebraska Press, 1991.

Guzmán, Ricardo Franco. "El regimen jurídico de la prostitución." *Revista de la Facultad de Derecho de México,* nos. 85–86 (1972): 85–134.

H. "Crónica del bueno tono." *Semana Literaria.* 2 (1848): 43–44.

Haber, Stephen, ed. *Political Institutions and Economic Growth in Latin America: Essays in Policy, History and Political Economy.* Hoover Institution on War, Revolution and Peace 458. Stanford, CA: Stanford University Press, 2000.

Hall, William Henry Bullock. *Across Mexico in 1864–5.* London: Macmillan, 1866.

Halperín Donghi, Tulio. *The Contemporary History of Latin America.* Latin America in Translation/En Traducción/Em Tradução. Durham, NC: Duke University Press, 1993.

Halperín Donghi, Tulio, Iván Jaksić, Gwen Kirkpatrick, and Francine Masiello, eds. *Sarmiento: Author of a Nation.* Berkeley: University of California Press, 1994.

Hardoy, Jorge E. "Theory and Practice of Urban Planning in Europe, 1850–1930: Its Transfer to Latin America." In Hardoy and Morse, *Rethinking,* 20–49.

Hardoy, Jorge E., and R. M. Morse, eds. *Rethinking the Latin American City.* Washington, DC: Woodrow Wilson Center, 1993.

Hardy, Robert William Hale. *Travels in the Interior of Mexico in 1825, 1826, 1827, and 1828.* London: H. Colburn and R. Bentley, 1829.

Harris, Max. *Carnival and Other Christian Festivals: Folk Theology and Folk Performance.* Joe R. and Teresa Lozano Long Series in Latin American and Latino Art and Culture. Austin: University of Texas Press, 2003.

Harrison, Carol E. *The Bourgeois Citizen in Nineteenth-Century France: Gender, Sociability, and the Uses of Emulation.* Oxford: Oxford University Press, 1999.

Harwich Vallenilla, Nikita. "Venezuelan Positivism and Modernity." *Hispanic American Historical Review* 70, no. 2 (May 1990): 327–44.

Hazard, Samuel. *Cuba with Pen and Pencil*. Hartford, CT: Hartford Publishing, 1871.

Hernández, José. *El gaucho Martín Fierro*. Buenos Aires: Librería Martín Fierro, 1894.

———. *The Gaucho Martín Fierro*. English translation by Frank Carrino, Alberto Carlos, and Norman Mangouni. New York: State University of New York Press, 1974.

———. *El gaucho Martín Fierro/La vuelta de Martín Fierro*. Edited by Luis Sainz de Medrano. Madrid: Cátedra, 1979.

———. *Martín Fierro, edición crítica*. Edited by Elida Lois and Angel Núñez. Madrid: Fondo de Cultura Económica, 2001.

. Hunefeldt, Christine. *Liberalism in the Bedroom: Quarreling Spouses in Nineteenth-Century Lima*. University Park: Pennsylvania State University Press, 2000.

Hutchinson, Thomas Joseph. *Two Years in Peru, with Exploration of Its Antiquities*. Vol. 1. London: Sampson, Marston, Low and Searle, 1873.

Ibarra, Domingo. *Colección de bailes de sala: Y método para aprenderlos sin ausilio de maestro, dedicada a la juventud mexicana*. Mexico City, 1862.

Iglesias Utset, Marial. *A Cultural History of Cuba during the U.S. Occupation, 1898–1902*. Latin America in Translation/En Traducción/Em Tradução. Chapel Hill: University of North Carolina Press, 2011.

Irwin, Robert McKee, Edward J. McCaughan, and Michelle Rocio Nasser, eds. *The Famous 41: Sexuality and Social Control in Mexico, c. 1901*. New Directions in Latino American Cultures. New York: Palgrave Macmillan, 2003.

Isaacs, Jorge. *María: Novela americana*. Paris: Garnier Hermanos, 1898.

———. *María*. Edited by Donald McGrady. Madrid: Ediciones Cátedra, 1995.

———. *Obras completas*. Vol. 1. Edited by María Teresa Cristina. Bogotá: Universidad Externado de Colombia, 2006.

Iturriaga, Enrique, and Juan Carlos Estenssoro. "Música y sociedad peruana en el siglo XIX." In Astete, *100 años*, 36–49.

Jiménez, Ivan Molina. "Cultura por unos pocos pesos: Libros e imprentas en Costa Rica, 1750–1914." In Castañeda, *Del autor al lector*, 359–82.

JME [commentator]. "Policía." *El Siglo XIX*, August 16, 1844, 2.

Kale, Steven. *French Salons: High Society and Political Sociability from the Old Regime to the Revolution of 1848*. Baltimore: Johns Hopkins University Press, 2004.

Karush, Matthew, and Oscar Chamosa, eds. *The New Cultural History of Peronism: Power and Identity in Mid-Twentieth-Century Argentina*. Durham, NC: Duke University Press, 2010.

Keen, Benjamin. *A History of Latin America*. 9th ed. Boston: Wadsworth Cengage Learning, 2013.

Kinsbruner, Jay. *The Colonial Spanish-American City: Urban Life in the Age of Atlantic Capitalism*. Austin: University of Texas Press, 2005.

Koebel, W. H. *Modern Argentina: The El Dorado of To-Day; With Notes on Uruguay and Chile*. London: F. Griffiths, 1907.

Kofman, Andrey. "La copla española en América Latina." *La Colmena* 79 (July–September 2013): 65–78.

Laera, Alejandra, "Cronistas, novelistas: La prensa periódica como espacio de profesionalización en la Argentina." In Carlos Altamirano, *Historia de los intelectuales*, 495–523.

Lafforgue, Jorge, ed. *Teatro rioplatense (1886–1930)*. Biblioteca Ayacucho 8. Caracas: Biblioteca Ayacucho, 1977.

Lafragua, Jose María. *Memoria de la primera secretaria del estado y del despacho de relaciones interiores y esteriores de los Estados Unidos Mexicanos*. Mexico City: Imprenta de Vicente Garcia Torres, 1847.

Lagomaggiore, Francisco. *América literaria: Producciones selectas en prosa y verso, coleccionadas y editadas*. Buenos Aires: Imprenta de "La Nación," 1883.

Lara y Pardo, Luis. *La prostitución en México*. Estudios de Higiene Social. Paris: Librería de la Vda de C. Bouret, 1908.

Lasso, Marixa. *Myths of Harmony: Race and Republicanism during the Age of Revolution, Colombia 1795–1831*. Pitt Latin American Series. Pittsburgh: University of Pittsburgh Press, 2007.

Lastarria, José Victorino. *Miscelanea literaria*. Santiago: Imprenta y Libreria del Mercurio, 1855.

Lecount, Cynthia. "Carnival in Bolivia: Devils Dancing for the Virgin." *Western Folklore* 58, nos. 3–4, Studies of Carnival in Memory of Daniel J. Crowley (Summer–Autumn 1999): 231–52.

Legislatura de la provincia de Córdoba. *Estatutos de la Sociedad Filarmónica Cosmopolita de Córdoba*. In *Compilación de leyes, decretos, acuerdos de la excma: Cámara de Justicia y demás disposiciones de carácter público dictadas en la Provincia de Córdoba*, vol. 31. Córdoba, Argentina: Imprenta y Encuadernación "La Italia," 1903.

Leonard, Irving Albert. *Books of the Brave: Being an Account of Books and of Men in the Spanish Conquest and Settlement of the Sixteenth-Century New World*. Berkeley: University of California Press, 1992.

León, Marco Antonio. *La cultura de la muerte en Chiloé*. 2nd ed. Ensayos y Estudios. Santiago: RIL Editores, 2007.

"Leyes i decretos del supremo gobierno." *Anales de la Universidad de Chile* 9 (1852): 571–72.

Lizardi, José Joaquín Fernández de. *Don Catrín de la Fachenda/Noches tristes y día alegre*. Edited by Rocío Oviedo and Almudena Mejías. Madrid: Cátedra, 2001.

———. *The Mangy Parrot: The Life and Times of Periquillo Sarniento; Written by Himself for His Children*. Translated by David Frye. Indianapolis: Hackett, 2004.

Lois, Elida, and Angel Núñez. "Advertencia editorial." In Hernández, *Martín Fierro*, v–vii.

Londoño Vélez, Santiago. *Historia de la pintura y el grabado en Antioquia*. Señas de Identidad. Medellín, Colombia: Editorial Universidad de Antioquia, 1995.

———. *Testigo ocular: La fotografía en Antioquia, 1848–1950*. Fotografía. Medellín, Colombia: Biblioteca Pública Piloto de Medellín: Editorial Universidad de Antioquia, 2009.

López, Lucio Vicente. *La gran aldea: Costumbres bonaerenses*. Buenos Aires: M. Biedma, 1884.

López Anaya, Jorge. *Arte argentino: Cuatro siglos de historia (1600–2000)*. Buenos Aires: Emecé Editores, 2005.

López Casillas, Mercurio. *José Guadalupe Posada: Illustrator of Chapbooks, with Charming Covers, Choice Illustrations and Vignettes*. Mexico City: Editorial RM, 2005.

López Martinez, Héctor. *Plaza de Acho: Historia y tradición, 1766–1944*. Lima: Fondo Editorial del Congreso del Perú, 2005.

López Rojas, Luis Alfredo. *Historiar la muerte (1508–1920)*. Colección Visiones y Cegueras. San Juan, Puerto Rico: Editorial Isla Negra, 2006.

López Tamés, Román. *Introducción a la literatura infantil*. Murcia, Spain: Universidad de Murcia, Secretariado de Publicaciones, 1990.

Losada, Leandro. "Sociabilidad, distinción y alta sociedad en Buenos Aires: Los clubes sociales de la elite porteña (1880–1930)." *Desarrollo Económico* 45, no. 180 (January–March 2006): 547–72.

Low, Setha. *On the Plaza: The Politics of Public Space and Culture*. Austin: University of Texas Press, 2000.

Lozano, Tomás. *Cantemos al Alba: Origins of Songs, Sounds, and Liturgical Drama of Hispanic New Mexico*. Edited and translated by Rima Montoya. Albuquerque: University of New Mexico Press, 2007.

Ludmer, Josefina. *The Corpus Delicti: A Manual of Argentine Fictions*. Illuminations. Pittsburgh: University of Pittsburgh Press, 2004.

———. "The Gaucho Genre." In González Echevarría and Pupo-Walker, *Cambridge History*, 608–31.

———. *The Gaucho Genre: A Treatise on the Motherland*. Durham, NC: Duke University Press, 2002.

Lyons, Martyn. *Reading Culture and Writing Practices in Nineteenth-Century France*. Studies in Book and Print Culture. Toronto: University of Toronto Press, 2008.

Macera, Pablo. *Pintores populares andinos*. Lima: Fondo del Libro del Banco de Los Andes, 1979.

Madden, Richard Robert. *The Island of Cuba: Its Resources, Progress, and Prospects, Considered in Relation Especially to the Influence of Its Prosperity on the Interests of the British West India Colonies*. London: C. Gilpin, 1849.

Majluf, Natalia. "Pancho Fierro: Entre el mito y la historia." In Majluf, *Tipos del Perú*, 16–50.

———, ed. *Tipos del Perú: La Lima criolla de Pancho Fierro*. Madrid: Ediciones El Viso; New York: Hispanic Society of America, 2008.

"Manifesto of the Mexican Congress." In Conway, *U.S.-Mexican War*, 28–30.

Mansilla, Lucio V. *Reglamento para el ejercicio y maniobras de la Infanteria del Ejército argentino*. Buenos Aires: Librerias de Mayo, 1875.

Manthorne, Katherine E. "'Brothers under the Skin': Blanes's Gauchos and the Delineation of the Frontier Types of the American West." In Fundación Bunge y Born, *Art*, 151–200.

Manuel, Peter. *Caribbean Currents: Caribbean Music from Rumba to Reggae*. Philadelphia: Temple University Press, 1995.

———, ed. *Creolizing Contradance in the Caribbean*. Studies in Latin American and Caribbean Music. Philadelphia: Temple University Press, 2009.

Marco, Luis, and Eugenio de Ochoa, recops. *Repertorio completo de todos los juegos.* Madrid: De Bailly-Bailliere e Hijos, 1897.

Marcoy, Paul. *Travels in South America from the Pacific Ocean to the Atlantic Ocean.* New York: Scribner, Armstrong, 1875.

Mariscal, Elisa, and Kenneth Sokoloff. "Schooling, Suffrage, and the Persistence of Inequality in the Americas, 1800–1945." In Haber, *Political Institutions,* 159–218.

Martí, José. *La edad de oro.* Mexico City: Fondo de Cultural Económica, 1992.

———. "Our America." In Martí, *Selected Writings,* 288–95.

———. *Selected Writings.* Edited and translated by Esther Allen. New York: Penguin, 2002.

———. "Tres héroes." In Martí, *La edad de oro,* 32–37.

Martínez, Alberto. *Censo general de población, edificación, comercio e industrias de la ciudad de Buenos Aires.* Buenos Aires: Compañía Sudamericana de Billetes de Banco, 1906.

Martínez Ortega, Bernardo. "El cólera en México en el siglo XIX." *Revista Ciencias, Universidad Nacional Autónoma de México,* no. 25 (1992): 37–40.

Martínez Silva, Juan Manuel. *Arte Americano: Contextos y formas de ver, terceras jornadas de historia del arte.* Valparaiso: RIL Editores, 2006.

Masiello, Francine. "Introduction." In Gorriti, *Dreams and Realities,* xv–liv.

Matto de Turner, Clorinda. *Bocetos al lapiz de americanos celebres: Tomo primero.* Lima: Imprenta Bacigalupi, 1890.

———. *Tradiciones cuzqueñas: Leyendas, biografías y hojas sueltas.* Arequipa, Peru: Imprenta de La Bolsa, 1884.

Mayer, Brantz. *Mexico as It Was and as It Is.* New York: J. Winchester, 1844.

McElroy, Keith. *Early Peruvian Photography: A Critical Case Study.* Studies in Photography 7. Ann Arbor, MI: UMI Research Press, 1985.

McGrady, Donald. "Introducción." In Isaacs, *María* [Cátedra], 13–43.

Mejía Pavony, Germán. "Los itinerarios de la transformación urbana: Bogotá, 1820–1910." *Anuario Colombiano de Historia Social y de la Cultura* 24 (1997): 101–20.

Mejías-López, Alejandro. *The Inverted Conquest: The Myth of Modernity and the Transatlantic Onset of Modernism.* Nashville: Vanderbilt University Press, 2009.

Memoria en que el secretario de la Sociedad Filarmónica Mexicana da cuenta de los trabajos de la junta directiva en el año de 1872. No. 21, a cargo de Juan M. Rivera. Mexico City: Imprenta de las Escalerillas, 1873.

"Memorias científicas y literarias." *Anales de la Universidad de Chile* 41 (1872): 78.

Mendoza, Vicente. *El romance español y el corrido mexicano: Estudio comparativo.* Mexico City: Universidad Nacional Autónoma de México, 1997.

Mendoza, Vicente T., and Virginia R. R. de Mendoza. *Folklore de la región central de Puebla.* Mexico City: Centro Nacional de Investigación, Documentación e Información Musical "Carlos Chávez," 1991.

Mendoza de Arce, Daniel. *Music in Ibero-America to 1850: A Historical Survey.* Lanham, MD: Scarecrow Press, 2001.

Menéndez Alarcón, Antonio V. *Power and Television in Latin America: The Dominican Case.* New York: Praeger, 1992.

Menéndez Pidal, Ramón. *Romancero hispánico: Teoría e historia.* Madrid: Espasa-Calpe, 1953.

————. *Los romances de América y otros estudios*. Madrid: Espasa-Calpe, 1972.

Merino Montero, Luis. "La Sociedad Filarmónica de 1826 y los inicios de la actividad de conciertos públicos en la sociedad civil de Chile hacia 1830." *Revista Musical Chilena* 60, no. 206 (December 2006): 5–27.

Meza, Ramón. "José el de las Suertes." In Bueno, *Costumbristas cubanos*, 511–14.

Michelson, Bruce. *Printer's Devil: Mark Twain and the American Publishing Revolution*. Berkeley: University of California Press, 2006.

Mikkelsen, Carol, ed. *Spanish Theater Songs: Baroque and Classical Eras*. Translated by René Aravena. Van Nuys, CA: Alfred, 1998.

Millares Carlo, Agustín. *Repertorio bibliográfico: De los archivos mexicanos y de los europeos y norteamericanos de interés para la historia de México*. Mexico City: Universidad Nacional Autonoma de México, 1959.

Millington, Mark. "Transculturation: Contrapuntal Notes to Critical Orthodoxy." *Bulletin of Latin American Research* 26, no. 2 (April 2007): 256–68.

Mraz, John. *Looking for Mexico: Modern Visual Culture and National Identity*. Durham, NC: Duke University Press, 2009.

Muchitango, El Abate D. [pseud.]. "Ordenanzas para los bayles de contradanza." *Diario de Madrid*, nos. 347–48 (December 13–14, 1795): 2107 and 2111–12.

Mumford, Lewis. *The City in History: Its Origins, Its Transformations, and Its Prospects*. New York: Harcourt, Brace and World, 1961.

Muñiz, Manuel A. *Higiene pública: Reglamentación de la prostitución*. Lima: Imprenta del Comercio, 1887.

Nabarz, Payam. *The Mysteries of Mithras: The Pagan Belief that Shaped the Christian World*. Rochester, VT: Inner Traditions, 2005.

Nari, Marcela M. A. *Políticas de maternidad y maternalismo político: Buenos Aires, 1890– 1940*. Buenos Aires: Editorial Biblos, 2004.

Navarrete, Carlos. *El romance tradicional y el corrido en Guatemala*. Mexico City: Universidad Nacional Autónoma de México, Instituto de Investigaciones Antropológicas, 1987.

Navarro Viola, Alberto. *Anuario bibliográfico de la República Argentina, 1879*. Buenos Aires: Imprenta del Mercurio, 1880.

Navarro Viola, Miguel. *La biblioteca popular de Buenos Aires*. Vol. 3. Buenos Aires: Imprenta del Mercurio, 1878.

Nemo, pseud. "Rossini." *El Renacimiento: Periódico Literario* 1 (1869): 11–12, 35–37, 75–76, and 137–38.

Nolasco Cruz, Pedro. *Murmuraciones: Artículos de crítica social i literaria*. Santiago: El Independiente, 1882.

————. "La música." In Nolasco Cruz, *Murmuraciones*, 105–9.

Nouzeilles, Gabriela, and Graciela Montaldo, eds., *The Argentina Reader: History, Culture, Politics*. Durham, NC: Duke University Press, 2002.

Núñez, Estuardo, comp. *Cuatro viajeros alemanes al Perú*. Translated by Ernesto More. Lima: Universidad Nacional Mayor de San Marcos, 1969.

Obarrio, Mariano. "Ordenanza reglamentaria de la prostitución sancionada el 5 de enero de 1875." In Buenos Aires, *Digesto de ordenanzas*, 293–300.

Oehmichen, Cristina. "El carnaval de Culhuacán: Expresiones de identidad barrial." *Estudios sobre las Culturas Contemporáneas* 4, no. 14 (Spring 1992): 163–80.

Olaechéa, Manuel Adolfo. *Cuestiones prácticas de higiene y medicina legal*. Barcelona: Establecimiento Tipográfico de J. Balmas Planas, 1893.

Olavarría y Ferrari, Enrique de. *Reseña histórica del teatro en México*. Vol. 3. Mexico City: La Europa, 1895.

Olsen, Dale, and Daniel Sheehy, eds. *The Garland Handbook of Latin American Music*. 2nd ed. New York: Routledge, 2008.

Ortega, Julio, and Celia del Palacios, coords. *México trasatlántico*. Guadalajara: Fondo de Cultura Económica, Universidad de Guadalajara, 2008.

Ortemberg, Pablo. "La entrada de José de San Martín en Lima y la proclamación del 28 de julio: La negociación simbólica de la transición." *Histórica* 33, no. 2 (2009): 65–108.

Ortiz, Fernando. "The Afro-Cuban Festival of the 'Day of the Kings.'" *Inter-America* 4 (1921): 322–33.

———. "The Afro-Cuban Festival 'Day of the Kings.'" Annotated and translated by Jean Stubbs. In Bettelheim, *Cuban Festivals*, 1–41. A revised version of the article first published in *Inter-America*.

———. *Contrapunteo cubano del tabaco y el azúcar: Advertencia de sus contrastes agrarios, económicos, históricos y sociales, su etnografía y su transculturación*. Caracas: Biblioteca Ayacucho, 1978.

Osborn, Harold, ed. *The Oxford Companion to Art*. Oxford: Clarendon Press, 1970.

Overmyer-Velázquez, Mark. *Visions of the Emerald City: Modernity, Tradition, and the Formation of Porfirian Oaxaca, Mexico*. Durham, NC: Duke University Press, 2006.

Oyuela, Calixto. *Trozos escogidos de literatura castellana: Desde el siglo XII hasta nuestros días (España y América)*. Buenos Aires: A. Estrada, 1885.

Páez, Adriano. "Crítica de *María*." In *Revista Argentina*, 9:251–57. Buenos Aires: Imprenta Americana, 1870.

Pachas Macedo, Sofía. *Las artistas plásticas de Lima, 1891–1918*. Lima: Seminario de Historia Rural Andina, Universidad Nacional de San Marcos, 2008.

Palau, Melchor. *Cantares populares y literarios, recopilados*. Barcelona: Montaner y Simón, 1900.

Pallares Peñafiel, Vicente, and J. Trajano Mera. "Notas literarias y bibliográficas: Clases de dibujo." *La Revista Ecuatoriana* 1, no. 2 (February 28, 1889): 78.

Palma, Ricardo. "De esta capa, nadie escapa." In Palma, *Tradiciones peruanas completas*, 856–65.

———. *Peruvian Traditions*. Translated by Helen Lane and edited by Christopher Conway. New York: Oxford University Press, 2004.

———. "Santiago el volador." In Palma, *Peruvian Traditions*, 110–16.

———. "Tauromaquia (apuntes para la historia del toreo)." In Palma, *Tradiciones y artículos*, 228–40.

———. *Tradiciones peruanas completas*. Madrid: Aguilar, 1964.

———. *Tradiciones y artículos históricos*. Lima: Imprenta Torres Aguirre, 1899.

Palomeque, Alberto. *Mi año político: Discurso parlimentario*. Vol. 3. Montevideo: Imprenta El Progreso, 1891.

Parada, Alejandro. "El orden y la memoria en una librería porteña de 1829: El catálogo de la Librería Duportail Hermanos." *Información, Cultura y Sociedad*, no. 7 (December 2002): 9–80.

Paredes, Américo. "The 'Décima' on the Texas-Mexican Border: Folksong as an Adjunct to Legend." *Journal of the Folklore Institute* 3, no. 2 (August 1966): 154–67.

———. *A Texas-Mexican Cancionero: Folksongs of the Lower Border*. Austin: University of Texas Press, 1995.

———. *"With His Pistol in His Hand": A Border Ballad and Its Hero*. Austin: University of Texas Press, 1982.

Pastor Ríos, Justo. "*María* y Jorge Isaacs." *Caras y Caretas* 8, no. 349 (June 10, 1905): 23.

Payno, Manuel. *El fistol del diablo: Novela de costumbres mexicanas*. Mexico City: Conaculta, 2000.

Pellettieri, Osvaldo, dir. *De Eduardo de Filippo a Tita Merello: Del cómico italiano al "actor nacional" argentino (II)*. Buenos Aires: Galerna, 2003.

———, dir. *De Sarah Bernhardt a Lavelli: Teatro francés y teatro argentino, 1890–1990*. Buenos Aires: Galerna, 1993.

Peñafiel, Antonio. *Anuario estadístico de la república mexicana*. Mexico City: Oficina Tipografía de la Secretaría de Fomento, 1894.

Pereira, Antonio. *Cosas de antaño: Bocetos*. Montevideo: Varzi, 1893.

Pérez, Juan. *Almanaque estadístico de las oficinas y guía de forasteros y del comercio de la Republica para 1875*. Mexico City: Imprenta del Gobierno, 1874.

Pérez, Louis A., Jr. "Between Baseball and Bullfighting: The Quest for Nationality in Cuba, 1868–1898." *Journal of American History* 81, no. 2 (1994): 493–517.

———. *The Structure of Cuban History: Meanings and Purpose of the Past*. Chapel Hill: University of North Carolina Press, 2013.

Pérez Bugallo, Rubén. *Cancionero popular de Corrientes*. Buenos Aires: Ediciones del Sol, 1999.

Pérez Oyarzun, Fernando, and José Rosas Vera. "Cities within the City: Urban and Architectural Transfers in Santiago de Chile, 1840–1890." In Almandoz Marte, *Planning*, 109–38.

Pérez Salas, María Esther. *Costumbrismo y litografía en México: Un nuevo modo de ver*. Monografías de Arte 29. Mexico City: Universidad Nacional Autónoma de México, Instituto de Investigaciones Estéticas, 2005.

Picón Febres, Gonzalo. *La literatura venezolana en el siglo XIX*. Fuentes para la Historia de la Literatura Venezolana 4. Caracas: Presidencia de la República, 1972.

Pinch, Adela. "Sensibility." In Roe, *Romanticism*, 49–61.

Pinto Espinosa, Andrés. "La apropiación de la copla y su renovación formal, dentro del canto popular en Chile." *Revista Chilena de Literatura*, no. 78 (April 2011).

Podestá, Guido A. "La reescritura de Juan Moreira: La política del decorum en el teatro argentino." *Latin American Theatre Review* 25, no. 1 (Fall 1991): 7–19.

Podestá, José J. *Medio siglo de farándula: Memorias*. Editorial Galerna, 2003.

Portal, Ismael. *Cosas limeñas: Historia y costumbres*. Lima: Tipografía "Unión" A. Giacone, 1919.

Pratt, Mary Louise. *Imperial Eyes: Travel Writing and Transculturation*. 2nd ed. New York: Routledge, 2008.

Prieto, Guillermo. "*María*: Novela americana por Jorge Isaacs." In Isaacs, *María* [Garnier], 419–21.

———. *Memorias de mis tiempos*. Paris and Mexico City: Librería de la Viuda de C. Bouret, 1906.

———. *Obras completas*. Vol. 2, *Cuadros de Costumbres 1*. Mexico City: Conaculta, 1993.

Prince, Carlos. *Lima antigua*. Biblioteca Popular. Lima: Imprenta del Universo de C. Prince, 1890.

Proctor, Robert. *Narrative of a Journey across the Cordillera of the Andes and of a Residence in Lima and other Parts of Peru in the Years 1823 and 1824*. London: Archibald Constable, 1825.

Puebla. *Código de procedimientos y ley orgánica del departamento judicial del estado de Puebla: Conteniendo todas las adiciones y reformas que se les han hecho hasta la fecha, y las demas leyes que sobre procedimientos se han expedido hasta el día*. 2nd ed. Puebla, Mexico: Tipografía del Liceo de Artes de la Sagrada Familia, 1899.

Pupo-Walker, Enrique. "The Brief Narrative in Spanish America: 1835–1915." In González Echevarría and Pupo-Walker, *Cambridge History*, 490–535.

Rama, Angel. *The Lettered City*. Post-Contemporary Interventions. Durham, NC: Duke University Press, 1996.

Ramírez, Serafín. *La Habana artística: Apuntes históricos*. Havana: Imprenta del E. M. de la Capitanía General, 1891.

Ramos, Julio. *Divergent Modernities: Culture and Politics in 19th Century Latin America*. Post-Contemporary Interventions. Durham, NC: Duke University Press, 2001.

Raygada, Carlos. *Guía musical del Peru*. 2 vols. Lima: Fénix, 1964.

Rearick, Charles. *Paris Dreams, Paris Memories: The City and Its Mystique*. Stanford, CA: Stanford University Press, 2011.

Restrepo, Jorge, and David Aponte, eds. *Guerra y violencias en Colombia: Herramientas e interpretaciones*. Bogotá: Pontificia Universidad Javeriana-Bogotá, 2009.

Reyes Carballido, Martha. "Las sociedades e instituciones filarmónicas en Matanzas durante el siglo XIX." *Revista de la Biblioteca Nacional Jose Martí* 84, nos. 1–2 (January–June 1993): 7–16.

Ribera, Adolfo Luis. "La pintura." In *Historia general del arte*, 113–21.

Ripamonti Montt, Valentina. "Academia de pintura en Chile: Sus momentos previos." *Intus-Legere Historia* 4, no. 1 (2010): 127–53.

Rivera, Jorge B. "Ingreso, difusión e instalación modelar del Martín Fierro en el contexto de la cultura argentina." In Hernández, *Martín Fierro*, 545–75.

Rock, David. *Argentina, 1516–1987: From Spanish Colonization to the Falklands War*. Rev. and exp. ed. Berkeley: University of California Press, 1987.

Rodríguez, Olavo Alén. "Cuba." In Olsen and Sheehy, *Garland Handbook*, 105–25.

Rodríguez Castro, María. "Oir y leer: Tabaco y cultura en Cuba y Puerto Rico." *Caribbean Studies* 24, nos. 3–4 (1991): 221–39.

Rodríguez Prampolini, Ida. *La crítica de arte en México en el siglo XIX*. Mexico City: Imprenta Universitaria, 1964.

Roe, Nicholas, ed. *Romanticism: An Oxford Guide*. New York: Oxford University Press, 2005.

Rojas, Armando. "Muerte y resurrección de las estatuas." *Boletin Histórico* [Venezuela], no. 21 (1969): 333–45.

Rojas, José María. *Biblioteca de escritores venezolanos contemporáneos*. Caracas: Rójas Hermanos, 1875.

Rojas Líbano, Macarena. "Estudio de las percepciones de la obra de Magdalena y Aurora

Mira Mena en la pintura chilena del siglo XIX." PhD diss., Universidad de Chile, 2006.

Rojas Rojas, Rolando. *Tiempos de carnaval: El ascenso de lo popular a la cultura nacional (Lima, 1822–1922)*. Serie Colección Popular 4. Lima: Instituto Francés de Estudios Andinos: Instituto de Estudios Peruanos, 2005.

Rosenblat, Rosa, and Angela Blanco Amores. "Diez años de actividad teatral en Buenos Aires, 1852–1862." *Cursos y Conferencias* 16, nos. 181–83 (1947).

Rosselli, John. "Latin America and Italian Opera: A Process of Interaction, 1810–1930." In *Culturas musicales del mediterráneo y sus ramificaciones*, vol. 1. Special issue, *Revista de Musicología* 16, no. 1 (1993): 139–45.

Rossi, Vicente. *Cosas de negros*. Nueva Dimensión Argentina. Buenos Aires: Taurus, 2001.

Roumagnac, Carlos. *Los criminales en México*. Mexico City: Tipografia "El Fenix," 1904.

Rudé, George F. E. *Europe in the Eighteenth Century: Aristocracy and the Bourgeois Challenge*. History of Civilisation. London: Weidenfeld and Nicolson, 1972.

Ruhl, Arthur. "The Lhasa of South America." *Everybody's Magazine* 29, no. 5 (November 1913): 591–603.

Ruschenberger, W. S. W. *Three Years in the Pacific; Including Notices of Brazil, Chile, Bolivia, and Peru*. Philadelphia: Carey, Lea and Blanchard, 1834.

Sachs, Curt. *World History of the Dance*. Translated by Bessie Schonberg. New York: Seven Arts, 1952.

Salazar Vergara, Gabriel. *Labradores, peones y proletarios: Formación y crisis de la sociedad popular chilena del siglo XIX*. Colección Estudios Históricos. Santiago: Ediciones Sur, 1985.

Salvador, José María. *Efímeras efemérides: Fiestas cívicas y arte efímero en la Venezuela de los siglos XVII–XIX*. Caracas: Universidad Católica Andrés Bello, 2001.

Samper Agudelo, Miguel. *La miseria en Bogotá*. Bogotá: Imprenta de Gaitán, 1867.

Sánchez Zinny, E. F. *Integración Del Folklore Argentino: Ensayo Sobre El Folklore de Las Zonas Bonaerense, Pampeana, y Patagónica*. Buenos Aires: Editorial Stilcograf, 1968.

Santa Cruz, Nicomedes. *La décima en el Perú*. Lima: Instituto de Estudios Peruanos, 1982.

———. *Obras completas*. Vol. 2, *Investigación (1958–1991)*. Compiled by Pedro Santa Cruz Castillo. Digital ed. Buenos Aires: LibrosEnRed, 2004.

Santoni, Pedro. "Salvas, Cañonazos, y Repiques: Celebrating the Pronunciamiento during the U.S.-Mexican War." In Will Fowler, *Celebrating Insurrection*, 114–51.

Sarmiento, Domingo Faustino. "El camino de la fortuna, o sea vida, y obras de Benjamin Franklin." In Sarmiento, *Obras*, 45:153–57.

———. "Escuelas nocturnas." In Sarmiento, *Obras*, 28:209–10.

———. *Facundo: Civilization and Barbarism; The First Complete English Translation*. Translated by Kathleen Ross. Latin American Literature and Culture 12. Berkeley: University of California Press, 2003.

———. "Lucía de Lamermoor." In Sarmiento, *Obras*, 2:201–5.

———. *Obras de D. F. Sarmiento*. Vol. 2, *Artículos críticos y literarios, 1842–1853*. Buenos Aires: Felix Lajouane.

———. *Obras de D. F. Sarmiento*. Vol. 45, *Páginas Literarias*. Buenos Aires: Imprenta y Litografía "Mariano Moreno," 1900.

————. *Obras de D. F. Sarmiento*. Vol. 28, *Ideas pedagógicas*. Buenos Aires: Imprenta y Litografía "Mariano Moreno," 1899.

————. "La opera italiana en Santiago." In Sarmiento, *Obras*, 2:187–94.

————. "El teatro como elemento de cultura." In *Obras de D. F. Sarmiento*, vol. 1, *Artículos críticos y literarios, 1841–1842*, 271–75. Santiago: Imprenta Gutenberg, 1887.

Scavizzi, Giuseppe. Sections of "Institutes and Associations." In *Encyclopedia of World Art*, 8:158–66. New York: McGraw-Hill, 1963.

Schechter, John Mendell. *The Indispensable Harp: Historical Development, Modern Roles, Configurations, and Performance Practices in Ecuador and Latin America*. World Musics. Kent, OH: Kent State University Press, 1992.

Schneider, Luis Mario. "La muerte angélical, el velorio de los angelitos en Malinalco." In Aceves, "El arte ritual," 58–59.

Scobie, James. "The Paris of South America." In Nouzeilles and Montaldo, *Argentina Reader*, 170–80.

Segur, Count [Louis-Philippe]. *Memoirs and Recollections of Count Segur*. Boston: Wells and Lilly, 1825.

Seibel, Beatriz. *Historia del circo*. Biblioteca de Cultura Popular 18. Buenos Aires: Ediciones del Sol, 1993.

————. *Historia del teatro argentino: Desde los rituales hasta 1930*. Buenos Aires: Corregidor, 2002.

Seigel, Micol. "Cocoliche's Romp: Fun with Nationalism at Argentina's Carnival." *TDR: The Drama Review* 44, no. 2 (Summer 2000): 56–83.

Serrano Barquín, Héctor, ed. *Imágen y representación de las mujeres en la plástica mexicana: Una aproximación a su presencia en las artes visuales y populares de 1880 a 1980*. Toluca: Universidad Autónoma del Estado de México, 2005.

Shumway, Nicolas. *The Invention of Argentina*. Berkeley: University of California Press, 1991.

Siliceo, Manuel. "La Sociedad Filarmónica Mexicana." *La Armonía: Órgano de la Sociedad Filarmónica Mexicana* 1, no. 1 (November 1, 1866): 1–3.

Silva, Renán. "Prácticas de lectura, ámbitos privados y formación de un espacio público moderno: Nueva Granada a finales del antiguo régimen." In François-Xavier Guerra, *Los espacios públicos*, 80–106.

Silva Hernández, Margarita. "Las fiestas cívico-electorales en San José y el reconocimiento de la autoridad de los elegidos (1821–1870)." *Revista de Historia*, no. 27 (1993): 31–50.

Silva Valdés, Fernán. *Lenguaraz: Colección de cosas de nuestra tierra*. Buenos Aires: G. Kraft, 1955.

————. "Recuerdos de 'Fausto' y 'Martín Fierro.'" In Silva Valdés, *Lenguaraz*, 175–80.

Simmons, Merle E. *The Mexican Corrido as a Source for Interpretive Study of Modern Mexico, 1870–1950*. Bloomington: Indiana University Press, 1957.

Singhal, Arvind, Rafael Obregon, and Everett M. Rogers. "Reconstructing the Story of Simplemente María, the Most Popular Telenovela in Latin America of All Time." *International Communication Gazette* 54, no. 1 (August 1995): 1–15.

Sociedad Económica de Amigos del País. *Memoria de la junta general de la Sociedad Económica del estado de Guatemala*. Guatemala City, 1845.

Sociedad Filarmónica de Bogotá. *Reglamento de la Sociedad Filarmónica.* Bogotá: Imprenta de J. A. Cualla, 1847.

Sociedad Unión. *Reglamento interior de la parte activa de la sección filarmónica de la Sociedad Unión.* La Paz: Tipografía de "El Imparcial," 1889.

Socolow, Susan Migden. *The Bureaucrats of Buenos Aires, 1769–1810: Amor Al Real Servicio.* Durham, NC: Duke University Press, 1987.

Solís Miranda, José Antonio. *El libro de los juegos infantiles olvidados: Unos juegos que solo precisaban unos sencillos materiales and mucha imaginación.* La Coruña, Spain: El Arca del Papel Editores, 2001.

Sosa, Francisco. *Escritores y poetas sud-americanos.* Mexico: Oficina Tipográfica de la Secretaría de Fomento, 1890.

Sowell, David. *The Early Colombian Labor Movement: Artisans and Politics in Bogotá, 1832–1919.* Philadelphia: Temple University Press, 1992.

Speckman Guerra, Elisa. "Cuadernillos, pliegos y hojas sueltas en la imprenta de Antonio Vanegas Arroyo." In Clark de Lara and Speckman Guerra, *La república,* 391–414.

Spence, James Mudie. *The Land of Bolivar; or, War, Peace and Adventure in the Republic of Venezuela.* London: Low, Marston, Searle and Rivington, 1878.

Spencer Espinosa, Christian. "Imaginario nacional y cambio cultural: circulación, recepción y pervivencia de la zamacueca en Chile durante el siglo XIX." *Cuadernos de Música Iberoamericana* 14 (2007): 143–76.

Squier, Ephraim George. *Peru: Incidents of Travel and Exploration in the Land of the Incas.* London: Harper, 1877.

Stabler, Jane. "The Literary Background." In Roe, *Romanticism,* 27–37.

Staël, Madame de. *The Influence of Literature upon Society.* Boston: W. Wells and T. B. Wait, 1813.

Staples, Anne. "La lectura y los lectores en los primeros años de vida independiente." In Colegio de México, *Historia de la lectura,* 94–126.

Starr, Frederick. *Catalogue of a Collection of Objects Illustrating the Folklore of Mexico.* London: Nutt, 1899.

Stastny, Francisco. "Pancho Fierro y la pintura bambocciata." In Colección Ricardo Palma, *Acuarelas de Pancho Fierro,* 19–28.

Sturman, Janet Lynn. *Zarzuela: Spanish Operetta, American Stage.* Music in American Life. Urbana: University of Illinois Press, 2000.

Subercaseaux, Bernardo. *Historia del libro en Chile: Desde la colonia hasta el bicentenario.* 3rd ed. Santiago: LOM Ediciones, 2010.

Taft, Robert. *Photography and the American Scene: A Social History, 1839–1889.* New York: Dover, 1964.

Tala, Pamela. "La cultura popular, la poesía popular y la décima." *Revista Chilena de Literatura* 78 (2011).

Tenenbaum, Barbara A. "Streetwise History: The Paseo de la Reforma and the Porfirian State, 1876–1910." In Beezley, Martin, and French, *Rituals of Rule,* 127–50.

Thompson, Guy P. "The Ceremonial and Political Roles of Village Bands, 1846–1974." In Beezley, Martin, and French, *Rituals of Rule,* 307–42.

Tinajero, Araceli. *El Lector: A History of the Cigar Factory Reader.* Translated by Judith E. Grasberg. Austin: University of Texas Press, 2010.

Toft, Robert. *Bel Canto: A Performer's Guide*. New York: Oxford University Press, 2013.

Toro, Fermín. *Descripción de los honores fúnebres consagrados a los restos del libertador Simon Bolivar*. Caracas: En la Imprenta de V. Espinal, 1843.

Torres, George, ed. *Encyclopedia of Latin American Popular Music*. Santa Barbara, CA: ABC-CLIO, 2013.

Tovey, David G. "José Mariano Elízaga and Music Education in Early Nineteenth-Century Mexico." *Bulletin of Historical Research in Music Education* 18, no. 2 (January 1997): 126–36.

Ultimo Harabica [Abelardo Gamarra]. *Algo del Perú y mucho de pelagatos por el Tunante*. Lima: Imprenta de C. Prince, 1905.

Uribe, Eloisa. "1843–1860." In Uribe and Lombardo de Ruiz, *Y todo*, 67–111.

Uribe, Eloisa, and Sonia Lombardo de Ruiz, coords. *Y todo . . . por una nación: Historia social de la producción plástica de la ciudad de México, 1781–1910*. 2nd ed. Mexico City: Instituto Nacional de Antropología e Historia, 1987.

Valdés, Mario J., and Djelal Kadir, eds. *Literary Cultures of Latin America: A Comparative History*. Vol. 2. New York: Oxford University Press, 2004.

Valenzuela, Jesus. *Mis recuerdos: Manojo de rimas*. Mexico City: Consejo Nacional para la Cultura y Artes, 2001.

Valero de Tornos, J. "Zola." *La Ilustración Española y Americana* 29, no. 43 (November 22, 1885): 307.

Van Young, Eric. "The Limits of Atlantic World Nationalism in a Revolutionary Age? Imagined Communities and Lived Communities in Mexico, 1810–1821." In Esherick, Kayali, and Van Young, *Empire to Nation*, 35–67.

Vargas, J. Enrique. "Ligeras reflexiones sobre la higiene pública de Lima." *Anales de la Universidad Mayor de San Marcos de Lima* 25 (1898): 257–82.

Vega, Carlos. "Contradanza y pericón." *La Prensa* (Buenos Aires), October 1, 1939.

———. *Danzas y canciones argentinas: Teorías e investigaciones; Un ensayo sobre el tango*. Buenos Aires: G. Ricordi, 1936.

Velasco del Real, Octavio. *Viaje por la América del Sur*. Barcelona: Grande Establecimiento Tipoglitográfico Editorial de R. Molinas, 1892.

Ventura de Molina, Jacinto. *Los caminos de la escritura negra en el Río de Plata*. 2nd ed. Edited by William G. Acree Jr. and Alex Borucki. Colección El Fuego Nuevo 7. Madrid: Iberoamericana, 2010.

Vergara y Vergara, José María. *Artículos literarios de José María Vergara y Vergara*. London: J. M. Fonnegra, 1885.

———. "Juicio crítico." In Vergara, *Artículos literarios*, 55–61.

Vicuña Cifuentes, Julio. *Romances populares y vulgares, recogidos de la tradición oral chilena*. Santiago: Imprenta Barcelona, 1912.

Vicuña Mackenna, Benjamín. *Pájinas de mi diario durante tres años de viajes: 1853–1854–1855*. Santiago: Imprenta del Ferrocarril, 1856.

———. *La transformación de Santiago: Notas e indicaciones respetuosamente sometidas a la ilustre Municipalidad, al Supremo Gobierno y al Congreso Nacional por el intendente de Santiago*. Santiago: Imprenta de la Libreria el Mercurio, 1872.

Vidriera, Licenciado. [pseud.] "El gallero." In de Landaluze, *Los cubanos pintados*, 229–36.

Viqueira Albán, Juan Pedro. *Propriety and Permissiveness in Bourbon Mexico*. Translated by Sonya Lipsett-Rivera and Sergio Rivera Ayala. Latin American Silhouettes. Wilmington, DE: Scholarly Resources, 1999.

Voysest, Oswaldo. "Mercedes Cabello de Carbonera y la cuestión del Naturalismo en el Perú: Pautas para una interpretación de *Blanca Sol*." In Cabello de Carbonera, *Blanca Sol*, vii–xxiii.

Webber, Christopher. *The Zarzuela Companion*. Lanham, MD: Scarecrow, 2002.

Weber, William. *Music and the Middle Class: The Social Structure of Concert Life in London, Paris and Vienna between 1830 and 1848*. Burlington, VT: Ashgate, 2004.

Wood, R. Derek. "The Voyage of Captain Lucas and the Daguerreotype to Sydney." In Foucrier, *French*, 69–79.

Young, Richard, ed. *Music, Popular Culture, Identities*. New York: Rodopi, 2002.

Zamacois, Eduardo. *Tipos de café*. Madrid: Imprenta Plaza del Dos de Mayo, 1893.

Zañartu, Sady. *El Tile Vallejo y sus cuentos: De las andanzas del buscón copiapino cayetano vallejo, apodado el tile, ejemplo de mineros y espejo de narradores*. Santiago: Ediciones Fantasía, 1963.

Zapiola, José. *Recuerdos de treinta años: 1810–1840*. Santiago: Ahumada, 1902.

Zaragoza, Gonzalo. *Anarquismo argentino, 1876–1902*. Colección Nuestro Mundo, Serie Historia 47. Madrid: De la Torre, 1996.

Zárate, Armando. *Facundo Quiroga, Barranca Yaco: Juicios y testimonios*. Colección Política e Historia. Buenos Aires: Plus Ultra, 1985.

Zarco, Francisco. "Don Juan Cordero." In Rodríguez Prampolini, *La crítica de arte*, 284–301.

———. "Operas y toros." *La ilustración mexicana* 8 (1852): 592–95.

Zea, Leopoldo. *El Positivismo en México*. 2nd ed. Mexico City: Studium, 1953.

Zúñiga Saldaña, Marcela. "Licencias para imprimir libros en la Nueva España, 1748–1770." In Castañeda, *Del autor al lector*, 163–78.

INDEX

Page numbers in *italic* refer to figures.

censorship, 55
centralism, 13–14
Céspedes y Santa Cruz, Benjamín de, 40
Cevallos, Mariano "El Indio," 126
Chacallaza, Manuel Peña, 161
Charles IV (king of Spain), 16
Chateaubriand, François-René de, 77, 78,
    85–86
Chávez, Hugo, 202–3
Chávez, Valentín, 71
Chile
    academies of art in, 135, 137
    chinganas in, 47
    corrido in, 12–13
    mining in, 18
    popular songs in, 194–96
    poverty and crowding in, 34
    puppet theater in, 119–22
    War of the Pacific and, 17–18
    women artists in, 146, 147–48
    See also Santiago
Chilean Sociability (Bilbao), 10
chinaco y la china, El (Arrieta), 149
Chin-Chun-Chán (Medina and Elizondo),
    177
Chinese immigrants, 35, 36
chinganas, 47, *48*, 111, 119
cholera, 34
choral dancing, 178–181, *179*
Cicarelli, Alejandro, 137
cielitos, 71
cigar factories, 74–75
cinquillo, 184
Circo Criollo, 113–16
circus, 111–14
cities
    cafés in, 47–50, *51*
    clubs and associations in, 42–47, *45, 46,*
        68
    design of, 23–24
    further reading on, 207–8
    light and, 24–29
    modernity and, 23, 50–52
    monuments and, 29–32
    population of, 24–25
    poverty and crowding in, 32–37
    prostitution in, 37–42, *39*
    Republican fiestas in, 91–94
    urban ideal and, 15
    See also specific cities

civilization and barbarism
    cities and, 15, 23–25
    dance and, 178
    further reading on, 206–7
    modernity and, 199–200
    music and, 169–170
    print culture and, 53, 57, 84–85
    Quiroga and, 5–10
    theatricality and, 101
    views of, 10–12
Clavé, Pelegrín, 147
cleanliness, 97–98
Clemencia (Altamirano), 61–62
closed-couple dancing, 178–79, 182–83
clowns, 111–12, 113–16, 117–18, *118*, 126–27
Club del Progreso, 43–44
clubs, 42–47, 68
cockfighting, 122–24
Cocolicchio, Antonio (Cocoliche), 117–18,
    118
cócoras, 113
cofradías, 46, 197
Colección de bailes de sala (Ibarra), *179, 183*
Colombia
    academies of art in, 135–36
    conservative and liberal factions in, 14,
        33–34, 76
    exporting sectors in, 18
    literacy rates in, 54
    television in, 202
Colón, Jesús, 74–75
Columbus, Christopher, 31–32, 119–22, 136
comedia costumbrista, 108–11
Comercio, El (Peruvian newspaper), 69, 128,
    221n22
*Compendio del manual de urbanidad y buenas
    maneras* (Carreño), 96
Comte, Auguste, 10–11
Comte, Louis, 154
conservatism
    in Colombia, 14, 33–34
    versus liberalism, 13–14, 16–17
    modernity and, 15, 199–200
    print culture and, 55–56
conservative and liberal factions in
    in Colombia, 76
    filarmónicas and, 173
continente de los siete colores, El (Arciniegas),
    20
contradanse, 179–80, 183

Lombroso, Cesare, 40
López, Estanislao, 5
López, Javier, 162
López, José Hilario, 93
López, Lucio V., 43–44
López de Santa Anna, Antonio, 17
Los Reyes de Culhuacán, 103, 105
Lucia di Lammermoor (Donizetti), 170
Ludmer, Josefina, 223n80
Luján, Rafael, 144

"Mambrú se fue a la guerra" (song), 190–91
mandinga women, 106
Mangy Parrot, The (Lizardi), 56–57, 80–81
Manual de urbanidad y buenas maneras (Carreño), 13, 14, 96–101
Maquinista, El (Mexican newspaper), 71
Marcoy, Paul, 141–42
María (Isaacs), 63, 65, 75–80, 85–86
maromeros, 112
Martí, José, 11–12, 30, 66, 138
martial music, 186–88
Martín de la Guardia, Heraclio, 225n42
Martín Fierro (Hernández), 85
Marx, Karl, 74
Masonic lodges, 13
mass culture, 199–202
Matto de Turner, Clorinda, 70
Maximilian (emperor of Mexico), 162–63
Mayer, Brantz, 1–2
Mazzantini, Luis, 129
Medina, Rafael, 177
Melchior, 104
memento mori, 160–63, *161*
Mercurio Peruano (Lima newspaper), 53
merengue (*contradanza merengueada*), 184, 187
Merino, Ignacio, 136
mexicanos pintados por sí mismos, Los, 58, 59, 149
Mexico
    bullfighting in, 129
    caudillismo in, 17
    cigar factories in, 74–75
    conservative and liberal factions in, 14
    corridos in, 12–13, 191–92
    dance in, 177–78, 182
    Day of the Dead and, 164–65
    Federalism in, 17
    French invasion and occupation of, 17–18

literacy rates in, 54
mortuary photography in, 160–61, *161*
musical nationalism in, 201–2
national anthem of, 187–88
popular devotional art in, 142, *143*, 144–45, 150
Posada's Calaveras and, 163–66, *166*
poverty and crowding in, 34, 36
prostitution in, 38
puppet theater in, 122
telenovelas in, 201
village bands in, 174
women artists in, 146–47
Mexico City
    Academy of San Carlos in, 135, 136–38, 146–47
    Altamirano on, 15
    bookstores in, 64, 68
    cafés in, 47, 49, *51*
    clubs in, 44
    daguerreotypes in, 155
    design of, 24
    evangelistas and *tinterillos* in, 72–74
    filarmónicas in, 171, 172, 231n20
    'Haussmannization' of, 26
    infectious diseases in, 34
    Mayer's arrival in, 1–2
    monuments in, 31–32
    motion pictures in, 167
    newsboys and streetsellers in, *88*
    popular pastimes in, 111–13
    population of, 25
    poverty and crowding in, 36
    printing presses in, 54
    puppet theater in, 81
Michelangelo, 134
Michelena, Arturo, 138–39, *139*
milagros, 144
milonga, 185
minuet, 179
Mira, Aurora, 146
Mira, Magdalena, 146, 147–48
Miranda, Francisco de, 138–39, *139*
Miranda, Primitivo, 137
Miranda en La Carraca (Michelena), 138–39, *139*
miseria en Bogotá, La (Agudelo), 33–34
Mite, El (Mexican newspaper), 71
Mitre, Bartolomé, 61, 66, 86
modernity, 3–4, 15, 23, 50–52, 199–200